Understanding Rock

Understanding
Rock ESSAYS IN MUSICAL ANALYSIS

Edited by
JOHN COVACH & GRAEME M. BOONE

New York   Oxford
Oxford University Press
1997 OCM 36112257

Oxford University Press

Oxford   New York
Athens   Auckland   Bangkok   Bogota   Bombay   Buenos Aires
Calcutta   Cape Town   Dar es Salaam   Delhi   Florence   Hong Kong
Istanbul   Karachi   Kuala Lumpur   Madras   Madrid   Melbourne
Mexico City   Nairobi   Paris   Singapore   Taipei   Tokyo   Toronto   Warsaw

and associated companies in
Berlin   Ibadan

Copyright © 1997 by Oxford University Press, Inc.

Published by Oxford University Press, Inc.,
198 Madison Avenue, New York, New York 10016

Oxford is a registered trademark of Oxford University Press

Library of Congress Cataloging-in-Publication Data
Understanding rock : essays in musical analysis / edited by
   John Covach and Graeme M. Boone.
        p.   cm.
   Includes index.
   Contents: Progressive rock, "Close to the edge," and the
boundaries of style / John Covach — After sundown : the Beach Boys'
experimental music / Daniel Harrison — Blues transformations in the
music of Cream / Dave Headlam — "Joanie" get angry : k. d. lang's
feminist revision / Lori Burns — Swallowed by a song : Paul Simon's
crisis of chromaticism / Walter Everett — Little wing : a study in musical
cognition / Matthew Brown — Tonal and expressive ambiguity
in "Dark star" / Graeme M. Boone.
   ISBN 0-19-510004-2; ISBN 0-19-510005-0 (pbk.)
   1. Rock music—History and criticism.   2. Rock music—Analysis,
appreciation.
ML3534.U53   1997
781.66'0973—dc21   96-53475

9 8 7 6 5 4 3 2 1

Printed in the United States of America
on acid free paper

Preface

In the summer of 1974, the rock critic Lester Bangs was invited to type a review of a J. Geils Band concert onstage as part of the band's show. Jumping at the chance to jam with a favorite band and, at the same time, to storm the ultimate barrier between music and meaning, Bangs set up his typewriter next to the musicians as if it were another instrument. As he typed away in rhythmic and mental counterpoint to the music, he became more excited and frustrated until, at the song's climax, he smashed the table and finally stomped the typewriter itself in a fit of ecstatic rage.[1]

Is this the way it is, or should be, between rock music and the critical mind? Since the beginning of rock 'n' roll, opponents of the music, and some fans too, would have us think so. The plaint of rock's enemies is familiar: loud, raucous, drug ridden, and narcissistic, if not nihilistic, rock music causes degeneration in youth, transmitting social evils and subverting rational thought and responsibility; even worse, it is boring, annoying, bad music. The same, of course, was thought about earlier musical crazes that now seem tame and stodgy by comparison: swing, ragtime, the waltz, the minuet, the sarabande. Each of these did in fact threaten some perceived element of social order, and rock has posed its own distinct threats: arising in a time of social upheaval, it has reflected, accompanied, enabled, and at times even constituted the rumblings of that upheaval.

Partly for that very reason, however, a generation has grown up for whom this music is fundamental and necessary; partly also because it has simply been there, a central part of American life. It hardly seems coincidental that the election of 1992 should have climaxed with a sax-toting president and a rock anthem. In this and innumerable other ways, rock music has come of age: not in itself, for it sprang fully fledged from the bosom of postwar America, but rather as a cultural force internalized by the broadest spectrum of American society. In 1968, a *Star Trek* episode could shock us with a scene from after the year 2000, showing a rock band composed of elderly hippies (yipes!) whose wrinkles and gray hair clashed disturbingly with their peace symbols and bellbottoms. In 1997 such an image is no longer shocking at all: we see it on record covers all the time, a natural (no matter how ironic) course of events. In precise contrast to the *Star Trek* hippies, today's old rockers look happy, well adjusted, successful, rich. The counterculture is the culture.

Rock's social stigmata remain, of course, but they are integrated into an increasingly complicated status quo. In a time of unprecedented social and cultural eclecticism, the enduring American preoccupation with distinctions of highbrow versus lowbrow is greeted with ambivalence by a society for which it has lost its clarity and, for many, its relevance. In that respect, the doomsayers are right. Allan Bloom's call to America, to "grow up" beyond childish, blaring popular music, falls on the deaf ears of a public crowned with Walkmen.[2] In other respects, however, the doomsayers are wrong, as they always have been. Each younger generation grows up into, and through, its popular music, in pursuit of its own maturity. That music is a part of the American environment, and the music's changes will continue to reflect broader social changes, as they always have in the past. As American culture drifts inevitably further from its traditional Western European slant, it cannot but redefine and reinvent itself; but this does not mean that its diverse roots will be lost. Instead, they take on a new, and newly specific, relevance. Rock, country, jazz, hip-hop, classical, and other musics continue to influence each other and intertwine in smooth or rough combinations, just as their audiences do; and writers about music continue to absorb and reflect upon these developments.

Lester Bangs's essay offers a classic example of such reflection. Is it a violation of his experience that, following his J. Geils bacchanal, he should have sat himself down again, presumably at another typewriter, to write a story, and a parable, of it? It is that second act of writing, not the first, that brought his story into existence for us, the public who knows him only through reading him. His personal rock apocalypse was, after all, only a passing delirium whose darknesses proved compatible with, even essential to, his goals and responsibilities as a critic and a person. The same is true of the vast majority of rock experience. Writings about rock music profit from the opportunity to relate, and reflect on, remarkably broad and fresh varieties of musical and social activities, ranging from the most Dionysian and in-the-moment to the most Apollonian and coolheaded; to make sense of them through language; and to bring them into relationship with other aspects of personal and social life. To the extent that there remains a challenging, or even conflictual, relationship between rock music and traditional social values, the paradox of creation and destruction that Bangs sets down is likely to form an essential part of the best rock writing. As those values change, so will the music change, and so will the writing.

Seven years ago, at the time when this book was first conceived, academic attention to rock music was in a period of tremendous growth, the results of which now surround us clamorously. In bookshops throughout the country, the proportion of popular in relation to classical titles is expanding, and now includes academic studies as well as detailed transcriptions, histories, and biographies.[3] Meanwhile, academic job listings around the country show an unprecedented demand for popular specializations. These developments result in a new kind of irony, for there is, as yet, no clear "discipline" of rock studies, no consensus on what might constitute its focus or its limits, as a field of study or set of approaches; and it is not clear that there ever will or should be.[4] It is not that scholars have failed to attempt to address such questions. On the contrary, the interested reader is no longer lacking in stylistic overviews, encyclopedic histories, theoretical treatises, and college textbooks. But these manifold projects are beset from the outset by ideological and methodological controversies, while still lacking the solid underpinning of serious, close musical analysis that is needed if clear musicological understanding is to be obtained.

Conservatives doubt that rock music should be taught in universities at all, since the traditional focus of the humanities has been on canonical works in the European art tradition. Radicals doubt that analytical methods developed to describe such art music can appropriately be employed to address what is most meaningful in rock, since such analyses reinforce the musical work as an autonomous aesthetic object and produce interpretations foreign to the proper nature of the music. Such debates have their value and are, in any event, inevitable. But while some will see fit to pursue them to logical or extreme conclusions, others will continue, more quietly, to lay the groundwork that the field of rock musicology needs, if it is to find compatibility with the goals and assumptions of existing pedagogy. For it is the firm conviction of the writers in this book that that pedagogy, while in need of further reflection and modification (as it always is), provides strong and useful tools for analysis of rock music as it does for other music, and that, through such analysis, a better understanding of the music—not just the conditions surrounding it, but the music itself—can be gained. Like Lester Bangs, we have been through the music and have faith in its integrability, just as we have no doubt about the positive impact rock analysis can and will have on other musical analysis.[5]

Work on *Understanding Rock Music* began in 1990, after five of its contributors (Boone, Brown, Covach, Everett, and Headlam), all active in musicological and theoretical circles of academia, gave papers at a special session devoted to the analysis of rock music at the joint national meeting of the Society for Music Theory and the American Musicological Society in Oakland, California. The session was scheduled at 8:00 P.M. on Friday night, a time that seemed ironically appropriate: close to the heart of any rocker's schedule while, in academic conference terms, as dead as possible. To our knowledge, it was the first session ever devoted to rock music in either society; still today, sessions on the subject remain rare at the mainstream meetings.

The essays in the finished book are linked, and also opposed, by a number of themes. Beyond the avoidance of replication in subject matter and methodology, the editors have not found it necessary to ensure the presence of specific styles or approaches, nor of any particularly broad or "representative" variety. Instead, we have encouraged the authors to concentrate on music about which they feel strongly and to use whatever analytical materials seem most appropriate to their ideas about that music. As it happens, in the subject matter there is a focus on the era of the

1960s and '70s, a time when many of us were young and impressionable; every essay gives prominent attention to recordings made in that period. But the actual discussion ranges from early acoustic blues recordings to the '90s country rock of k. d. lang, and from the Beach Boys' a cappella doo-wop spinoffs to the psychedelic instrumental jamming of the Grateful Dead. In the process, a number of analytical issues germane to the study of rock are raised, and a breadth of analytical approaches comes into play.

In "Progressive Rock, 'Close to the Edge,' and the Boundaries of Style," John Covach explores the ways in which this Yes song, a landmark in the progressive-rock movement, fuses aspects of Western art music and early '70s rock. Heard by contemporaries as evoking an "alternative classical music," it is revealed through analysis as mixing features of both traditions, not only on a surface level but, more unexpectedly, on deeper structural levels as well.

Daniel Harrison, in "After Sundown: The Beach Boys' Experimental Music," is also concerned with the "art" boundaries of pop, which he explores through analysis of the tonal language of the Beach Boys. Discussing recordings from the period of "Good Vibrations," Harrison compares alternate versions and outtakes of songs in order to explain how the Beach Boys' music developed up through the unfinished landmark *Smile* LP and speculates on why that legendary album was never completed in the way group leader and composer Brian Wilson intended.

Both Walter Everett and Lori Burns employ Schenkerian techniques in their analyses, demonstrating in the process how features of musical structure can be seen to reflect issues addressed in the lyrics. At the same time, their approaches are directly opposed, since Everett's essay takes on a broad survey of music in order to make points about one songwriter's stylistic evolution, while Burns's focuses more closely on two songs in order to make connections between musical and social commentary. Everett's "Swallowed by a Song: Paul Simon's Crisis of Chromaticism" investigates the 1970s period in Paul Simon's songwriting, a time when Simon concentrated on chromatic techniques. Everett approaches Simon's music with particular attention to the composer's own commentary on it and frames his analysis of the 1970s songs by a telling consideration of Simon's preceding and following styles, both of which are marked by a predominant diatonicism. In Burns's essay, "'Joanie' Get Angry: k.d. lang's Feminist Revision," she presents an analysis of lang's 1991 cover version of Joanie Sommers's 1962 "Johnny Get Angry." The changes that lang makes in covering the tune provide a pointed commentary on the social assumptions contained in the original, a commentary made explicit in the video for lang's song. Burns's study reveals how transformations of the musical structure contribute to the song's effect, constituting a level of purely musical critique as well as a foil to its lyrics.

Matthew Brown also relies on Schenkerian theory to account for musical structure in his essay, "'Little Wing': A Study in Music Cognition." But he does so in a distinct way and to a different end. Brown's topic is the role that hierarchical tonal structures can play in a musical composition by Jimi Hendrix, as well as in its improvisations. But his point of departure is recent work in cognition, including the information-processing model and the idea of problem solving. By these means, Brown offers a new model for explaining how Hendrix approached tonal and motivic organization.

One of Brown's analytical concerns is the question of blues adaptation in rock style; in Dave Headlam's essay, "Blues Transformations in the Music of Cream," this becomes the central issue. Headlam approaches the blues-rock interface through one of its most important manifestations, the late-1960s British power trio Cream. Tracing its versions of such blues classics as "Cross Road Blues" and "Rollin' and Tumblin'" back to the original sources in Delta and Chicago blues, he illuminates the stylistic transformations in analytical terms and assesses their significance. With these analyses in mind, he then turns to consider the style of Cream's own blues compositions.

Graeme Boone, finally, takes a song by the Grateful Dead as the focus of his essay, "Tonal and Expressive Ambiguity in 'Dark Star.'" Countering a common perception of the Dead's music as aimless or disorganized, he uses harmonic, contrapuntal, and melodic analysis to reveal the means by which the Dead achieve musical and expressive cohesion, even as they incorporate extended and, to some extent, unpredictable improvisations into their music. The Dead's approach is, in conclusion, measured against the broader context and significance of the Deadhead movement.

Ultimately, the justification for any analytical program stems from one's own experiences. Like many now in the fields of musicology and music theory, the authors in this book were born in the decade of the birth of rock 'n' roll and grew up with it. Introduced to the serious study of organizing structures in art music, we naturally asked similar questions of popular music. Of what materials is it made? What makes it the way it is? Today's climate of heightened self-consciousness discourages scholars from taking their likes and dislikes for granted; but these are also times when people are making new and important discoveries simply by turning things around inside their own minds and connecting different parts of their own fragmented experience. This book is precisely the result of such a personal, interior movement, and for each author, it has yielded a different discovery. Ultimately, we find no better justification for analyzing rock music than this: it is part of us, and we like it.

Cambridge, Mass.   G. M. B.
Chapel Hill, N.C.   J. C.
January 1997

Notes

1. Lester Bangs, "My Night of Ecstasy with the J. Geils Band," in his *Psychotic Reactions and Carburetor Dung*, ed. Greil Marcus (New York: Vintage, 1988), 142–45. This review originally appeared in *Creem* (Aug. 1974).

2. Allan Bloom, *The Closing of the American Mind* (New York: Simon and Schuster, 1987), 68–81.

3. According to a subject search in *Books in Print*, the percentage of books devoted to popular music in the years 1980–89 represented 4% of the total of books on music. In the years 1990–96, this figure has risen to 7%.

4. Among recent arguments for the importance of the study of popular music, see Susan McClary and Robert Walser, "Start Making Sense! Musicology Wrestles with Rock," in *On Record: Pop, Rock, and the Written Word*, ed. Simon Frith and Andrew Goodwin (New York: Pantheon, 1990), 277–92; Susan McClary, "Terminal Prestige: The Case of the Avant-Garde

in Music Composition," *Cultural Critique* 12 (Spring 1989): 57–81; Richard Middleton, "'Change Gonna Come'? Popular Music and Musicology," in his *Studying Popular Music* (Milton Keynes: Open University Press, 1990), 102–26; and John Shepherd, "Musicology and Popular Music Studies," in his *Music as Social Text* (Cambridge: Polity Press, 1991), 189–223.

5. For a more detailed discussion of issues that arise in the analysis and music-historical assessment of popular music, see John Covach, "We Won't Get Fooled Again: Rock Music and Musical Analysis," *In Theory Only* 13, nos. 1–4 (1997): 119–36, reprinted in *Keeping Score: Music, Interdisciplinarity, Culture,* ed. Anahid Kassabian, David Schwarz, and Lawrence Siegel (Charlottesville: University Press of Virginia, 1997), 75–89; "Popular Music, Unpopular Musicology," in *Redefining Music,* ed. Nicholas Cook and Mark Everist (Oxford: Oxford University Press, 1997).

Acknowledgments

We would like to thank David Carson Berry, who expertly edited all of the musical examples contained in this collection. John Covach would like to thank the Music Program at the University of Rochester, the University of North Texas College of Music, and the University of North Carolina at Chapel Hill Department of Music for their institutional support of this project; special thanks go to Thomas Sovik at North Texas, who supported work on this project in ways too numerous to mention. Thanks also to Mary Davis for help with the index. Thanks finally to William Bolcom, Nicholas Cook, Allen Forte, Robert Hatten, Andrew Mead, David Neumeyer, and Brian Robison for their various forms of support. Thanks are also due to the publishers listed below for permission to use the excerpts as indicated.

Chapter 1
"Close to the Edge," by Jon Anderson and
  Steve Howe
© 1972 Warner-Tamerlane Publishing
  Corp.
All Rights Reserved
  Used by Permission
WARNER BROS. PUBLICATIONS U.S.
  INC., Miami, Fl. 33014

Chapter 2
"Don't Back Down," by B. Wilson
© 1964, Renewed 1992, Irving Music, Inc.
  (BMI)
All Rights Reserved   Intl. © Secured
Used by Permission

"California Girls," by B. Wilson
© 1965, Renewed 1993, Irving Music, Inc.
  (BMI)

Chapter 3

Chapter 4

Chapter 5

Contents

Contributors

Graeme Boone is assistant professor of music at the Ohio State University. He is the author
of *Patterns in Play: A Model for Text Setting in the Early French Songs of Guillaume Dufay*.

Matthew Brown is associate professor of music theory at the Eastman School of Music at
University of Rochester. He is the author of *Debussy: "Iberia."*

Lori Burns is assistant professor of music theory at the University of Ottawa.

John Covach is associate professor of music at the University of North Carolina at Chapel
Hill. He is coeditor of *In Theory Only*.

Walter Everett is assistant professor of music theory at the University of Michigan School of
Music. He is the author of *The Beatles as Musicians*.

Daniel Harrison is associate professor of music in the College Music Program at the University of Rochester and is associate professor of music theory at the university's Eastman
School of Music. He is the author of *Harmonic Function in Chromatic Music*. Harrison
appeared in the documentary film *I Just Wasn't Made for These Times*, devoted to the life
and music of Brian Wilson.

Dave Headlam is associate professor of music theory at the Eastman School of Music at the
University of Rochester. He is the author of *The Music of Alban Berg*.

Understanding Rock

1

Progressive Rock, "Close to the Edge," and the Boundaries of Style

JOHN COVACH

1

"Progressive rock," "classical rock," "art rock," "symphonic rock"—these labels have been used over the last twenty-five years by various authors to designate a style of popular music developed in the late 1960s and early 1970s, primarily by British rock musicians.[1] During this time groups such as King Crimson, the Moody Blues, Procol Harum, the Nice (and later Emerson, Lake, and Palmer), Gentle Giant, Genesis, Yes, Jethro Tull, Van der Graaf Generator, and Deep Purple attempted to blend late-'60s and early-'70s rock and pop with elements drawn from the Western art-music tradition.[2] This attempt to develop a kind of "concert-hall rock"—which was nevertheless still often performed in stadiums and arenas—was the result of a tendency on the part of some rockers and their fans to view rock as "listening music" (as opposed to dance music), an aesthetic trend that Wilfrid Mellers[3] attributes to the influence of the Beatles' *Sgt. Pepper's Lonely Hearts Club Band* of 1967.[4]

The early progressive rockers were not the first to employ musical elements generally associated with the "classical" or art-music tradition in their arrangements. The mid-1960s British-invasion groups, in an apparent attempt to surpass one another in eclecticism, began to use instruments and stylistic elements drawn from both the British music-hall and European art-music traditions. Music-hall elements are present, for instance, in Peter and Gordon's "Lady Godiva" (1966) and Herman's

3

Hermits' "I'm Henry VIII, I Am" (1965); concert-hall elements can be found in the use of a string octet in the Beatles' "Eleanor Rigby" (1966) and harpsichord in the Rolling Stones' "Lady Jane" (1966).[5] Expanding this trend in stylistic eclecticism to include what might be considered a kind of pop-music exoticism, Beatles guitarist George Harrison introduced the Indian sitar into rock music in "Norwegian Wood" (1965), and Harrison's musical exoticism was quickly imitated by other rock musicians. This mixture of 1960s pop with the Indian musical tradition can, of course, be viewed as an early instance of the "East meets West" trend that two years later became a basic component of the psychedelic movement.[6]

Considering the trend toward stylistic experimentation that was so much a part of mid- to late-1960s rock and pop, the combination of rock and art-music practice as it occurs in a tune such as Procol Harum's 1967 "A Whiter Shade of Pale" (literally Bach and rock) was not especially new for its time.[7] What was distinctive about the progressive-rock movement that arose out of the British-invasion scene, however, was an attitude of art-music "seriousness"—critics often called it pretentiousness—that many of these musicians brought to their music making. Among the most ardent fans of progressive rock at the time, there was the perception that these musicians were attempting to shape a new kind of classical music—a body of music that would not disappear after a few weeks or months on the pop charts, but would instead be listened to (and perhaps even studied), like the music of Mozart, Beethoven, and Brahms, for years to come. In their sometimes uncompromising adherence to what they took to be lofty art-music standards, progressive-rock musicians often seemed to be more interested in standing shoulder to shoulder with Richard Wagner or Igor Stravinsky than with Elvis Presley or Little Richard.[8]

Within the developing progressive-rock style of the late '60s and early '70s, groups often incorporated different aspects of art-music practice into their music. Some groups, like Yes and Jethro Tull, explored ways of creating pieces of extended length.[9] Peter Gabriel and Genesis incorporated aspects of opera into their innovative song texts, creating stage shows that evolved into the 1974 one-man rock opera, *A Lamb Lies Down on Broadway*.[10] Gentle Giant made extensive use of traditional contrapuntal writing in its compositions and arrangements, while King Crimson explored complex metrical schemes, atonality, and free-form improvisation.[11] Many groups showcased instrumental virtuosity: Keith Emerson and Rick Wakeman on keyboards, Steve Howe and Robert Fripp on guitar, Chris Squire and Michael Rutherford on bass, Bill Bruford, Carl Palmer, and Phil Collins on drums—all of these musicians set new performance standards on their respective instruments while incorporating some aspect of "classical" playing into their personal styles.

Historical accounts of progressive rock in the years that follow the rich period from about 1967 to 1977 tend to chronicle how the movement began to dissolve in the late 1970s. Progressive rock was one target of the punk and new-wave groups that gained popularity late in the decade; for many of these groups, the aesthetic call was for a return to simplicity—often cast as a return to the raw garage-band sound of the mid-1960s—and the "overproduced" albums of Yes and Emerson, Lake, and Palmer, for instance, represented just the kind of approach that most of these groups—on the surface, at least—rejected. Indeed, there is an obvious difference in aesthetic approach between late-1970s progressive-rock album tracks such as Yes's "Awaken" and ELP's "Pirates," on one hand, and early new-wave singles such as Talking Heads' "Take Me to the River" or Joe Jackson's "Is She Really Going Out with Him?"—not to mention the punk music of the Sex Pistols or the Ramones—on the other.[12]

Punk rock, in an effort perhaps to reestablish a directness of personal expression, tended to celebrate musical amateurism, and clearly such an aesthetic is antithetical to the drive to virtuosity and textural complexity found in the music of most progressive groups.[13] The simplicity of new-wave music, however, is often something of a deception. The music of Elvis Costello, Talking Heads, Joe Jackson, Devo, and other late-1970s new wavers is far more sophisticated that it may at first appear; most of this music is carefully written, arranged, and produced, and all this to the highest of pop-music professional standards. The perceived simplicity of this music ultimately boils down to a return to simpler formal types (mostly to the verse-refrain format of earlier pop) that in almost all instances respects the four-minute boundary of the pop single, an absence of extended instrumental soloing, and a relatively conservative harmonic vocabulary (especially when compared with that of progressive rock). New-wave groups also appealed to a new kind of musical simplicity by returning to the particular kinds of instruments used by 1960s rock groups: after a long absence from the rock stage and recording studio, Vox and Farfisa portable organs, Gretsch and Rickenbacker guitars, and Vox amplifiers were employed by many new wavers to evoke an earlier, simpler era in rock music.[14] Despite this return to less-sophisticated equipment, however, much new-wave music is actually more sophisticated in production terms than some progressive music of the same period.[15] Nevertheless, rock audiences still perceived new wave as simpler; it was understood as a return to basics, and as such, the new style had little use for any overt appeal to art music or art-music practice.

By the early 1980s, progressive rock was thought to be all but dead as a style, an idea reinforced by the fact that some of the principal progressive groups had developed a more commercial sound. Genesis, and especially drummer and post–Peter Gabriel lead vocalist Phil Collins, had more success in the 1980s with a mainstream rock approach than it had ever had in the 1970s playing progressive rock. In 1983, Yes scored its only number-one hit with "Owner of a Lonely Heart," written in part by South African pop-rock guitarist Trevor Rabin, who had replaced Steve Howe in the group.[16] Howe himself had left Yes to form Asia, along with ex-Yes keyboardist Geoff Downes, ex-King Crimson and UK bassist and vocalist John Wetton, and drummer Carl Palmer; Asia's 1982 single "Heat of the Moment" rose as high as number four on the Billboard charts, and the album on which this single appeared remained on the top forty album chart for thirty-five weeks, nine weeks at number one.[17] What went out of the music of these now ex-progressive groups when the more commercial sound came in was any significant evocation of art music: the Mellotrons and electric harpsichords were gone, replaced by distorted power-chord guitars;[18] the long and intricate tracks were replaced by tunes that would fit the radio pop-single format. But unlike the new wavers, who had (at least supposedly) returned to a 1960s brand of pop simplicity, the ex-progressive rockers moved more toward the rock mainstream that had existed in the 1970s when they were still playing progressive rock; they seemed far less influenced by the Animals or Iggy Pop and more influenced by Foreigner, Bad Company, and Led Zeppelin.

Despite this stylistic reorientation by its original practitioners, however, the progressive rock movement did not go under; rather, it went underground. Beginning in the early 1980s, a number of mostly British groups began performing and recording music that was clearly influenced by the music of the earlier progressive rockers; groups such as IQ, Twelfth Night, Pendragon, and especially Marillion tended to use Gabriel-era Genesis as the principal model in developing a style that has since been labeled "neo-progressive rock" (or simply "neo-prog"). Like the earlier music of the original progressive rockers, neo-prog also employs art-music practice within a rock context, though perhaps in a more indirect manner than did the original progressive rockers. Mellotron and synthesized string sounds, for example, saturate long and often intricately structured tracks that cover entire LP sides, but they seem to refer in many cases to those kinds of sounds as they can be found in 1970s Yes or Genesis and thus refer to the string section of a symphony orchestra only by way of this earlier music. Neo-prog bands of the 1980s never achieved the level of commercial success that the original progressive groups had enjoyed in the 1970s. The most successful neo-prog group of the 1980s was Marillion, who had twelve different singles reach the British top forty, three of these in the top ten.[19] But what success the neo-prog groups did enjoy was restricted to the United Kingdom and Europe, and none of these groups ever drew a significant level of attention in the United States.

Viewed within the historical context outlined thus far, neo-progressive rock might be viewed as a kind of stylistic and historical echo of progressive rock: it is less distinctive stylistically than its model and has had far less impact. But a recent resurgence of interest in progressive rock is likely to change this perception of neo-prog as well as the perception of progressive rock in general. Since the late 1980s, a number of new groups have appeared inside what might be termed the "progressive-rock underground"—a network of progressive-rock fans held together by Internet newsgroups and web sites, special magazines and fanzines devoted to progressive-rock music and the groups that play it, and mail-order businesses that distribute an impressive variety of new and old recordings.[20] These groups originate in Europe, Japan, and North America, and via the underground they are able to circulate their music to fans and listeners around the world.[21] The new progressive groups return not only to the early 1970s style of Genesis—as the neo-prog groups did—but also evoke the stylistic tendencies of King Crimson, Gentle Giant, ELP, Jethro Tull, and Yes.[22] Important to this chapter is the fact that with this return to the "classic" progressive-rock style comes a renewed fascination with engaging art-music practices in a rock context; like the originators of the style, this new generation of groups is grappling again with the problems of form, harmonic and melodic language, contrapuntal textures, instrumentation, and virtuosity that were so central to progressive rock in the 1970s.

Viewing the history of progressive rock over the course of three decades forces a rethinking of the commonly accepted historical accounts of the style; for instance, such an overview encourages one to see neo-prog not so much as an echo of the original progressive movement but rather as a significant link between the 1970s and the new resurgence of progressive rock that has been occurring in the 1990s. Considering this thirty-year view of progressive rock along with the careers of its originators also brings out another important point: progressive rock can be thought of as a style that is separable from the output of any particular group. In the 1980s, for instance, Genesis was playing music in a mainstream pop style while the progressive style that it had pioneered was underground, being sustained by other musicians. If progressive rock cannot then be reliably distinguished simply on the basis of who is recording and performing the music, it seems clear that it must be a stylistic category that depends on characteristics to be found in the musical texts themselves. As I have been implying throughout this introduction, one of the characteristics that is central to progressive rock is the evocation of art music within the context of rock and pop. But how art music is evoked in this music is a complicated problem, and it is this problem upon which this chapter will focus.

It is clear that the original progressive rockers were conscious of their attempt to fuse rock and art-music practices in their music. This is perhaps most obvious in the case of Keith Emerson, who, first with the Nice and later with ELP, consistently reworked familiar classical pieces in his often flamboyant keyboard style; Emerson was among the first to work with a symphony orchestra. In the liner notes to the Nice's *Five Bridges* of 1969, Emerson writes:

> On a journey from the almost Utopian freedom of our music to the established orthodox music school I met Joseph Eger [conductor of the Sinfonia of London on the album] who was travelling in the opposite direction.
>
> Since that meeting we have on occasions been catalysts in combining together the music from our different backgrounds forming sometimes a fusion, and other times a healthy conflict between the orchestra, representing possibly the establishment, and the [rock] trio, representing the non-establishment; ourselves having complete trust in a rebellious spirit and highly developed, broad minded, music brain whose reformed ideas in direction have been frowned upon, almost spat upon by so-called critics. That being Joseph Eger, the fighter.[23]

Emerson goes on to give brief descriptions of each of the five movements in his "Five Bridges Suite," a piece that covers all of the album's first side. While side two features arrangements of pieces by Sibelius, Tchaikovsky, and Bach, the "Five Bridges Suite" is an original composition, composed and scored by Emerson with lyrics by the band's bassist and vocalist, Lee Jackson. In these liner notes, it is clear that Emerson means to bridge rock and art music in this piece, and that, in fact, this is perhaps the central idea of the work.

Members of other progressive groups have remarked about the blending of rock and art-music practice in their music. For example, Jon Anderson, lead vocalist with Yes, once described the band's approach by saying, "We are rock musicians who borrow ideas from the classics—we sometimes emulate the structural form, just as [other] rock groups emulate jazz, soul, and rhythm and blues in their music ... We try to create music that is around us today in an orchestral way."[24] Lead guitarist Robert Fripp casts his aspirations for King Crimson in terms of his first hearing of *Sgt. Pepper* and specifically "A Day in the Life":

> I remember driving back from the hotel one night and on the radio I heard *Sgt. Pepper's* for the first time. I tuned in after they'd introduced the album. I didn't know what it was at first, and it terrified me—"A Day in the Life," the huge build-up at the end. At about the same time I was listening to Hendrix, Clapton with John Mayall's Blues-breakers, the Bartok String Quartets, Stravinsky's *The Rite of Spring*, Dvorak's *New*

World Symphony . . . they all spoke to me the same way. Perhaps different dialects, but it was all the same language. At that point, it was a call which I could not resist . . . From that point to this very day [1984], my interest is in how to take the energy and spirit of rock music and extend it to the music drawing from my background as part of the European tonal harmonic tradition. In other words, what would Hendrix sound like playing Bartok?[25]

The aspirations of these original progressive rockers to blend rock with classical music is readily apparent on the surface of their music; progressive rock of the late 1960s and early to mid-1970s borrows heavily and in a number of ways from the Western art-music tradition, and this characteristic is also obvious in the music of the progressive-rock groups that followed. It important to note, however, that progressive rock tends to borrow from "classical music" mostly as it is understood in the modern concert culture that promotes Western art music—a culture that can sometimes foster an image of the art-music traditition that is quite different from the ways in which that tradition is understood by musicologists and theorists. Making this distinction helps in accounting for how the borrowings that occur throughout progressive rock are often drawn freely from what scholars and other specialists would tend to view as very different styles; such diverse art-music charcteristics as baroque-era counterpoint, romantic-era virtuosity, and modernist rhythmic syncopation and sectional juxtaposition, for instance, seem to coexist comfortably and without any sense of historical incongruity within much progressive-rock music. One gets the sense that for these rock musicians, as well as for the audience for whom they compose, record, and perform their music, all of these borrowings are of the same kind: "classical."[26]

Considering the challenge that the original progressive-rock musicians established for their music, one might well wonder how successful these groups really were at blending 1960s and '70s pop and rock with classical music—two general styles that were at the time considered to be very disparate. In some instances it may seem as if progressive rock is simply rock music pasted over with a kind of art-music veneer, using classical-music instrumentation such as strings, pipe organ, or harpsichord to embellish musical structures that do not have much more in common with art music than does most other rock music of the time. Or inversely, progressive-rock musicians sometimes souped up classical music with a rock treatment—Keith Emerson's penchant for reinterpreting orchestral warhorses is perhaps the best-known example of this approach.[27] Both of these characterizations are, as it turns out, applicable to much progressive-rock music. But a more crucial issue, however, is whether these descriptions account for all progressive rock; and further, whether they account for all the ways in which art-music is evoked even for progressive-rock tracks in which they are indeed applicable. After noting the references to art music to be found on the surface of progressive-rock pieces, as well as in aspects of their performance, one might well wonder whether some deeper interaction with art-music practice might also be present in this music.

In order to explore these questions, I will focus on 1970s progressive rock, though certainly such an investigation could be expanded easily to include subsequent music in the style. This chapter will be further limited, for the most part, to a detailed discussion of a single piece by Yes entitled "Close to the Edge"; rock historians have tended to view Yes as one of the principal groups within the progressive-rock movement of the 1970s and have also tended to view "Close to the Edge" as one of the group's most important tracks. I will be concerned with exploring the ways in which this 1972 composition shares structural features and compositional practices with Western art music of the eighteenth and nineteenth centuries. By analyzing the piece according to criteria typically applied to Western art music (that is, formal, harmonic, rhythmic, motivic, and text-music analysis), I hope to demonstrate not only that the piece is a hybrid of rock and art music at the surface level, but also that the underlying structure of the work exhibits features common to both common-practice art music and the British-invasion pop from which the progressive-rock style emerged.

2

In September 1972, the British group Yes released its fifth album, *Close to the Edge*.[28] This album followed relatively close on the heels of the fourth album, *Fragile*, which had been released in January 1972, and the third album, called simply *The Yes Album*, released in March 1971.[29] The development of the Yes sound over the eighteen months that separate *The Yes Album* from *Close to the Edge* is dramatic. Personnel changes within the group played a major role in the band's growth; guitarist Steve Howe joined the group for *The Yes Album*, and multikeyboardist Rick Wakeman joined the group for *Fragile*. One may note that the song arrangements across these three albums become increasingly sophisticated over this short period. In fact, the *Close to the Edge* LP may be considered a significant point of arrival in the development of the Yes group; drummer Bill Bruford, who left the group after the recording of this album, has remarked that this LP "is absolutely my favorite. No doubt about it. To me, everything I did with the group was leading up to *Close to the Edge*."[30]

The *Close to the Edge* album contains three songs. All of side one is taken up with the title track. Side two contains "And You and I" and "Siberian Khatru." The title track, "Close to the Edge," will be the focus of the analytical discussion that follows. This piece constituted the most extended work that the group had recorded up to that time. The liner notes divide the piece into four sections labeled "A Solid Time of Change," "Total Mass Retain," "I Get Up, I Get Down," and "Seasons of Man."[31] Note that in the formal diagram (see fig. 1.1) the piece is divided into four large sections, marked A A' B A". This division corresponds to the four-part division indicated on the album jacket. Note also that figure 1.1 indicates that the piece opens with a substantial instrumental introduction that occurs after a gradual crescendo of taped bird and stream sounds; these same taped sounds also fade out at the end of the track.

The words and music to "Close to the Edge" were written by guitarist Howe and lead vocalist Anderson, and the track was arranged by the entire group. According to Howe, the song began by putting together parts of two preexistent songs: one by Howe that became the basis for the chorus and one by Anderson that formed the basis for the verses. Howe also provided the harmonic progression for the B section from yet another song.[32] The lyrics to "Close to the Edge" reveal the influence of Hermann Hesse's novel *Siddhartha*. The chorus, for example, contains the lyrics "Close to the edge, down by the river," followed by "seasons will pass you by, I get up, I get down." These lyrics likely refer to the river that plays such a crucial role in Hesse's novel and to the spiritual enlightenment that comes to Siddhartha as he communes with the river in the novel's final chapters. It is clear that the taped bird and water sounds that begin and end "Close to the Edge" are meant to suggest the river's edge, but I will also argue below that some of the fundamental ideas portrayed in Hesse's novel play an important role in the overall structure of the song.

Before discussing the structural aspects of the piece, however, I would like to consider a short excerpt that could be considered, following the discussion above, a surface instance of classical borrowing. This passage, which is here called the "Close to the Edge fugato," occurs at approximately 8:00.[33] As example 1.1 shows, the Coral electric sitar[34] and electric bass begin a pseudobaroque figure in C major and are joined by the pipe organ playing three statements of a melodic figure; this organ figure is a thematic transformation of the "Close to the Edge" theme (discussed below) that occurs earlier in the piece. The initial statement of the organ figure is imitated at the octave and at the fifteenth as these three statements of the figure ascend registrally.

While this passage is not likely to be mistaken for authentic baroque music, the texture, instrumentation, and counterpoint make clear the reference to the baroque style.[35] The kind of stylistic reference observed in this passage can be found in numerous passages throughout Yes arrangements during the early 1970s; the classical-guitar introduction to "Roundabout," the extended passage for solo piano in "South Side of the Sky," and the harpsichord solo in "Siberian Khatru" are other examples.[36] These stylistic references to art music have played a major role in prompting scholars and critics to label Yes music "classical rock" or "art rock," and I will return below to the important role played by this kind of stylistic intertextuality in Yes music. For present purposes it is sufficient to note that this example constitutes an instance of what I will term "stylistic reference" to Western art music. The discussion that follows, however, will explore a more fundamental kind of reference to art music that occurs in the structure of this work.

3

Figure 1.1 interprets the overall formal design of "Close to the Edge" as falling generally into a four-part scheme, with two large A sections followed by a contrasting B section and a return of the A section. Each A section begins with what I have designated an A-dorian verse; the final A section has two verse passages of structural importance. These verse passages begin at 3:54, 6:03, 14:59, and 15:53. Before considering these verses further, however, it may be helpful to address my use of the phrase "dorian mode." In using this term to describe the tonality of these passages, I am mostly prompted by a desire to avoid viewing the harmonic activity in the verse against the model of the traditional major-minor system (see fig. 1.2). According to the traditional model derived from common-practice-period European art music,

Example 1.1. "Close to the Edge" fugato

the chord progression A-minor – G-major – A-minor – B-minor that occurs in the verse and the general lack of a structurally significant leading-tone G# would be considered deviations from the tonal norm; thus, "modal" in this case could possibly signal an aesthetically significant departure from standard practice. But in rock music from about the mid-1960s forward, both this chord progression and the use of the natural seventh scale degree constitute stylistic norms; indeed, if the more conventional progression i – V – i – ii° were to occur in the verse, it would constitute a significant stylistic deviation. Thus, dorian mode is used in this instance to designate a harmonic environment that is typical within rock music.[37]

There are, however, other passages in this piece that can be viewed productively against the common-practice tonal model, and invoking traditional tonal procedures is a key component in creating both stylistic and structural references to classical music. If we recall the "Close to the Edge" fugato discussed above, for instance, one can see readily how important it is that such a passage be considered in the context of art-music practice. In the fugato, it is more a case of employing a contrapuntal combination of thematic elements to create the reference to art music than of overtly employing traditional harmony and voice leading; but other passages could be cited in which common-practice voice leading and harmonic progression are employed and in which detecting their presence plays a crucial role is establishing the stylistic reference. For instance, the church organ passages beginning at 12:10 and 12:27, the beginnings of which are shown in example 1.6 and discussed later, are clear instances of creating stylistic references to art music through the use of traditional voice leading and harmony. While the use of church organ in itself creates a reference to art music, the harmonic progression and voice leading are almost stereotypically "classical." There is nothing problematic about employing standard analytical techniques to such a passage.

Consider again the verse passages, specifically the first verse passage beginning at 3:54, after the substantial instrumental introduction (see ex. 1.2). The Coral electric sitar (along with the lead vocal) is in 12/8 meter, while the bass (along with the drums) plays in 3/2. Because rock listeners tend to take their tempo and metric bearings from the drums and bass, a listener is not likely to hear this passage in

Figure 1.1. Formal diagram of "Close to the Edge"

	Timing	Description	Key
Intro	0:00 – 0:56	stream and bird sounds	
	0:56 – 1:21	3-8ve ascending bass scale	e (d#-harm.)
	1:21 – 2:00	bass ostinato, 9x's to fermata	
	2:00 – 2:13	bass and guitar ostinato, 2x's to fermata	
	2:13 – 2:58	bass ostinato then ascending scale to lead-in fermata	
	2:58 – 3:54	"Close to the Edge" theme	D/d
A	3:54 – 4:22	intro and verse	a dorian
	4:22 – 4:53	verse and chorus 1	
	4:53 – 5:24	bridge	F
	5:24 – 6:03	bridge, chorus 1 (+ "I get up")	F to C
A'	6:03 – 6:33	intro and verse	a dorian
	6:33 – 7:09	verse and chorus 2	
	7:10 – 7:24	bridge	G
	7:25 – 7:59	bridge, chorus 1 (+ "I get up")	G to D
	8:00 – 8:28	"Close to the Edge" fugato	C
B	8:28 – 9:48	static interlude	E
	9:48 – 10:35	verse	
	10:35 – 11:19	verse	
	11:20 – 12:10	verse	
	12:10 – 12:47	church organ interlude	
	12:47 – 13:04	partial verse	
	13:04 – 14:11	church organ interlude and fanfare	
	14:11 – 14:59	"Close to the Edge" theme reset	F#
A"	14:59 – 15:30	instr. verse (organ solo) w/ chorus 2	a dorian
	15:30 – 15:52	instr. verse (organ) w/ chorus 2	
	15:53 – 16:17	verse	
	16:17 – 16:33	verse	
	16:33 – 17:36	bridge, chorus 1 (+ I get up, extended)	Bb to F
	17:36 – 18:38	fade to bird and stream sounds	

Figure 1.2. Dorian-mode harmonic progression in A-section verse

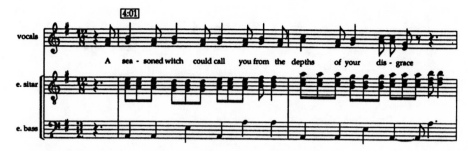

Example 1.2. Polymetric scheme between parts in A-section verse

terms of polymeter and is much more likely to hear the first verse in 3/2; consequently, the listener will perhaps interpret the rhythmic figures in the electric sitar and vocals as highly syncopated within the metric context of 3/2.

On the return of the verse passage at the start of the second A section (6:03ff.), the metric dissonance set up (or at least suggested) in the earlier passage is further developed (see ex. 1.3). While the Coral sitar (and vocals) remain in 12/8, the bass (and drums) are now in 4/2. But the repeating lengths, or "cycles," of these two metric levels no longer align, and the parts move in and out of synchronization according to a predictable pattern; that is, after eight bars of 12/8 and six bars of 4/2, the parts once again begin together. Unlike in the previous passage, the listener will now likely have great difficulty reducing the rhythmic patterns in the sitar and vocals to syncopations within 4/2, owing mostly to the lack of an aligned downbeat at the beginning of each measure.

After the lengthy B section, the A section returns at 14:59ff. with an instrumental verse, in this case a Rick Wakeman Hammond organ solo. One may note on the recording that Wakeman takes his metrical cue from the bass and drums, which are back in 3/2 as they were earlier. The electric guitar, now playing the part previously played on the Coral sitar, remains in 12/8 as before.

Following the organ solo the vocals return for the verse at 15:53ff. (see ex. 1.4), and there are some important changes in this passage. The piano is now doubling the Coral sitar and with the vocals and sitar is in 12/8. The bass part is very similar to the line that occurs in the second A section, except that bassist Chris Squire has trimmed the figure metrically so that it is no longer in 4/2 but in 3/2. This change thus aligns the new figure with the beginning of each 12/8 bar. While previously the

Example 1.3. Nonaligned meters between parts in A'-section verse

Example 1.4. Realigned meters in A"-section verse

3/2 meter seemed to dominate, now the 12/8 seems to take over, or at least to compete more effectively for the listener's metric orientation.

By directly comparing these four verse passages with one another in sequence, the techniques of variation at work across these passages become apparent. It is certainly not exceptional for rock musicians to rearrange the instrumentation in a tune from verse to verse, adding and changing parts along the way. In fact, it is fairly typical for rock arrangements to add something new to each statement of the verse, usually building up the arrangement to drive toward the ending. But in "Close to the Edge" one observes something more sophisticated than just building up an arrangement: here a musical issue is taken up. In the first A section the two metric levels are established or at least suggested. In the second section (A') these levels clearly establish a metric dissonance. In the third statement (organ solo, A") there is a return to the metric structure of the first verse statement; and in the fourth statement (vocal verse, A") the metric dissonance set up by the second statement is reconciled as the parts become aligned metrically. Over the course of the piece, therefore, verse sections do not simply return, they also develop; and, of course, variation according to some principle of development is a well-documented feature of much eighteenth- and nineteenth-century art music.[38] Thus we can see, in the unfolding of these four verses across some fifteen minutes of music, a long-range developmental strategy at work that invokes a familiar art-music practice. It is important to point out as well that the music involved in this development makes no significant stylistic reference to classical music on the surface; it is rather at the level of large-scale structure that the reference to art music is to be found. Stylistic and structural reference to art music can thus be seen to be independent of one another.

The preceding discussion has suggested that "Close to the Edge" falls basically into a four-part scheme. This scheme is supported by the return of the A sections and the presence of a contrasting B section and can be seen to refer back to rock song form through the use of strophic verse and chorus (or refrain). The use of bridge material to extend the verse sections is also traceable to rock sources.[39] In addition, the overall A A' B A" scheme can be traced back to the thirty-two-bar song form found in so many Tin Pan Alley tunes.[40] But it is also possible to detect features of an overarching two-part design, with the second section beginning at what I have labeled B in figure 1.1; and thinking of this piece in terms of a large two-part structure makes possible the further extension of the preceding argument suggesting the working out of a large-scale strategy. This two-part formal perspective hinges on interpreting the second part of the song as constituting, to some degree, a recomposition of the first part. In order to support that view, one must view the B

Example 1.5. E-F motive in the introduction

section as in some way reworking—or at least recalling in some significant way—
the long instrumental introduction that begins the piece.

Let us take a closer look at the introduction (0:56ff.). The bass part for most of
the introduction—that is, up to what has been termed the "Close to the Edge
theme"—is based on an ascending scale that might be called the second mode of D
harmonic minor and that forms the basis of the bass's opening material.[41] In the
first subsection of the introduction, Chris Squire plays this scale in a slow stepwise
ascent over the three octaves available to him on his Rickenbacker electric bass; he
pauses in this steady ascent only twice, both times on the "tonic" pitch-class E. The
guitar plays an angular figure based on the half step E–F (see ex. 1.5). As the introduction continues the bass falls into an ostinato pattern based on the exotic E scale,
as guitarist Steve Howe improvises using scalar patterns freely derived from the D-
minor scale patterns.[42]

Now let us now compare the opening of the introduction with the beginning of
the B section (8:28ff.). The B section opens with a static section in E (again, not the
traditional E major, though the E-major pitch-class collection is the basis for it). In
contrast to the multivoice texture and exotic E tonality of the introduction, here one
notes a tonal stasis and a floating, "focusless" texture in which sounds fade in and
out of the soundscape. This section arrives through the motivic F–E half step played
by the bass.

At 9:48 a new verse begins that ultimately forms the focus of the B section. This
new material does not seem to be a recomposition of previous material in an obvious way, but I will return to an analysis of these B-section verses below. As the third
B-section verse comes to its conclusion, an organ interlude begins that restates the
half-step motive of the introduction, here transposed down a half step to occur at
E–D♯ (see ex. 1.6). As the interlude continues, the half-step motive is transposed to
F–E, recalling the pitch level of the introduction. The motive then returns to E–D♯
at the end of the interlude. This organ interlude returns after the "I get up, I get
down" vocal climax of the B section, where it is extended somewhat (see 12:10ff.).

A third associative connection between the introduction and the B section may
be found in the "Close to the Edge theme" that appears in both sections, as well as in
the material that leads up to that theme. Consider the passage that introduces the
theme in the introduction (2:45ff.; see ex. 1.7). With the E–F motive as the bottom
voice in a compound melodic figure, the top voice ascends A–B♭–C–D. Now compare that passage with the keyboard fanfare that directly precedes the return of the

Example 1.6.   E–D♯ and F–E motive in B-Section church-organ interlude

"Close to the Edge" theme (13:50ff.); example 1.8 shows the synthesizer part. By comparing examples 1.7 and 1.8, one may note that the second passage is motivically derived from the first: the common compound melodic figuration and the stepwise ascent of the top voice make the reference very clear.

Let us turn now to the "Close to the Edge theme" itself as it appears in the introduction (2:58ff.; see ex. 1.9). The theme appears four times in the introduction, alternately in D major and D minor. The same theme appears at the end of the B section in a transformed but easily identifiable form (14:11ff.). The return of the "Close to the Edge" theme at the end of the B section and the transformation of the material that leads up to that return constitute a recomposition of the latter portion of the introduction. The recall of the half-step motive, both transposed and at its original pitch-class level, constitutes a significant recall of the first portion of the introduction. Considering, in addition, the common tonic E shared by the introduction and the B section, the overarching two-part scheme becomes more attractive analytically than it might at first appear. In addition, the final return of the A section can be viewed as a kind of telescoped return of the initial two A sections, with the organ solo serving as the return of the first A section and the vocal verses serving as the return of

Example 1.7.   E–F motive in the lead-in to the "CLose to the Edge" theme

Example 1.8.   Synthesizer lead-in to the reset "Close to the Edge" theme

Example 1.9. "Close to Edge" theme in the introduction

the second A section. The metric analysis presented earlier tends to support this reading of the final A section: the instrumental verses correspond metrically to the first A
section, and the vocal verses correspond to the second section.

This large two-part division in "Close to the Edge" corresponds to a similar formal division that occurs in other songs from both the *Close to the Edge* and *Fragile*
albums. "Heart of the Sunrise" begins with a substantial instrumental introduction
that returns and is developed with new material. "And You and I" features a return
of the guitar introduction, which serves as a clear divider in an overall two-part
design. Despite these similarities in structural design, however, no previous Yes
number achieves the scale and complexity of "Close to the Edge," and in this sense
the track constitutes a new point of arrival in terms of formal design—a point
toward which, following Bill Bruford's remarks above, the previous music seemed to
be leading.

But, as mentioned above, the structure of the song can in part be seen to enact in
musical terms certain ideas that are central to the Hermann Hesse novel that
inspired the lyrics. *Siddhartha* is set in India during the time of Buddha and chroni-
cles the life of the young Brahmin Siddhartha from about the age of eighteen to the
age of sixty. Throughout the novel Hesse returns to two themes that have some
bearing on "Close to the Edge": the contrast of the world of the spirit and intellect
with that of the senses and the idea that the unity of all things is experienced in a
realm of timelessness. The book consists of twelve chapters laid out according to a
three-part scheme of four chapters each, in which Siddhartha experiences the life of
the ascetic, life in the material and sensual world (as a successful merchant), and
enlightenment by the river.[43] The river serves as a symbol of timelessness throughout the novel and is the central image around which the story unfolds.

I do not want to claim that "Close to the Edge" should be understood as a portrayal of the novel, its story, or any of its characters; Jon Anderson has been quick to
deny any notion that his lyrics always tell a story or articulate a philosophical point
of view.[44] Rather, I want to focus on the notion that the piece both plays out the
dialectic of the material and physical versus the spiritual and intellectual, as well as
suggest that the piece also captures an aspect of the timelessness that is so central to
the novel. Let us begin by considering the contrast between the verse and bridge sections in the song. Each verse is set in A dorian; the melody in the voice is chantlike

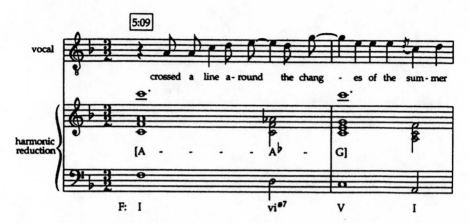

Example 1.10. A–A♭–G motive in the A-section bridge

and, as was discussed earlier, a certain amount of rhythmic and metric tension is present (see ex. 1.2). The bridge sections, by contrast, are in major keys (though in different keys at each appearance), with a far more conventional melodic contour in the voice; there is no unusual rhythmic tension, and the harmonic progression suggests that traditional voice leading is operative (see ex. 1.10). One could, then, view the verse as in some way capturing a kind of chaotic and perhaps primitive material realm, while the bridge stands for a more refined and even more life-affirming spiritual realm. The lyrics in these sections tend to reinforce this interpretation; consider, for instance, the following lyrics from the A-section verse:

> A seasoned witch could call you from the depths of your disgrace
> And rearrange your liver to the solid mental grace
> And achieve it all with music that came quickly from afar
> Then taste the fruit of man recorded losing all against the hour

These images tend to focus on being lost amid the confusion of material existence, contrasting "the depths of your disgrace" with the prospect of attaining "the solid mental grace." Perhaps, as in the novel, the "music that came quickly from afar" is the holy Om pronounced by the river itself.

By contrast, the bridge lyrics tend to be concerned more with images of a higher and simpler vision. Consider these lyrics drawn from the A-section bridge:

> Getting over all the times I had to worry
> Leaving all the changes far from far behind
> We relieve the tension only to find out the master's name

The chorus then follows with:

> Down at the end, round by the corner
> Close to the edge, just by the river
> Seasons will pass you by
> I get up, I get down
> Now that it's all over and done, now that you find, now that you're whole

In the bridge the tension of the chaotic material world is left "far from far behind," and enlightenment is reached when one "finds out the master's name." In the chorus we learn that all of this occurs "close to the edge, just by the river" and that in this timeless vision, "seasons will pass you by." The recurring lyric "I get up, I get down" could refer to the heights and depths of the human experience; certainly in Hesse's novel, Siddhartha experiences both in their fullest pain and glory.

The passage that runs "now that it's all over and done," however, suggests a topic that lyricist Anderson has described as one of the initial impulses of the song. In a radio interview, Anderson remarked: "The lyrical content became a kind of dream sequence in a way. The end verse is a dream that I had a long time ago about passing on from this world to another world, yet feeling so fantastic about it that death never frightened me ever since. I think in the early days when I was small I used to be frightened of this idea of not being here; where else can there be if there isn't a 'here'? And it just seemed a matter of course that death [is just as much] a beautiful experience for a man to physically go through as being born is."[45] One of the crucial scenes in *Siddhartha* is a near-death scene in which Siddhartha, thoroughly disgusted with himself after twenty years of life as an increasingly wealthy but also increasingly decadent merchant, decides to drown himself in the river:

> A chilly emptiness in the water reflected the terrible emptiness in his soul. Yes, he was at the end. There was nothing more for him but to efface himself, to destroy the unsuccessful structure of his life, to throw it away, mocked at by the gods. That was a deed which he longed to commit, to destroy the form which he hated! Might the fishes devour him, this dog of a Siddhartha, this corrupted and rotting body, this sluggish and misused soul! . . .
>
> With a distorted countenance he stared into the water. He saw his face reflected, and spat at it; he took his arm away from the tree trunk a little, so that he could fall headlong and finally go under. He bent, with closed eyes—towards death.
>
> Then from a remote part of his soul, from the past of his tired life, he heard a sound. It was one word, one syllable, which without thinking he spoke indistinctly, the ancient beginning and ending of all Brahmin prayers, the holy Om, which had the meaning of "the Perfect One" or "Perfection." At that moment, when the sound of Om reached his Siddhartha's ears, his slumbering soul suddenly awakened and he recognized the folly of his action.[46]

On the surface it is not immediately clear what Anderson's fascination with death as a "beautiful experience" and Siddhartha's narrow escape from it could hold in common. But in the novel, this scene occurs at just the point at which Siddhartha gives up a life of material wealth to become a simple ferryman on the river; the near suicide thus marks a point at which Siddhartha transcends material concerns to devote himself to a spiritual lifestyle. In a similar way, Anderson's vision of death is also a transformation into a higher consciousness and—in this case—into a purely spiritual state. The intersection between this important scene from the novel and Anderson's dream is the idea that there is a point of transition from the material to the spiritual; the verse and bridge, in both strictly musical terms and in the lyrics, can be seen to enact this crucial dialectical tension.

The same kind of contrast that occurs between the verse and chorus sections can be seen to be present at a much larger structural level, and extending this idea of playing out the dialectical tension between the material and spiritual realms further reinforces the reading of the piece as a two-part form. Consider the introduction; with its exotic E tonality and overtly complicated—perhaps overly complicated— texture, it suggests the chaotic nature of the material world. As Howe's lead lines scurry frantically up and down the register of the guitar, the bass slowly unfolds the ascending scale and then breaks into a frenzied ostinato. This apparent chaos is interrupted twice by radical disruptions: vocal sonorities on "ah." The third disruption leads to the "Close to the Edge" theme, and through it, out of the introduction and on to the song proper. Now contrast this introduction with the B section: it is also centered on E, but here there is no frantic musical scurrying about; instead, a sustained and floating texture is achieved. Diatonic pitches fade in and out of the texture as Mellotron lines blend with melodic fragments from the guitar, acoustic piano, electric bass, and synthesizer bass pedals, all in a rich sea of reverb. Thought of in terms of the contrast discussed above, we can see that it is the introduction that captures the senseless whirr of the physical world and the B section that suggests the contrasting order, and perhaps even for a moment the timeless unity, of Siddhartha's spiritual vision.

As discussed above, there are a number of associations between the B section and the introduction; but the previous discussion deferred analysis of the three verses that occur in this B section, focusing instead on the church organ interlude, the fanfare, and the resetting of the "Close to the Edge" theme. But the verses can also be seen to be related to earlier material. A simple instance of this can be found in the piano chords that introduce the B-section verse. As example 1.11 shows, the upper voice of these chords articulates an alternation between F# and E, and this can be thought of as a major-key transformation of the opening E−F motive; this is all the more significant when one recalls that the organ interlude also recalles the E−F motive. But a more significant connection can be found between the harmonic progression found in the B-section verses and that of the A-section bridge and its variants. As example 1.10 shows, the harmonic progression of the first A-section bridge features a chromatic filling in of a major second, producing an A−A♭−G line in F major; this same filled-in second occurs in the A'-section bridge in G major (B−B♭−A) and in the A" bridge in B♭ (D−D♭−C). In the B-section verses, this chromatic filling in is taken up and expanded to span the interval of a fourth, from E down to B (see ex. 1.12).[47] This filled-in fourth occurs in each case directly after the articulation of the F#−E motive and thus combines the transformed motive from the introduction with an expanded one from the bridge.

The connections both to the introduction and to the bridge sections are important in a consideration of how the dialectic operative between verse and bridge sections can be seen to be in effect between the introduction and B section. The transformation of the E−F motive to E−F# in the B section can be seen as reinforcing the notion of a transformation from the material realm into the spiritual one. The expansion of the filled-in seconds to filled-in fourths creates a stronger association between the B-section verses and the bridge sections. Since the bridge sections have been interpreted as characterizing the spiritual vision, it is possible to see the B-section verses as also suggesting the spiritual realm. The B-section verse lyrics gen-

Example 1.11. F♯–E motive leading to the B-section verse

erally support this interpretation; consider, for instance, the following verse (the
third of the three) from the B section:

> In charge of who is there, in charge of me
> Do I look on blindly and say I see the way
> The truth is written all along the page
> How old will I be before I come of age for you
> I get up, I get down

Here, as in the bridge lyrics discussed above, there is the sense of participating in a
mystical vision of the higher order of things—a vision very similar to ones that Siddhartha experiences in the latter third of the novel as he learns to listen to the river.

In terms of formal design, the B section can thus be seen to be a reworking of the
introduction in an additional way to the ones described earlier in this chapter: the B
section is a reinterpretation of the introduction in terms of an idea that is central to

Example 1.12. Filled-in fourth motive in the B-section verse

the Hesse novel. In this section, one might posit that the material realm (of the introduction) is transformed into the spiritual one, or, better, the spiritual nature of the material world is revealed through this transformation—and all of this is supported in terms of the music itself. As in Hesse's novel, perhaps, one sits by the river and understands the ultimate unity of all things.

The theme of timelessness is present in the lyrics of the bridge sections, as well as in the lyrics and music of the B section. But there is an even larger-scale way in which the music can be seen to enact this idea. As was mentioned earlier, the piece fades in with bird and stream sounds and fades out with these same sounds at the end. Thinking about the overall structure of the piece, we can see that the first of the two large sections begins on E and ends, with the "Close to the Edge" fugato, at 8:28; this last subsection is in the key of C, but the final note in the guitar and bass figuration is F, which leads directly to the low E that begins the B section, and with it, the second large section of the piece. At its approximate midpoint then, the E–F motive is literally present as a way of reinitiating the music.

At the end of the second large section the last chorus is in F major, though the final chord of the piece is a IV in F, a Bb-major sonority. Still, that the piece ends in F is significant: if one were to loop the music from the end back to the beginning, the E–F motive, now thought of in terms of two key centers, would connect up the end with the beginning in a way that would parallel the way in which the first large section leads to the second (though, admittedly, this latter connection occurs in terms of pitch classes and not key centers). The piece then might be seen as a kind of loop or wheel at the largest level of formal structure.[48] Clearly, that the piece emerges out of taped sounds that suggest the timeless river of Hesse's novel, and that it retreats back into those same taped sounds, already indicates that the entire piece can itself be thought of as a kind of vision; and perhaps like the visions that occur in Arnold Schoenberg's *Erwartung* or *Die Glückliche Hand*, the almost seventeen minutes of music that make up "Close to the Edge" are really a kind of expansion of a mere moment in chronological time—the moment at which Siddhartha's soul awakens as he hears the holy Om. That the form of the piece at the largest level could then be seen to be circular further reinforces the overall connection of the music to Hesse's text: while at one level the piece unfolds in chronological time—and in so doing develops musical materials dynamically and teleologically—at another, perhaps higher level, the piece turns back on itself and explodes a moment in chronological time. It might be better to say that all the successive moments of chronological time collapse back into a larger synchronic vision.

4

The preceding analysis suggests that there are a number of features in the structure of "Close to the Edge" that correspond to structural features in Western art music: the piece unfolds a large-scale formal design reinforced by tonal, thematic, and rhythmic return and development. The piece can also be seen to take up central issues within the Hesse novel that in part inspired it. The lyrics reflect a concern with these issues, and the musical material itself can be seen to participate in projecting these issues in music-structural and -formal terms. At the largest level of structure, I would like to argue for a large circular form, divided at the approximately halfway point by a second beginning that transforms the first. It is also clear that in other ways one can detect elements of the thirty-two-bar AABA form so prevalent in popular song in this century, as well as elements of the strophic verse-refrain (with bridge) structure that is common in much rock music. Thus this analysis supports the claim that the fusion of classical and rock in this particular Yes piece is not restricted to surface features; indeed, in many of the passages upon which my analysis depends, there is no clear stylistic reference to art music on the surface at all. A fusion of the two styles of music occurs in the domain of structure, and at even the deepest level of formal structure "Close to the Edge" can be seen to resemble the formal structures of large works from the art-music tradition.

I do not want to claim, however, that this piece, by virtue of its use of structural modes of organization that are in some cases more characteristic of art music than of mainstream 1970s rock music, somehow thereby becomes art music in any traditional sense of this term. In fact, the essence of the aesthetic appeal of "Close to the Edge" is that it balances stylistically and structurally between the art music and rock worlds; "Close to the Edge" pushes at the stylistic boundary of 1970s rock by evoking the world of classical music, but ultimately it does not cross over into that world. It is, rather, the maintenance of this very tension between these two widely disparate styles that accounts for the compelling aesthetic effect of "Close to the Edge"; a reconciliation of these forces that would attempt to securely place the piece in either the world of rock music or that of art music would surely weaken the dynamic effect of the song.

By focusing my discussion on the structure of this piece, I also do not mean to imply that the stylistic intertextuality that occurs on the surface of the work is somehow subordinate aesthetically. These intertextual references—which, it should be noted, are by no means restricted to references to Western art music—play a crucial role in the aesthetic experience of a piece of Yes music. In fact, by working exclusively from the variety of stylistic references that occur in Yes music, one might just as easily label passages "jazz rock," "Latin rock," or even "country rock" or "folk rock."[49] But it is stylistic reference to art music that most distinguishes progressive rock from other styles of popular music, and this is an important and distinctive feature of Yes music. As the preceding analysis has shown, the networks of stylistic and structural reference in "Close to the Edge" can be distinguished from one another; certainly both networks are present in the work and are mutually reinforcing, but they can also be seen in many cases to be operating relatively independently.

"Close to the Edge," then, is a piece that challenges the listener's sense of stylistic boundary. And the piece not only challenges the often tacitly assumed line that may be supposed to separate rock music from art music; its attempt at stylistic fusion also led the group to test the boundaries of popular acceptance within the rock music community of musicians, critics, and listeners. After the recording of Close to the Edge, Yes began work on its seventh album, Tales from Topographic Oceans, released in January 1974.[50] Tales was a double LP that featured one song on each side and thus four songs on the scale of "Close to the Edge." Playing on the title of the earlier album, critics attacked the new release as going "over the edge."[51] But Tales *from Topographic Oceans* takes up structurally where "Close to the Edge" left off and can be viewed in retrospect as a logical outgrowth of the musical concerns that had produced the earlier albums.[52] While "Close to the Edge" was inspired by Hesse's novel, *Tales from Topographic Oceans* was inspired by a commentary on the four Vedas that Anderson found in a footnote in Paramahansa Yogananda's *Autobiography of a Yogi*.[53] Despite constituting a logical extension of "Close to the Edge," both musically and in terms of lyrics, *Tales* was not a popular success, and the Yes drive toward complexity and expansiveness led it to a fork in the road where one path must have seemed to lead to artistic growth and satisfaction and the other to continued commercial success.[54] The direction that Yes decided to go is clear from its next studio album:[55] the first side of *Relayer* contains a single track, "The Gates of Delirium," inspired by Tolstoy's *War and Peace*. Thus the *Close to the Edge* album cannot be seen as the ultimate point of arrival in the group's drive to blend art music and rock. The LP does emerge historically, however, as the album with which Yes pushed its classical-rock fusion to the limits of popular acceptance, thus defining at least one boundary of commercial rock in the 1970s.

Other progressive groups followed a path similar to the one taken by Yes: Both Jethro Tull's *A Passion Play* and Genesis's *A Lamb Lies Down on Broadway* were attacked by critics as overindulgent; yet both albums might be seen as logical extensions of the albums that preceded them. Yes, then, was not the only group to push at both the boundaries of rock and art music as well as at the boundaries of commercial success. This brings us back to some of the central questions that were posed earlier in this chapter concerning progressive rock generally: how successful is this music at blending rock and art-music practice? And does this stylistic interaction occur only at the surface of the music or also at a deeper, structural level?

In the case of "Close to the Edge," this analysis has shown that the interaction between styles does indeed occur in the domains of large-scale structure and form. I have also suggested along the way that this piece extends formal structures to be found in earlier Yes music and that such structural concerns are evident in the pieces that follow "Close to the Edge." Others have suggested that the music of Jethro Tull, Genesis, ELP, King Crimson, and Gentle Giant also engages the art-music tradition in ways that affect form and structure.[56] But as suggestive as this research is, work on the progressive rock repertory is still in the preliminary stages; much more detailed analytical work needs to be done to more fully substantiate claims for large-scale structure and form in 1970s progressive rock in a broad sense. And, as I outlined above, two decades of progressive rock music have followed the first wave of the 1970s; most of this music is yet to be accounted for historically, let alone music-analytically. This chapter, then, may be seen as taking another step toward a fuller consideration of progressive rock—a fuller consideration that I am confident will continue to unfold in academic writing in popular music over the next several years.

Notes

An earlier version of this chapter was delivered at the 1992 conference "Popular Music: The Primary Text," held at Thames Valley University, London, 3–5 July.

1. For the use of "classical rock," see David P. Szatmary, *Rockin' in Time: A Social History of Rock and Roll*, 2d ed. (Englewood Cliffs, N. J.: Prentice-Hall, 1991), 201–2. For "art rock," see Charles T. Brown, *The Art of Rock and Roll*, 2d ed. (Englewood Cliffs, N. J.: Prentice-Hall, 1987), 179–92; Katherine Charton, *Rock Music Styles: A History*, 2d ed. (Madison, Wisc.: Brown & Benchmark, 1994), 192–206); David Joyner, *American Popular Music* (Madison, Wisc.: Brown & Benchmark, 1993), 279–86; Allan F. Moore, *Rock: The Primary Text* (Buckingham: Open University Press, 1993), 79–87; Joe Stuessy, *Rock and Roll: Its History and Stylistic Development*, 2d ed. (Englewood Cliffs, N. J.: Prentice-Hall, 1994), 274–300; and Ed Ward, Geoffrey Stokes, and Ken Tucker, *Rock of Ages: The Rolling Stone History of Rock and Roll* (Englewood Cliffs, N. J.: Rolling Stone Press, 1986), 480–83. For "progressive rock," see Edward Macan, *Rockin' the Classics: English Progressive Rock and the Counterculture* (New York: Oxford University Press, 1997), and Jon Pareles and Patricia Romanowski, *The Rolling Stone Encyclopedia of Rock and Roll* (New York: Rolling Stone Press, 1983), 447–48. For "symphonic rock," see Dan Hedges, *Yes: The Authorised Biography* (London: Sidgwick and Jackson, 1981), 62.

In this study I will use the term "progressive rock," principally because those involved in the recent resurgence of interest in this style (as discussed briefly in the text later) have adopted this term universally.

2. Macan provides a thorough account of the history of progressive rock during this period in his *Rockin' the Classics.*

3. See Wilfrid Mellers, *Twilight of the Gods: The Music of the Beatles* (New York: Viking Press, 1973), 86. Mellers also states this position succinctly in the Beatles video documentary *The Compleat Beatles* (Delilah Films, 1982).

4. The Beatles, *Sgt. Pepper's Lonely Hearts Club Band,* Parlophone 7027/Capitol 2635 (1967). In his essay in this book, Dan Harrison explores the relationship between the Beatles and the Beach Boys in the period surrounding the release of the Beatles' *Sgt. Pepper,* the Beach Boys' "Good Vibrations," and the ill-fated *Smile* LP.

5. Peter and Gordon, "Lady Godiva," Capitol 5740 (1966); Herman's Hermits, "I'm Henry VIII, I Am," MGM 13367 (1965); the Beatles, "Eleanor Rigby," on *Revolver*, Parlophone 7009/Capitol 2576 (1966); and the Rolling Stones, "Lady Jane," London 902 (1966). For a consideration of the use of classical-music instrumentation in late British-invasion and psychedelic music, see my "Stylistic Competencies, Musical Humor, and 'This is Spinal Tap,'" in *Concert Music, Rock, and Jazz since 1945: Essays and Analytical Studies,* ed. Elizabeth West Marvin and Richard Hermann (Rochester, N. Y.: University of Rochester Press, 1995), pp. 402–24.

6. The Beatles, "Norwegian Wood," on *Rubber Soul,* Parlophone 3075/Capitol 2442 (1965). David Pichaske (*A Generation in Motion: Popular Music and Culture in the Sixties* [New York: Schirmer, 1979], 96) considers the Maharishi Mahesh Yogi and his contact with the Beatles (among others) to be an important factor in directing the attention of late-'60s popular culture to Eastern religion and music. Later in his book Pichaske (171) quotes sitar virtuoso Ravi Shankar on the blending of Indian music and religion with hippie culture. According to Shankar, aspects of Indian culture were understood in a very superficial way, leading to gross distortions of these imported musical elements. For an interesting, if informal, discussion of the relationship between Eastern mysticism and psychedelic drugs in Beatles music, see Davin Seay with Mary Neely, *Stairway to Heaven: The Spiritual Roots of Rock 'n' Roll* (New York: Ballantine Books, 1986), 123–55.

7. Procol Harum, "A Whiter Shade of Pale," Deram 7507 (1967). Richard Middleton

(*Studying Popular Music* [Buckingham: Open University Press, 1990], 30) reports that the basic harmonic progression and organ melody in this tune are borrowed from a Bach cantata. Considering the stylistic eclecticism outlined here, it is perhaps not surprising to find Charlie Gillett (*Sound of the City: The Rise of Rock and Roll*, 2d ed. [New York: Pantheon, 1983], 394–95) pointing out that Percy Sledge's "When a Man Loves a Woman" (Atlantic 2326 [1966]) was "a vital inspiration behind the arrangement."

8. For a discussion of these attitudes about progressive rock, see Ward, Stokes, and Tucker, *Rock of Ages*, 480–82. Some idea of the kinds of things that were being written at the time can be found in a review by music critic Robert Sheldon, "Yes: Rainbow Theatre," *London Times*, 23 Nov. 1973. In assessing a Yes performance of its then recently released *Tales from Topographic Oceans* (discussed later), Sheldon is effusive about the historical importance of the music. He writes that Yes's music might best be termed "rockophonic" and that side three of the two-LP release will be studied twenty-five years hence as a turning point in modern music. In an interview with lead vocalist Jon Anderson and bassist Chris Squire that appeared less than a month later, Anderson uses the term "rockophonic," suggesting that he had read Sheldon's review. See Chris Welch, "Yes Weather the Storm," *Melody Maker*, 15 Dec. 1973. A more moderate summary of progressive rock's relation to the art-music tradition can be found in "Rock Goes to College," *Time*, 23 Sept. 1974, 90–91. A perceived air of pretentiousness among progressive-rock musicians is likely what prompts John Rockwell to dismiss Yes's music as "convoluted pop mysticism." See his "The Emergence of Art Rock," in *The Rolling Stone Illustrated History of Rock and Roll*, ed. Anthony DeCurtis, James Henke, and Holly George-Warren (New York: Random House, 1992), 493–94. Discussing the Moody Blues, Rockwell pronounces: "Although Moody Blues devotees seemed to think they were getting something higher toned than mere rock, they were kidding themselves: Moody Blues records were mood music, pure and regrettably not so simple. There's nothing wrong with that, of course, except for the miscategorization into something more profound" (494).

9. Yes's music is discussed later. For extended pieces by Jethro Tull, see *Thick as a Brick*, Reprise 2072 (1972), and *A Passion Play*, Chrysalis PV 41040 (1973). The formal design of *Thick as a Brick* is discussed by Nors S. Josephson in his "Bach Meets Liszt: Traditional Formal Structures and Performance Practices," *Musical Quarterly* 76/1 (1992): 67–92; see pp. 75–77 especially. Josephson views this piece as a cyclical variation form. For a discussion of the use of a number of art-music practices in progressive rock, see Edward Macan, "'The Spirit of Albion' in Twentieth-Century English Popular Music: Vaughan Williams, Holst, and the Progressive-Rock Movement," *Music Review* 53/2 (1992): 100–125.

10. Genesis, *A Lamb Lies Down on Broadway*, Atco SD2-401 (1974). Genesis's rock opera was not the first, however; the first rock opera was the Who's *Tommy* (Decca 7205 [1969]). The Who album made a tremendous impact on members of Genesis; remembering the period surrounding the recording and release of the group's first album, *From Genesis to Revelation* (Decca SKL 4990 [1969]), ex-Genesis lead vocalist Peter Gabriel relates how excited he was that one reviewer compared him to Who lead vocalist Roger Daltry: "That was the best review we got. It was incredibly exciting because it [*Tommy*] was my bible at the time." See Spencer Bright, *Peter Gabriel: An Authorised Biography* (London: Headline, 1989), 35.

11. Several cuts from the many Gentle Giant albums could be brought forward to illustrate the group's employment of traditional contrapuntal practice, but an especially good example is the first section of "On Reflection" (*Free Hand*, Capitol ST-11428 [1975]), a four-voice fugal exposition. Allan Moore discusses Gentle Giant's music briefly in his *Rock: The Primary Text*, 100–103. A transcription of "On Reflection" by Geir Hasnes appears in *Proclamation: The Occasional Gentle Giant Newsletter* 3 (Aug. 1993): 36–40. King Crimson's music is discussed in detail in Eric Tamm, *Robert Fripp: From King Crimson to Guitar Craft* (Boston: Faber and Faber, 1990).

12. Yes, "Awaken," on *Going for the One*, Atlantic 19106 (1977); Emerson, Lake, and Palmer, "Pirates," on *Works, Volume 1*, Atlantic 7000 (1977); Talking Heads, "Take Me to the River," Sire 1032 (1978); and Joe Jackson, "Is She Really Going Out with Him?" A&M 2132 (1979). That the new-wave songs were released as singles and the progressive songs were album tracks also betrays part of the aesthetic difference between these two styles: new-wave artists returned to the pop-single format of the 1960s, while progressive rockers had always tended to produce album tracks of extended duration.

13. For a detailed discussion of the punk-rock movement in Britain, see Dave Laing, *One-Chord Wonders: Power and Meaning in Rock* (Milton Keynes: Open University Press, 1985). Greil Marcus was among the first to write about punk rock from the American side; see his "Anarchy in the UK," in *The Rolling Stone Illustrated History*, 594–607.

14. Of course, this return to the use of earlier and in many ways less sophisticated musical instruments was accompanied by a return to mid-1960s fashions. Perhaps the most extreme instance of this is the return of the beehive hairstyle sported by Cindy Wilson and Kate Pierson of the new-wave B-52s. For a discussion of the new-wave movement, see Ken Tucker's "Alternative Scenes: America," and "Alternative Scenes: Britain," both in *The Rolling Stone Illustrated History*, 573–78 and 579–85.

15. A comparison of, say, Yes's *Going for the One* with the Cars' first album, *The Cars* (Elektra 6E-135 [1978]), reveals that the Cars album is at least as well recorded and produced as the Yes one. Interestingly, Roy Thomas Baker produced this Cars album and later briefly worked with Yes on an album project that was never finished owing to a temporary break-up of the band in 1980. See Hedges, *Yes*, 128.

16. Yes, "Owner of a Lonely Heart," Atco 99817 (1983). This single appears on Yes's *90125* (Atco 90125 [1983]), which was produced by Trevor Horn. Horn had joined Yes to replace vocalist Jon Anderson for Yes's *Drama* album (Atlantic 16019 [1980]), along with Geoff Downes, who replaced Rick Wakeman. Together and aside from Yes, Horn and Downes constituted the techno-pop band called The Buggles and recorded two albums: one before they joined Yes (*The Age of Plastic*, Island ILPS 9585 [1980]) and one after (*Adventures in Modern Recording*, Carrere PZ 37926 [1981]). The Buggles' video to their "Video Killed the Radio-Star" has the distinction of being the first video ever played on MTV. Needless to say, the addition of the techno-pop Buggles to the Yes line-up was seen as a drastic departure by many progressive-rock fans, though the *Drama* LP remains very much within the progressive-rock style. The Buggles subsequently rerecorded a track they had done with Yes, "Into the Lens," renaming it "I Am a Camera"; this second version appears on *Adventures in Modern Recording*, and a comparison of the two highlights the differences between the Buggles and Yes styles.

17. Asia, "Heat of the Moment," Geffen 50040 (1982), which also appears on the album *Asia*, Geffen 2008 (1982). The second Asia album, *Alpha* (Geffen 4008 [1983]), spent eleven weeks on the top forty album chart; the single from that album, "Don't Cry" (Geffen 29571 [1983]), rose as high as number ten on the singles charts.

18. The Mellotron is an instrument that employs a standard keyboard to control taped sounds; the standard sounds employed in the late '60s and '70s tended to be orchestral strings, choral voices, and recorders. As one presses down on each key, one actually triggers a tape of, for instance, orchestral violins playing that pitch. For a thorough description of the Mellotron, as well as all of the synthesizers that played such a crucial role in the music of the original progressive rockers, see Mark Vail, *Vintage Synthesizers: Groundbreaking Instruments and Pioneering Designers of Electronic Music Synthesizers* (San Francisco: Miller Freeman Books, 1993).

19. Marillion's "Kayleigh" (EMI Maril 3 [1985]) went to number two, while "Lavender" (EMI Maril 4 [1985]) rose as high as number five and "Incommunicado" (EMI Maril 4 [1987]) to number six. Their third album, *Misplaced Childhood* (EMI MRL 2 [1985]), reached

number one in the British album charts and remained in the top one hundred for forty-one weeks.

20. A short listing of some of the new progressive groups would include Anekdoten, Landberk, and Ånglagård (Sweden); White Willow (Norway); Devil Doll and Deus ex Machina (Italy); Happy Family (Japan); and Cairo, Magellan, and echolyn (U.S.). But even the most cursory glance through progressive-rock magazines such as *Progression, i/e,* or *Exposé*—or through the mail-order catalogs of the Laser's Edge (New Jersey), ZNR Records (Kentucky), or Syn-Phonic (California)—will reveal the tremendous number of currently active progressive-rock groups. Greg Walker's January 1996 Syn-Phonic catalog lists approximately 2,000 CDs by groups, both active and defunct, from thirty-five countries around the world.

21. It is difficult to assess the current size of the progressive-rock underground community, but it would seem that it is still small by the standards of the popular-music industry. Almost all of the new progressive groups record either for small independent labels or release their music themselves. One notable exception to this is the American group echolyn, whose recent *as the world* CD (Sony BK 57623 [1995]) was released by the corporate giant Sony.

22. An interesting development in the mid-1990s has been the return of some of the original principal groups to the progressive-rock style. ELP returned to the scene with their *Black Moon* CD (Victory 383 480 003–2 [1992]), featuring a characteristic reworking of music from Prokofiev's ballet *Romeo and Juliet.* King Crimson's recent CDs, *Vrooom* (Discipline Records 9401 2 [1994], *Thrak* (Virgin 7243 8 40312 2 9 [1995]), and *B'Boom: Official Bootleg—Live in Argentina 1994* (Discipline Records 9503 [1995]), in many ways constitute an unmistakable return to their early-1970s style. At current writing, reunion albums are being planned by Gentle Giant, UK, and Yes (featuring the 1970s group members).

23. Keith Emerson, liner notes to the Nice, *Five Bridges,* Mercury SR-61295 (1969).

24. Jon Anderson, "Yes Split to Stay Fresh" (interview), in *Manchester Evening News,* 7 Dec. 1973. In the recent Yes video documentary, *Yesyears: A Retrospective* (Atco Video 50250–3 [1991]), keyboardist Rick Wakeman also remarks that during the early to mid-1970s Yes attempted to construct its songs according to structural principles drawn from Western art music.

25. This quotation appears in Tamm, *Robert Fripp,* 30–31. These remarks originally appeared in Bill Milkowski, "Fripp: I Take My Iconic Role of Being Robert Fripp, Public Guitarist, Quite Seriously," *Guitar World* 5/5 (Sept. 1984): 28. After correspondence with Fripp, Tamm has edited these remarks slightly and Tamm's version is quoted here.

26. How these musicians came to form their ideas about what makes music "classical" is an interesting sociomusicological question that lies beyond scope of this chapter. Edward Macan deals with this issue in some detail in chap. 6 of his *Rockin' the Classics.*

27. See, for instance, Emerson, Lake, and Palmer's *Pictures at an Exhibition* (Cotillion 66666 [1971]), which is not only based on Mussorgsky's piece but includes "Nut Rocker," a version of the march from Tchaikovsky's ballet *The Nutcracker* as an encore. In this case, ELP is actually covering a version done by the American instrumental group B. Bumble and the Stingers; this earlier version (Top Rank JAR 611 [1962]) hit number one in the British charts in April 1962.

28. Yes, *Close to the Edge,* LP format: Atlantic 19133 (1972); original CD format: Atlantic SD 19133–2 (n.d.); digitally remastered on CD: Atlantic 82666–2 (n.d.). A different digital remastering can be found on the *Yesyears* retrospective box set (Atco 7 91644–2 [1991]). All of these are versions of the same studio recording. Live versions of "Close to the Edge" can be found on Yes, *Yessongs,* LP: Atlantic SD 3–100 (1973), CD: Atlantic 82682 (n.d.); Anderson, Bruford, Wakeman, and Howe, *An Evening of Yes Music Plus,* Caroline HER 006 (1994); and a wide variety of bootleg recordings. The two commercially released live versions can also be

found on the following videos, which correspond to the audio versions: *Yessongs*, VidAmerica 7033 (1984), and *An Evening of Yes Music Plus*, Griffin GVAB-108 (1994). An abridged arrangement of the piece for symphony orchestra can be found on *Symphonic Music of Yes*, RCA Victor 09026–61938–2 (1993).

29. Yes, *The Yes Album*, Atlantic 19131 (1971), and *Fragile*, Atlantic 19132 (1972).

30. Hedges, *Yes*, 68. Bruford left Yes to join King Crimson and was replaced by Alan White, who had played with numerous high-profile musicians—including John Lennon—in the period leading up to 1972.

31. On the original CD release, the lyrics, which had been printed on a green inner sleeve of the LP, were omitted, apparently a casualty of repackaging. The more recent digitally remastered version restores the lyrics, but not as they were packaged on the LP version.

32. Hedges, *Yes*, 68–69. Hedges quotes Howe to the effect that Howe's original song was "partially about the longest day of the year." Howe goes on to remark that "when you're writing for Yes, the whole integrity of holding on to things disappears. If the lick fits, you use it."

33. Timings are keyed to the studio version of "Close to the Edge" and will be given throughout as they occur on the original CD rerelease, which conforms to the newer digitally remastered version. To work from the digitally remixed version that is contained in the *Yesyears* box set, subtract 0:06 from each timing given.

34. The Coral electric sitar is an instrument manufactured by the Danelectro Company; it is tuned like a standard electric guitar, but a special bridge construction causes the instrument to produce a timbre somewhat like that of a sitar. See Tom Wheeler, *American Guitars: An Illustrated History*, rev. and updated ed. (New York: Harper Perennial, 1992), 16–21; for Steve Howe's discussion of this instrument, see his *The Steve Howe Guitar Collection* (San Francisco: GPI Books, 1993), 68–69.

35. See Robert Hatten, "The Place of Intertextuality in Music Studies," *American Journal of Semiotics* 3/4 (1985): 69–82, for a discussion of intertextuality in music. An extremely helpful survey of the uses of this term in literary criticism can be found in Thais E. Morgan, "Is There an Intertext in this Text? Literary and Interdisciplinary Approaches to Intertextuality," *American Journal of Semiotics* 3/4 (1985): 1–40. For applications of the concept of intertextuality to rock-music analysis, see my "Stylistic Competencies, Musical Humor, and 'This is Spinal Tap'" as well as "The Rutles and the Use of Specific Models in Musical Satire," *Indiana Theory Review* 11 (1990): 119–44. See also Philip Tagg, "Analyzing Popular Music: Theory, Method, and Practice," *Popular Music* 2 (1982): 37–67, which addresses this issue from a slightly different angle.

36. "Roundabout" and "South Side of the Sky" appear on *Fragile*; "Siberian Khatru" appears on *Close to the Edge*.

37. For a discussion of modes in rock music, see Moore, *Rock*, 47–50, as well as his "Patterns of Harmony," *Popular Music* 11/1 (1992): 73–106, and "The So-Called 'Flattened Seventh' in Rock," *Popular Music* 14/2 (1995): 185–201.

38. I am assuming a familiarity on the reader's part with the standard kinds of claims made by most twentieth-century music analysts about music in the "great German tradition"; clearly this literature is too vast for me to adequately reference here. For those less familiar with such claims, good introductions are provided by Nicholas Cook, *A Guide to Music Analysis* (New York: George Braziller, 1987), and Jonathan Dunsby and Arnold Whittall, *Music Analysis in Theory and Practice* (New Haven: Yale University Press, 1988).

39. For a discussion of typical formal elements in rock music, see Moore, *Rock*, 47–48.

40. For a discussion of standard form in popular songs, see Allen Forte, *The American Popular Ballad of the Golden Era, 1924–1950* (Princeton: Princeton Univrsity Press, 1995), 36–41, and Alec Wilder, *American Popular Song: The Great Innovators, 1900–1950*, ed. James T. Maher (Oxford: Oxford University Press, 1972), 56.

41. If one takes a D harmonic minor scale—D–E–F–G–A–B♭–C♯–D—and, without changing any of the notes, merely respells the scale beginning and ending with E instead of D, one arrives at the following scale: E–F–G–A–B♭–C♯–D–E.

42. For readers wary of the exotic E-minorish tonality I suggest here, it is also possible to interpret the music as emphasizing ii° in D minor. In either reading, a strong emphasis on pitch-class E reinforces the two-part design discussed in the passages that follow.

43. For commentary on *Siddhartha* and these themes as they occur in the novel, see Theodore Ziolkowski, *The Novels of Hermann Hesse: A Study in Theme and Structure* (Princeton: Princeton University Press, 1965), 146–77; Edwin F. Casebeer, *Hermann Hesse* (New York: Warner Books, 1972), 23–54; and Joseph Mileck, *Hermann Hesse: Life and Art* (Berkeley: University of California Press, 1978), 159–72. Casebeer's preface is especially interesting since it was written in 1972 (the same year "Close to the Edge" was released) and addresses the popularity of Hesse's work within the hippie counterculture.

44. According to Dan Hedges, Jon Anderson has remarked: "Sometimes I'd just use a series of tantalizingly sounding words, but sometimes I'd get deeper into meaning and statement . . . I've had incredible conversations and get letters from people telling me what they think my words are all about. Who knows? Maybe they're right." See Hedges, *Yes*, 51.

45. This passage is transcribed in Thomas J. Mosbø, *Yes, But What Does It Mean? Exploring the Music of Yes* (Miltin, Wisc.: Wyndstar, 1994), 48; Anderson makes these remarks in a recorded interview titled "Yes Music: An Evening with Jon Anderson," which was released in 1977 by Atlantic records for use by radio stations. Mosbø engages in careful and comprehensive interpretations of the lyric to dozens of Yes songs, and my interpretation of "Close to the Edge" differs from his in some aspects. He also provides an analytical listening guide to the piece, which, though it is not technically specific in the way that my figure 1.1 is, still constitutes a very helpful guide (especially for the nonmusician).

46. Hermann Hesse, *Siddhartha*, trans. Hilda Rosner (New York: Bantam, 1971), 88–89.

47. It is probably coincidental that the chromatically filled-in seconds in the three bridge sections, when taken together, constitute a filled-in fifth from D down to G. Still, one might argue that by taking only the bridge and B-section verses into consideration, the following systematic unfolding of materials takes place: filled-in second from A to G; another filled-in second from B to A, creating an overall filled-in major third from B to G in bridge passages; a filled-in fourth from E to B in the B-section verses; and a resumption of the bridge-passage expansion with the filled-in second from D to C, completing and overall filling the fifth D down to G across bridge sections.

48. In all of the live versions that I have been able to check, the group plays the bridge and chorus (from 16:33 forward on figure 1.1) one whole step lower than on the studio version; in live performance an extra measure is added to smooth out this key change. This is presumably done to reduce the strain on Anderson's voice during live performance of the song. Thought of in terms of the point I am making here about the structure, one might wonder why, if the key relationship between the opposite ends of the piece was so crucial, the group would opt for such a modulation; this would seem to undercut the pitch-specific focus of my analysis at this point. But one might just as easily wonder why this last section would have been recorded to end in F in the first place. It is certainly possible that ending in F was important to the group for structural reasons (and could be accomplished in the studio) but was impractical under the demands an almost nightly performance schedule.

49. The beginning of "Sound Chaser" (*Relayer*, Atlantic 19135 [1974]) is perhaps the most pronounced instance of jazz-rock, perhaps owing to the influence of keyboardist Patrick Moraz, who replaced Wakeman on this LP. "To Be Over" from this same LP features pedal-steel guitar playing by Steve Howe that is unmistakably derived from country and western styles. The ending of Yes's cover version of Paul Simon's "America" (Atlantic 45–2854

[1972]) is in a Latin-rock style. The recent box set *Yesyears* contains a Yes version of the Stephen Sondheim–Leonard Bernstein song "Something's Coming" (Broadway rock?); this tune was originally the B side of a 1969 UK single that featured "Sweetness" as the A side (Atlantic 584280).

50. Yes, *Tales From Topographic Oceans*, Atlantic 2–908 (1974). Yes's sixth release was the three-LP live collection *Yessongs* (Atlantic 100 [1973]).

51. See Chris Welch, "Yes—Over the Edge," *Melody Maker*, 1 Dec. 1973 (concert review of *Tales*). Another review that plays on the title of *Close to the Edge* in a review of *Tales* is Steve Peacock, "Yes—Close to Boredom," in *Sounds*, 1 Dec. 1973. Chris Welch continues his word-play in "Yes: Adrift on the Oceans," *Melody Maker*, 1 Dec. 1973 (album review of *Tales*).

52. In a 1974 interview, bassist Chris Squire discusses the composition of *Tales*, revealing that sides one and three of the LP are motivically related. See Peter Erskine, "Hello Squire: Interview by Peter Erskine," *Sounds*, 19 Jan. 1974.

53. Paramahansa Yogananda, *The Autobiography of a Yogi* (Los Angeles: Self Realization Fellowship, 1946). The obvious affinity between Hesse's novel and the brand of Hindu religious and mystical philosophy that permeates Paramahansa's book make it clear why Anderson would have been intrigued by it. There is a further connection between *Tales* and the Beatles' proto-progressive *Sgt. Pepper*: among the many faces appearing on the *Sgt. Pepper* album cover are those of Parmahansa, his guru Sri Yukteswar, and the mysterious Babaji.

54. For an interesting discussion of the kinds of conflicting pressures to which rock musicians are subject, especially with regard to what he refers to as a pop versus rock distinction, see Simon Frith, *Sound Effects: Youth, Leisure, and the Politics of Rock 'n' Roll* (New York: Pantheon, 1983), 61–88.

55. It is at least clear what direction four of the five members of Yes decided to take. Keyboardist Rick Wakeman left the group due to his own misgivings about the musical path the group was on. As mentioned above, Wakeman was replaced on *Relayer* by Swiss keyboardist Patrick Moraz.

56. See Josephson, "Bach Meets Liszt"; Macan, "'The Spirit of Albion'"; and Tamm, *Robert Fripp*.

2

After Sundown

The Beach Boys' Experimental Music

DANIEL HARRISON

Sometimes it happens in this crazy world that the cartoon becomes great art, the self-indulgent reveals generosity, the absurd comes to contain meaning, the silly shows profundity. Sometimes drinking songs end up as national anthems, young shepherds defeat giant warriors, and Hollywood personalities become leaders of the free world.

Sometimes raucous singing at an innocent party shows a keen artistic consciousness, and inscrutable, off-the-wall songs that fail as rock music succeed as chic, minimalist art music. Sometimes musicians who gain fame hymning to surfboards and hot rods, who record not in stereophonic splendor but in monophonic modesty—sometimes such a group succeeds in honing for a little while an edge that cuts open convention, prunes away proprieties, and clears the way for a music that both taps your foot and feeds your head.

1

Those who have only a top-forty acquaintance with the music of the Beach Boys might have smiled their way through the opening paragraphs of this piece. Surely, the Beach Boys as art rockers is a ridiculous proposition. Summertime is hardly the season of quiet contemplation, as the beach is conducive more to the sweating of erotic perfumes than to the cool meeting of minds. But one famous top-forty Beach Boys hit ought to give the reader pause: "Good Vibrations," widely acknowledged as one of rock music's greatest masterpieces, can hardly be dismissed as mindless beach fare. Indeed, its prominent images are not surf 'n' sun but sensory stimuli of near psychedelic intensity; the atmosphere is one not of roaring fun, but of deep yet seemingly improvised introspection. "Good Vibrations" clearly expresses another, far different sensibility from that of the Beach Boys' better-known top-forty hits. It is both so exotically different and yet recognizably within the Beach Boys' style that one cannot help but wonder about the existence of other like-minded works. What else happened when the surfboards were put up for the night?

Even from their inception the Beach Boys were an experimental group. They combined, as Jim Miller has put it, "the instrumental sleekness of the Ventures, the lyric sophistication of Chuck Berry, and the vocal expertise of some weird cross between the Lettermen and Frankie Lymon and the Teenagers" with lyrics whose images, idioms, and concerns were drawn from the rarefied world of the middle-class white male southern California teenager.[1] This choice of subject was itself a highly experimental act; instead of exploring typical adolescent topics as generally as possible—an artistic and marketing strategy that targets a wide audience—the Beach Boys refracted them through a very specific and, indeed, esoteric worldview. Full of the specialized slang of surfers and street racers, localized geographic and climatic references, and obsession with good times and fun, Beach Boys' songs proved highly attractive to teenagers across the world despite their apparent esotericism; being in on the ways of an elite and hip subculture as well as its thickly textured hedonism turned out to be a powerful engine for promoting escapism, fantasy, and frolic—prized commodities for any teenager.

While the unusual and, for a while, interesting combination of elements made the Beach Boys almost single-handedly responsible for a national surf-music fad in the early 1960s,[2] it was the profound vocal virtuosity of the group, coupled with the obsessional drive and compositional ambitions of their leader, Brian Wilson, that promised their survival after the eventual breaking of fad fever. On the first point, the original group of three brothers, a cousin, and a neighbor possessed a rare and wonderful vocal tightness. Comparison to other contemporary vocally oriented rock groups, such as the Association, shows the Beach Boys' technique to be far superior, almost embarrassingly so. They were so confident of their ability, and of Brian's skill as a producer to enhance it, that they were unafraid of doing sophisticated, a cappella glee-club arrangements containing multiple suspensions, passing formations, complex chords, and both chromatic and enharmonic modulations.[3] Some of these techniques are shown in example 2.1, an excerpt from Brian's arrangement of a Four Freshmen hit, "Their Hearts Were Full of Spring." The example gives the wispiest taste of the technical ability the Beach Boys had at their disposal; unable to be captured in the score is the sensitivity to blend and intonation that enabled the group to undertake such arrangements, as well as Brian's expert recording technique.[4]

Clearly, "Hearts" is not rock 'n' roll, so citing it can seem a bit disingenuous. Yet the point here is not that the Beach Boys made rock 'n' roll out of glee-club mater-

Example 2.1. Bobby Troup: "Their Hearts Were Full of Spring," arr. B. Wilson, mm. 1–8

ial, but that the harmonic resources and the compositional sophistication of that repertory (relative to the rock 'n' roll of the early 1960s) were available to them, and that they could bring these to their original works.

The easiest point of transfer for these sophisticated techniques was the ballad, generally identifiable by slow tempo in compound duple meter. The Beach Boys added their own stylistic signature to this common genre: a falsetto lead melody over both an unobtrusive instrumental accompaniment and a thick choral texture. "Surfer Girl," "In My Room," and "Warmth of the Sun" are perhaps the best-known exemplars of the Beach Boys' ballad style, and in each of these one finds at least one harmonic or formal twist not native to rock 'n' roll. Example 2.2, for instance, which illustrates the harmonic and rhythmic structure of "Warmth of the Sun," shows a self-consciously intrepid root motion by tritone from vi to ♭III. The problems in carrying off such a remote chord change are mitigated by the larger-scale modal mixture. As the analysis shows, the tritone motion marks the entry point of minor mode; major returns subtly upon the entrance of ii⁷ and more firmly upon the resolution of the augmented-minor seventh chord at the end of the first ending. Later in the song, VI is revisited—this time as a key—and again participates in modal mixture; the refrain begins upon a tonicized VI♯ (A major) and then slips into its natural version before progressing to G major as V of C. Needless to say, the voice leading carrying out these chord changes is clean and classically correct.

"Warmth of the Sun," as well as the other ballads, shows its stylistic and genre origins most clearly. But even the least distinguished of the Beach Boys' early up-tempo rock 'n' roll songs show traces of structural complexity at some level; Brian was simply too curious and experimental to leave convention alone. Consider in this regard example 2.3, which shows the harmonic structure of an otherwise ephemeral

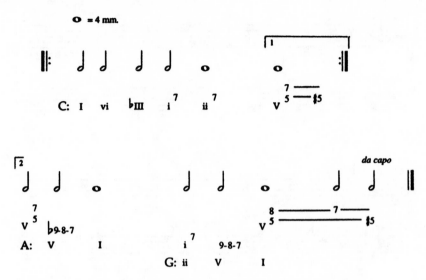

Example 2.2. "Warmth of the Sun," comp. B. Wilson. Harmonic analysis

surf-music work, "Don't Back Down." Of interest here is obviously not the harmonic structure of the individual structural components, which is quite conventional, but the large-scale modulatory plan that takes the A-major verses into B♭-major refrains and back again. Though half-step key relationships are common in rock 'n' roll—they afford a dramatic and expressive use of tonality, as well as a minimal change in range for the vocally untrained lead singer—the manner in which the Beach Boys carried out this key change is quite complex. The analysis shows a chromatic modulation that depends upon modal mixture: an F-major chord as ♭VI of A major pivots to become V of B♭, a shift marked with an asterisk in the example. The dramatic effect of the F-major pivot chord is strengthened by its unexpected shortness: it lasts only a measure, while previous harmonies filled out at least two measures. The new B♭ tonic thus rushes in a full measure sooner than expected based on the preceding hypermetrical structure of the verse. The return to A major is handled in a different, though equally interesting way. Example 2.4 shows a transcription of the last three measures of the refrain, which then connect to the opening of the verse. The refusal of I in favor of IV in measure 2 is followed by a passing

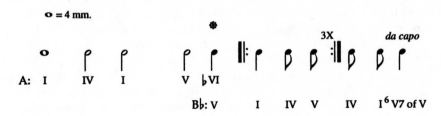

Example 2.3. "Don't Back Down," comp. B. Wilson. Harmonic analysis

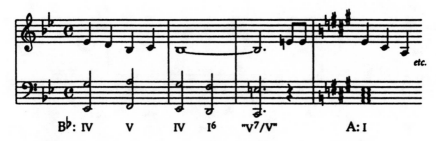

Example 2.4. "Don't Back Down," transcription of mm. 5–8 of refrain

motion that reaches a major-minor seventh over C in measure 3. (Temptingly ana-
lyzable as V⁷ of V in B♭, it is rather a passing chord whose ultimate goal is—or
rather should be—I in B♭.) Yet this unstable chord serves as the tentative conclusion
of the refrain. The E appearing on the fourth beat, far from harmonizing nicely with
the C-major-minor seventh, introduces itself as $\hat{5}$ in A, thus effecting a common-
tone modulation back to A. Again, as in the movement into B♭, a rhythmic irregu-
larity highlights the modulation; in this case, odd-even measure alternation of one
and two harmonies per bar (clearly seen in ex. 2.3) is broken, so that measure 2 of
the example (which is the seventh measure of the refrain) receives two harmonies,
the following measure, only one.[5]

The Beach Boys' initial commercial success gave Brian the prestige, resources,
and courage to carry out further stylistic experiments. The motivation for these
is complex. Certainly much must be attributed to Brian's innate musical curiosity.
But also at work here is the inherent stylistic constriction that created such narrow
genres as "surf" and "hot-rod" music. If they were to be anything more than a musical nine-days'-wonder, the Beach Boys had to find ways to broaden the range of
their lyrics, the structure of their songs, and the texture of their vocal and instrumental sounds.[6]

Glimmerings of change can be heard in the two 1965 albums, *The Beach Boys
Today!* and *Summer Days (and Summer Nights!!).*[7] The ballads and slower numbers
contain more complex lyrical expressions than before, treating such "un-fun" topics
as the loss of youthful innocence ("When I Grow Up") and emotional vulnerability
("She Knows Me Too Well"). But harmonic and formal innovations in these songs
are just as notable. In light of subsequent developments, one of the most interesting
technical experiments involves quick-changing, unpredictable, yet logical harmonic
relationships to access remote keys, thereby giving an illusion of a formal expanse
larger than the eight or so measures that actually contain it. The most famous example is the refrain of "California Girls," transcribed in example 2.5. Although on
paper it is easy enough to see that the structure is "logically" governed by a descending sequence, the effect in sound of this sequence is quite remarkable, largely
because arrivals at the third and fifth measures are so extraordinarily striking and
affecting. In fact, these moments are so arresting, so harmonically unusual, so unexpectedly expansive, that one is drawn away from hearing the passage as one would
normally listen for sequence—that is, as model and imitations in measures 1–2,

Example 2.5. "California Girls," harmonic structure of refrain

3–4, and 5–6—and is drawn instead to the connections between these units—to measures 2–3, 4–5, and 6–7. It is at these points where the expectations of the I–ii⁷ progression of the model (i.e., I–ii⁷ . . . V!) are thwarted and where harmonic structure seems to push apart the formal unit.[8] Though the refrain is actually no longer than expected given the hypermetrical behavior of the rest of the song, it gives the impression of being something larger. The harmonic innovations of the refrain simply reverberate far longer than the more prosaic progression of the verses.

The album that all but announced the renunciation of their early work was *Pet Sounds* (1966).[9] Even the title, in comparison with that of their previous album, *Summer Days (and Summer Nights!!)*, demonstrates a curious detachment from their usual themes.[10] The most obvious stylistic difference is the nature of the lyrics. Not a single reference to surfing or hotrodding appears in any song; instead, the album works out in song-cycle fashion a complex treatment of love and loneliness, moving between these two with an attitude that itself alternates between naive fantasy and budding cynicism. Though the subject matter is considerably removed from their earlier topics, the use of current and faddish idiom in the lyrics is familiar. This time, however, the specialized language of beach and garage is replaced by that of the nascent California counterculture of the 1960s, spiced with some leftover beatnik lingo.

Accompanying this change in the style of the lyrics is a broadening of the musical palette. Taking a cue from Phil Spector, Brian explored all manner of unusual instrumental combinations and percussion instruments.[11] "Caroline No," for example, seems to use harpsichord, guiero, alto flute, electric bass, and—outrageously—an empty and overturned plastic water jug as percussion instrument.[12] The showcasing of these unusual combinations was done at the expense of the traditional two-guitar, bass, and drum-set arrangement. The close vocal harmonies, however, the Beach Boys' central expressive vehicle, are still prominent, and they now find more congenial and expansive surroundings among the ambitious lyrical and accompanimental styles.

Pet Sounds was a showcase for a new style of lyrics and instrumentation. In terms of the structure of the songs themselves, there is comparatively little advance from what Brian had already accomplished or shown himself capable of accomplishing. Most of the songs use unusual harmonic progressions and unexpected disruptions of hypermeter, both features that were met in "Warmth of the Sun" and "Don't Back Down."

One of the songs on the album, however, does have a remarkable formal characteristic that can best be appreciated in light of the technique of "California Girls." "God Only Knows," because of its avoidance of root-position tonic and lack of cadential drive, seems the ultimate expression of the form-expanding illusions that Brian created in "California Girls." Example 2.6a presents the harmonic structure of the verse and refrain using figured-bass symbols and some rough realizations of the chords. A number of features of this structure are remarkable. First, note the extraordinarily weak versions of tonic favored in the progression. Ostensibly set in E major, there is not a single root-position E-major triad, the $\frac{6}{4}$ position being the privileged tonic form. (See the neighbor motion at chords five through seven that prolongs I $\frac{6}{4}$ in E.) Second—and working in tandem with the avoidance of E major in root position—the highly chromatic nature of the progression militates against the influence of E tonic and seems to leave the progression without any tonic support. The D-major $\frac{6}{4}$ that opens the verse signals the overall weakness of E tonic, and this signal is boosted at the following chord, a B-minor triad that in no way is heard as V of E. Finally, in the absence of a strong E tonic, A major seems to fill the vacuum at the tonal center, since it is the chord that begins the refrain, and since it receives a strong tonic charge upon the resolution of the chord preceding the refrain.[13] In addition, the opening chords of the verse, while nondiatonic to the nominative E-major tonic, *are* diatonic to A.[14]

The competition between E and A for tonic control is made clear during the break between verse 2 and the recapitulation of verse 1 lyrics. A bass-line sketch of the later portion of that section appears in example 2.6b, along with some analysis of phrase-joining technique. During the second half of the break, the harmonic progression of the verse is interpolated but transposed to the key of A; the asterisks in both examples 2.6a and 2.6b show this correspondence. During this interpolation, no words are sung, and the singers are involved in complicated contrapuntal play over the progression—in other words, the allusion to the harmonic structure of the verse is made subtle both by the transposition and by different melodic activity. Only when the music of the now A-major refrain is encountered do the voices return to their familiar words. Yet, at the end of the first sentence of the refrain, the progression elides with wonderful smoothness into the beginning of the E-major verse. The A-major refrain seems shunted aside as the E-major verse inserts itself into the musical flow, an impression conveyed visually by the phrase markings above example 2.6b. There is no moment in rock music more harmonically and formally subtle than this transition. It is the apex of Brian Wilson's first period of formal experimentation.

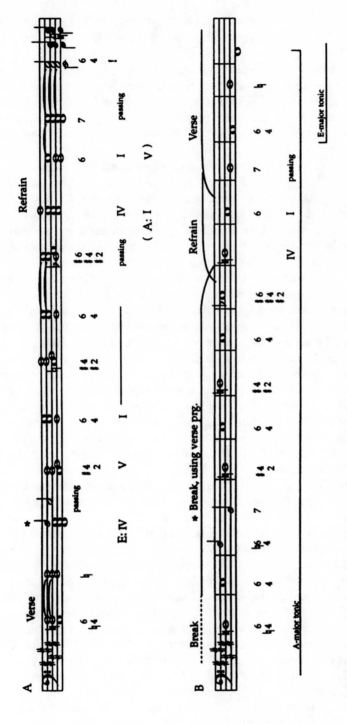

Example 2.6. Some aspects of harmonic structure in "God Only Knows"

Two significant and complementary projects were undertaken around the time of *Pet Sounds*, though to call the album *Beach Boys Party!* a project is perhaps a misnomer, and many critics might quibble with the label "significant."[15] Made in response to record-company demands for new material, *Party* was an exercise in minimalistic production that was ostensibly recorded during a party at bandmate Mike Love's house. (Recording-studio logs indicate otherwise.) The performances seem unrehearsed, the instrumental support is minimal (acoustical guitar, bongo drums, tambourine), and fooling around (laughing, affected singing, background conversation) pervades every track. Compositionally, the album is a compilation of fun-to-sing music composed mostly by others.[16] The significance of *Party* is twofold. First, the seeming inattention to production niceties, the extraordinarily thin instrumentation, and the loose, relaxed ensemble would all be incorporated into the albums of the very experimental and noncommercial period from 1967 to 1970. Here, they appear in fun; later, they accompany more complex expressions.

Second, while the Beach Boys give other groups' material bona fide performances—even if the general performance atmosphere is hardly reverent—the two songs of their own are given savagely satirical treatments. "I Get Around," for example, is given new lyrics appropriate for singing by a social maladroit ("doofus" is the term that comes to mind), not by the cool persona who throws off the original lyrics.[17] A comparison of the two can offer only the barest hint at the change in tone:

Original lyrics	Lyrics on Party
I'm gettin' bugged drivin' up and down the same old strip. I gotta find a new place where the kids are hip.	I'm getting awfully mad, driving down the street. I just don't want to be bugged, sitting next to my sweets.
My buddies and me are gettin' real well known. Yeah, the bad guys know us and they leave us alone.	The other guys are pretty tough so those other cats over there, better not get rough.
We always take my car 'cause it's never been beat, and we've never missed yet with the girls we meet.	We always take my car although it's a heap, and we never get turned down by the chicks we pick up on the street.

While hilarious, the biting-the-hand-that-feeds-you treatment of their own work presages a more coordinated rejection of their early work that occurred after "Good Vibrations."

2

And it is to "Good Vibrations"—the second project of the period—that we now turn, for it represents the most successful intersection of the Beach Boys' commercial appeal with Brian's artistic ambitions.[18] The trajectory suggested by *Pet Sounds* clearly is followed upon here, in that the instrumentation, lyrics, and general atmosphere are markedly different from those in the earlier music. (This, of course, is also the case with *Party*, but for different reasons.)

"Good Vibrations" represents a significant change with respect to *Pet Sounds* in the treatment of form. Whereas in "God Only Knows," for example, Brian attempted a seamless if repetitive form by suppressing both tonic strength and cadential drive, in "Good Vibrations" he creates the opposite—a highly articulated and contrastive march of formal units that simply breaks apart the traditional verse-and-refrain format of rock 'n' roll. The formal techniques of "California Girls" and "God Only Knows" simply were not dramatic enough to accommodate the type of expression Brian had in mind. This change in formal structure is linked directly to a new compositional technique that Brian began using during *Pet Sounds*. Beach Boys commentator David Leaf writes:

> Beginning with *Pet Sounds*, Brian's recording methods changed considerably from his past work. Rather than going into the studio with a completed song, Brian was writing music in the manner of an impressionistic painter. Brian, according to [Tony] Asher [principal lyricist for *Pet Sounds*], "used to go in and record [instrumental] tracks. We didn't know what they were going to be. They didn't even have melodies. They would just be a series of chord changes that Brian liked, with some weird or not-so-weird instruments. Then, we would bring these back [to the house] and play them and kind of write a melody to them and then write some lyrics."[19]

Brian himself explained the process this way: "I had a lot of unfinished ideas, fragments of music I called 'feels.' Each feel represented a mood or an emotion I'd felt, and I planned to fit them together like a mosaic."[20] "Good Vibrations" was the first piece where this mosaic effect was felt most strongly, since six different—and mostly disparate—"feels" are assembled. Example 2.7 shows these through an overview of the formal, harmonic, and metrical structure of the song.

"Good Vibrations" begins without introduction[21] in a traditional verse and refrain format, though the harmonic relationship between the two is more sophisticated than normal; the verses are set in Eb minor, while the refrain begins in the relative major, Gb. Yet the relationship is even more complex: the verse emphasizes descending harmonic motion through scale degrees still controlled by a single tonic, while the refrain marches upward through scale degrees heard as individual keys. Differences in metrical structure highlight this opposition, since the verse has a regular one-harmony-per-measure harmonic rhythm, while the refrain is more expansive, starting with a four-measure harmony followed by two-measure groups. Already, we can sense in this complicated relationship between such stock formal players as verse and refrain the mosaic effect to which Brian alluded earlier.

The verse and refrain form goes through two cycles before it is broken by the appearance of episode 1. This section begins disjunctively, in that the Bb harmony concluding the refrain, which, in the context of the verse, had acquired a dominant charge, is now maintained as a tonic. Over the course of the next ten measures (6 + 2 + 2)—unexpectedly long in light of previous patterns—the upper and lower dominants are visited and prolong Bb as the local tonic (or can one still detect the lingering dominant charge from the end of the refrain? The ambiguity here is exquisite). Bb is rudely abandoned, however, when a new, pianissimo "feel" is spliced in to

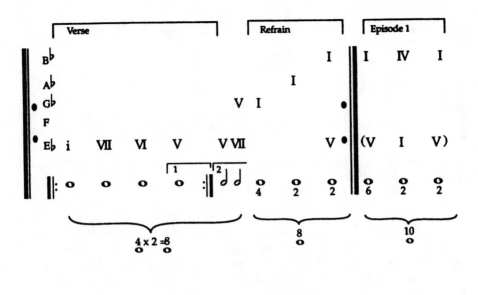

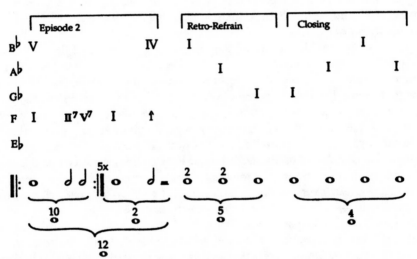

Example 2.7. Formal and harmonic structure of "Good Vibrations"

become episode 2, set in the key of F.[22] At this point, it is clear that "Good Vibrations" is not developing along the lines of any predictable formal pattern. The radical disjunctions in key, texture, instrumentation, and mood between episodes 1 and 2 are astounding and arresting. The appearance of episode 1 was unusual enough but could be explained as an extended break between verse and refrain sections. Episode 2, however, makes that interpretation untenable, and both listener and analyst must entertain the idea that "Good Vibrations" develops under its own power, as it were, without the guidance of overdetermined formal patterns. Brian's own description of the song—a three-and-a-half-minute "pocket symphony"—is a telling clue about his formal ambitions here.

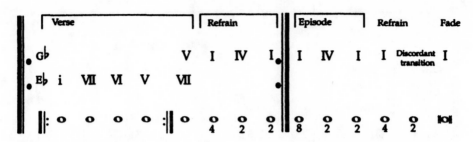

Example 2.8. Formal and harmonic structure of early version of "Good Vibrations," released on Capitol CDP 7 93696 2

The structure of the song is rounded off by the reappearance of the refrain music, though, as example 2.7 shows, it marches through its transpositional structure in retrograde, beginning in B♭ and concluding in an unexpectedly short, one-measure G♭ presentation. There follows a short section of vocalizing in three-part counterpoint. The transpositional structure of this section artfully refers both to the original refrain, in that it reproduces upward transposition, and to the retrograde version just heard, as it falls back one step from the B♭ apex to settle upon A♭, the concluding key of the song.

"Good Vibrations" luxuriates in harmonic variety, exemplified by the fact that the song begins and ends not only in different keys but also in different modes. Further, all seven scale degrees of the opening E♭-minor tonic are activated on some level in the song. The verse, for example, is structured by the time-honored ground-bass tetrachord, a descent from $\hat{8}$ to $\hat{5}$ in minor, while the refrain marches upward from $\hat{3}$ to $\hat{5}$. The only scale degree of the opening E♭-minor key not activated in the verse and refrain, $\hat{2}$, receives twelve measures worth of emphasis in episode 2.

In light of Brian's compositional technique of assembling various feels as if creating a mosaic, it is instructive to compare the released version of "Good Vibrations" with an early, rough version that Brian assembled and that was released only on a recent Capitol Records CD.[23] The formal structure of the rough version is mapped in example 2.8. One can see immediately that both the harmonic variety and the formal innovation marking the released version are severely attenuated here. The harmonic structure of the verse is the same as in the released version, as is the modulation to the relative major at the start of the refrain.[24] The refrain itself, however, has quite a different harmonic structure, essentially the one used in episode 1. (The metric structure, 4 + 2 + 2, is the same.) Because no transpositional ascent to B♭ occurs in this refrain, the connection back to the verse lacks the sureness found in the released version, where E♭ minor, the key of the verse, is easily be reached by descending-fifth motion from the B♭ apex.

In addition to the differences in the treatment of verse and refrain, the rough version is considerably more conventional in formal treatment after the end of the verse-and-refrain cycle. Though the basic outlines of episode 1 are present in the rough version, the episode is orchestrated differently (a Jew's harp is quite prominent here but is missing in the released version) and is also set in G♭, which contributes to the general harmonic stasis inaugurated in the refrain. The episode is followed by a truncated reprise of the refrain music, which thus makes the episode more of a traditional break than a true episode. We get a glimmering that Brian is interested in episodic effects when the reprised refrain is interrupted by two measures of discordant break—essentially a sudden shift into three different keys by three different parts. This break then gives way to the refrain again and is followed by a long fade. Since the break is neither long enough nor integrated well with the rest of the song, it is unable to function as a true episode, and the rough version of "Good Vibrations" thus seems more a funky rhythm-and-blues number than a pocket symphony.[25]

Good Vibrations" was phenomenally successful and placed the Beach Boys next to the Beatles in popularity among listeners and leadership among peers. But the cost, in both monetary and spiritual resources, was enormous. Brian himself estimates that the song cost "somewhere between $50,000 and $75,000" to produce, which he points out was "then an unheard amount for one song."[26] More significantly, Brian's obsession with outdoing previous achievements now could only enter an extremely dangerous phase, as topping what many esteem one of rock music's greatest compositional achievements became his next goal.

The sad story of what happened after "Good Vibrations" is well known: *Smile*, the album that the group worked on after "Good Vibrations" (and the first album since *Pet Sounds*), died aborning after months of intense and contentious labor. Brian simply could not motivate the group for the project, which contained very experimental—and hence commercially dangerous—material.[27] First, lyricist Van Dyke Parks abandoned the project after Mike Love expressed frustration at the inscrutable lyrics Parks was penning for the project. Then Brian, left without a lyricist and with too many songs not yet assembled, gave up work, thoroughly discouraged. The final tooth knocked out from *Smile* was the appearance of the Beatles' *Sgt. Pepper's Lonely Hearts Club Band*, an achievement that Brian believed (rightly or wrongly) he could not surpass.[28] The demise of *Smile* marked the beginning of a fifteen-year emotional collapse for Brian.

Considering just the compositional problems involved in the *Smile* project—without, of course, downplaying the complex psychological issues at work—it becomes clear that Brian had too many individual feels to keep track of, and that, moreover, finding the right fit for the appropriate pieces was too difficult. David Anderle, the chief executive of the Beach Boys' recording company, Brother Records, describes Brian's compositional process during *Smile*: "He was always interchanging parts. 'Cause at one point, he'd say 'OK. This is "Surf's Up" or this is "Bicycle Rider" or "Vegetables".' And then a night or two later, maybe the first verse and chorus of what had been 'Bicycle Rider' was all of a sudden the second verse of something else. It was continually changing at that point. A lot of those titles were at that point really just the tracks without the lyrics put on. That's why it was so easy to interchange."[29]

The differences between the released and rough versions of "Good Vibrations" discussed above give some clue about the nature of the problems. But an even more telling demonstration involves the one song that Brian did manage to pull together after "Good Vibrations": "Heroes and Villains."[30] All the feels for this song had been gathered by January 1967, and for the next few months Brian assembled various versions of the song, some of which are fully mixed and ready for release. One of these was included on the same Capitol Records CD that contains the rough version of "Good Vibrations." Though the alternate version of "Heroes and Villains" maintains the harmonic structure of the verse and has a few other feels in common with the released version, it is quite a different song. The alternate version lacks a refrain but has two lengthy sections (episodes) not found in the released version. These endow the alternate version with a formal structure more like that of "Good Vibrations" than that found in the released version and make the alternate version of "Heroes and Villains" a more compelling song than the actual release. Interestingly, Brian mixed versions of "Heroes and Villains" even more lengthy and complex than the alternate, one of which is reputedly twelve minutes long. That there were apparently at least three complete and ready-to-release versions of the same song gives some indication of the hesitation Brian must have felt in his compositional process. As a gauge of how thorny the problem must have been for Brian, consider what Beethoven might have done had he composed the three *Leonore* overtures at the same time instead of separately and with the benefit of having judged their effectiveness in public performance; which one would he have released first?

Despite the demise of *Smile* and Brian's catastrophic loss of competitive nerve, the Beach Boys were still obligated to Capitol Records for more albums. The album released instead of *Smile*, titled *Smiley Smile*, was similar in name only to the abandoned project. In all other respects, it was a completely different undertaking, which Carl Wilson pithily described as a "bunt instead of a grand slam." The depth of production that marked "Good Vibrations," as well as *Pet Sounds* and "Heroes and Villains," is missing in *Smiley Smile*; in its place is a deliberately understated and loose-limbed production style reminiscent of *Party*. It seems that, in the throes of discouragement, this was the only this kind of production effort Brian could manage. Or, perhaps more accurately, it was the only one the Beach Boys themselves could manage; the production of *Smiley Smile* is credited to the entire group, not to Brian alone—the first album in which Brian is not credited as the sole producer since *Surfin' U.S.A.*[31] This change in production regime gives eloquent testimony to Brian's abdication from the leadership position in the group.

Musically, *Smiley Smile* is a mixed bag. Two songs assembled under the previous production regime, "Good Vibrations" and "Heroes and Villains," are included, and these contrast markedly with the remaining nine songs, which are all at least a minute shorter than these two and considerably less dense in instrumentation and texture. Some of these nine were new compositions for *Smiley Smile* and thus were not part of *Smile*, but others (such as "Vegetables") incorporated some *Smile* feels among newly recorded material.

At heart, the artistic problem of *Smiley Smile* is one of mixing a compositional technique designed for one production style—that of "Good Vibrations"—with the very different style of *Party*. In other words, while the complex overdubbings and mixings that gave "Good Vibrations" a supremely rich texture are missing in *Smiley Smile*, the unusual harmonic and formal devices showcased in that song, as well its subtle and arch lyrics, were retained. Without the slick production, however, these techniques made for songs that seemed arid and obscure to most listeners. *Smiley Smile* sold poorly and reached only forty-first position on *Billboard*'s charts.[32]

What was a listener to do, for example, with a song like "Whistle In"? Lasting for only a minute and six seconds, it consists solely of a repeated harmonic progression, I–V/V–V, supporting the words, "Remember the day, remember the night; all day long (whistle in)." There is a lead singer and a softer background singer (who only sings the "whistle in" line); three other background voices enunciate words from the lyrics; and the whole is supported instrumentally by a very soft honky-tonk piano and somewhat louder bass guitar.[33]

What about "Fall Breaks and Back to Winter (W. Woodpecker Symphony)," which is just as enigmatic as "Whistle In"? Formally, it consists of two alternating units, one an unstable vamp over a V^9 of F and the other based on a stable and static F-major chord. The voices merely vocalize without lyrics, and the instrumentation seems to be two harmonicas, Hammond organ, electronic bass, wood blocks, wind chimes, tubular bell, one bass voice—lowered to an indeterminate pitch in the production stage—singing an occasional "wop," and two voices singing "ooh." The subtitle is obviously a reference to a harmonica lick in the stable F-major section, which sounds like the laugh of the cartoon character.

While these two songs are the oddest on the album in terms of style and structure, they have worn well over the years and can be profitably thought of as a kind of protominimal rock music. The lack of formal or harmonic development makes the listener focus upon other qualities such as instrumentation, timbre, and reverberation. A concentrated listening effort thus goes quickly to subtle details. Other songs, while not so weird, invite the same listening sensibility. "With Me Tonight," for example, begins with a repetitive a cappella feel structured by a I–IV–I progression. This introduction gives way to verse material, but not before it seems to be allowed to go on for longer than it should. That is, a voice from the control room saying "good" (as in "good take") is clearly heard over the studio speakers after the singers finish the first part of the introduction. While one might think that this is an editing mistake, it turns out that the control-room voice comes in exactly one beat after the singers conclude, and that it is delivered with a vocal richness that is itself musical and interesting. Moreover, since the song moves along in sixteen-measure units, and since the "Good" falls on beat four of measure 12, the seemingly out-of-place control-room voice actually provides a crucial formal link to the final four measures of the introduction. That is, the control-room voice—by accident or design—is truly part of the song and acts as a punctuation point in the form. It does not seem intrusive at all. In fact, it was only after many hearings that I understood what the voice was saying and thereby discovered the origin of this punctuation point; I had long assumed that it was produced in the studio as an original part of the feel.

One of the most interesting compositions on *Smiley Smile* is "Wonderful," a song that shows traces of work done during the *Smile* project (Van Dyke Parks is cocredited as lyricist). Some aspects of structure are shown in example 2.9a. In a basic sense, the song is set in a typical Beach Boys fashion: a series of opening verses followed by a break and concluding with a final verse. In "Wonderful," however, this conventional form goes unrecognized. Two very short and seemingly unrelated sections break up the flow of the form, obscuring the relationship among parts. Also,

[A]

A	A'	A				B	A	
Verse 1	Verse 2	Verse 3	Discordant transition	Codetta	(laughing)	Verse 4	Codetta
F C	F C	F C		A♭	E♭ D♭	F C	A♭
7 mm.	8 mm.	7 mm.	1 m.	1 m.	9 mm.	7 mm.	1 m.

[B]

Example 2.9. Formal, melodic, and harmonic structures in "Wonderful"

the middle section ("break") is quite episodic, being set in a different key and tempo. Finally, texture, instrumentation, and harmonic structure are all so absorbing that little attention is left to give to form. The foreground impression, thus, is that "Wonderful" is as formally diverse as "Good Vibrations."

Consider the melody of the verse, shown in example 2.9b. A more difficult, crabbed, tonally vague, and unfocused tune in the repertory of pop music is hard to imagine. That it is sung almost in a whisper (with a decrescendo into an actual whisper in the fourth verse) only adds to its fascination; the understated virtuosity here is nigh overwhelming. Its instrumental support is a pianissimo Hammond organ joined by a honky-tonk piano in the second verse, a somewhat louder electronic bass, and an off-key harmonica so soft that it seems to be the result of tape bleedthrough.[34] Yet this off-key (and off-meter as well) harmonica becomes the focus of attention during the "discordant transition" (see example 2.9a) as it grates uncomfortably against the organ, which is finishing off its material from the verse.

The middle section, as was already mentioned, is set in a different key and tempo. But it is also set in a different style and manner. It has no lyrics and consists only of doo-wop syllables supported by honky-tonk piano and set against a backdrop of group laughter and animated conversation, something introduced in a more light-hearted vein in *Party*. In "Wonderful," however, the technique is more self-conscious and arty. For example, the background has two levels of organization (if it can be called that). Undergirding the whole is a *Party*-like chatter whose conversational contents are indecipherable. Layered on top of the chatter are voices whose words can occasionally be understood.[35] One voice in particular seems loosely coordinated with harmony and rhythm, so that its squeals and giggles subtly alight upon chord members. Thus, in this section "Wonderful" affects the looseness of *Party* but is really just as controlled as the rest of the song.

As the preceding discussion has clearly suggested, *Smiley Smile* is not a work of rock music—at least as rock music was understood in 1967. Listening with ears that have heard other music besides rock, one cannot help but be struck by a self-conscious break with tradition, by the attempt to cut away convention and to explore new—and difficult to understand—musical territory. In this light, *Smiley Smile* can almost be considered a work of art music in the Western classical tradition, and its innovations in the musical language of rock can be compared to those that introduced atonal and other nontraditional techniques into that classical tradition. The spirit of experimentation is just as palpable in *Smiley Smile* as it is in, say, Schoenberg's op. 11 piano pieces.

Yet there is also a spirit of tentativeness in *Smiley Smile*. We must remember that it was essentially a Plan B—that is, the album issued instead of *Smile*. Had Brian been able to finish work on *Smile*, there would have surely been the same confidence in innovation and technique that marks "Good Vibrations," "Heroes and Villains," and other works begun during the *Smile* project. Another source of tentativeness no doubt was the anticipation that both Capitol Records and, later, the buying public would at least be baffled, at most irritated by *Smiley Smile*. The marketplace exerts tremendous force on an art so dependent upon expensive technology as rock music. Whereas a Schoenberg could have notated his compositions cheaply on paper and waited for sympathetic performers to play them, Brian Wilson composed in a recording studio that charged by the hour, employed professional musicians, and required the services of a record company to mass produce and distribute his work. Commercial failure simply cannot be tolerated in this regime, and a work like *Smiley Smile* has no place in it. Schoenberg could persevere in writing music according to his muse; the Beach Boys, after *Smiley Smile*, could not.[36]

To some extent, this situation explains why most of the albums after *Smiley Smile* gradually back away from its artistic implications, a retreat that corresponds exactly to Brian's progressive retirement from the group and into deep mental illness. Indeed, within a few months after *Smiley Smile* was released, the Beach Boys released another album, *Wild Honey*, which was considerably less experimental than both *Smiley Smile* and—significantly—"Good Vibrations." *Wild Honey* was a self-conscious attempt by the Beach Boys to regroup as a rock 'n' roll band and to reject the mantle of recording-studio auteurs that Brian had made them wear. Without

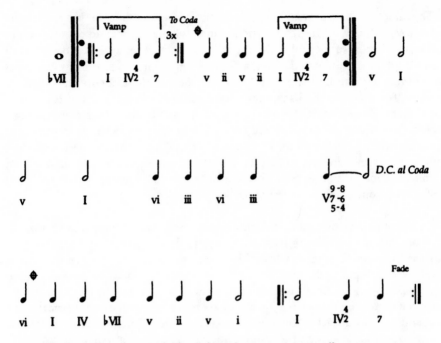

Example 2.10. "Let the Wind Blow," formal structure. N.B. All upper-case roman numerals denote major-minor seventh chords over the scale degree in question; lower-case roman numerals denote minor-minor seventh chords

Brian's drive, of course, they could no longer be those auteurs, hence *Wild Honey*. Carl Wilson again: "*Wild Honey* was music for Brian to cool out by."[37]

None of the music on *Wild Honey* has any of the enigmatic weirdness of "Whistle In" or "Fall Breaks and Back to Winter." The album also has no virtuosic mesmerizer like "Wonderful" or "Wind Chimes." Generally, the songs are neither harmonically nor formally adventurous, and they come across as simple, fun-to-sing, and unambitious rhythm and blues—a far different impression than that left by *Smiley Smile*. But the production regime is the same as in *Smiley Smile*: the instrumentation is spare and unusual (organ, honky-tonk piano, and electronic bass seem again to be the instrumental core), complex overdubbings are eschewed, and the overall density of sound is lower than that in the pre–*Smiley Smile* era.[38] In *Wild Honey*, this simple production style seems suited to the simple music.

"Let the Wind Blow" is the most arresting and compositionally assured song on the album, and it echoes the formal and harmonic technique of "God Only Knows." Example 2.10 displays a formal diagram of the song along with some notations about harmonic structure. The A section has an unusual twenty-measure rhythmic structure broken up into $(4 \times 3) + 4 + 4$, where the last four-measure unit contains the same vamp material as the four-measure units in the (4×3) segment. The listener is thus confused about whether measure 17 marks the beginning of the A-section repeat or not. There being no harmonic seam between the actual end of the section at measure 20 and the return to measure 1, the listener cannot detect that the four-measure *concluding* segment is not, in fact, part of the *opening* segment. At the second run-through of the A section, this confusion is heightened because the concluding segment does not connect to the opening but continues into the B section, giving the impression of a sudden attenuation of a formal unit after only one measure.

Looking at the song as a whole, it becomes clear that the reappearance of the vamp is always a somewhat surprising event. For example, while the twenty-measure A section is comprised of consistent four-measure units (it is their disposition that is surprising), the B section lasts for only fifteen measures, a three-measure unit at its conclusion being responsible for the odd hypermetric structure. Thus, the A' section and its vamp come in one measure too early, assuming that sixteen measures is the expected, normal length of the B section. A similar surprise occurs at the end of the A' section, where an extra measure of concluding A-minor harmony disrupts the hypermeter, this time making the vamp come in a measure too late. Moreover, there is no palpable harmonic connection at this point; a subtle change of mode alone signals the return of the vamp.

One commentator has considered the 1968 album *Friends*[39] to be "a return to *Smiley*'s dryness, minus the weirdness."[40] The opening song, "Meant for You," certainly corroborates this impression. All of forty-one seconds, the song functions as an overture to the album, announcing that "these feelings in my heart are meant for you," that is, the audience. Set in a slow tempo with only one eight-measure phrase followed by a fade, "Meant for You" does indeed hark back to the experimental style of *Smiley Smile*. But the remaining songs on the album have few of the formal or harmonic quirks of the earlier album, though there is no lack of clever and interesting effects, such as the bass harmonica line in "Passing By" or the repetitive monophonic organ line in the break of "Be Here in the Morning."

On *Smiley Smile*, Brian is credited in all eleven songs; on *Wild Honey*, the extent of Brian's involvement drops a bit—he was composer or co-composer of nine of the eleven tracks; *Friends* shows yet another decline in his contribution: eight out of twelve. (Dennis Wilson contributed two songs to *Friends* that showed him to be a close student of Brian's post–*Smiley Smile* style.) Clearly, as Brian's mental health deteriorated, he became less and less able to contribute new material. So, for *20/20*, the album made after *Friends*, the Beach Boys resurrected two songs of Brian's that had been partly assembled during the *Smile* era.[41] "Our Prayer," a sixty-five-second wordless vocalise in a vaguely sacred a cappella style, was actually recorded in 1966, with some additional finishing vocals added two years later. An exquisite exercise of harmonic virtuosity, "Our Prayer" allowed the Beach Boys once again to show off the vocal abilities and stylistic influences earlier demonstrated on such songs as "Their Hearts Were Full of Spring."

The remaking of the song "Cabinessence," all feels of which were recorded in 1966 for inclusion on *Smile*, was more complicated. Apparently, Brian had done a great deal of preliminary assembly work but had not been able to come up with a consistent plan for final assembly. "Reportedly," writes David Leaf, "there were twenty-five different mixes and combinations of that song all put on separate acetate discs before they [i.e., the Beach Boys during the production of *20/20*] put out one version. To add to the confusion, the song in its released form contains portions of 'Who Ran the Iron Horse' and 'The Grand Coolie Dam.'"[42] It is true that "Cabinessence" seems lyrically disorganized and more episodic than even the alternate version of "Heroes and Villains," but it does have that aura of manic brilliance that characterized Brian's work before the collapse of *Smile,* and thus this narrative problem is easily forgiven and forgotten. The contrast between these songs and Brian's five newly composed songs for *20/20* is stark and poignant.

The 1970 album, *Sunflower,* marks the end of the experimental songwriting and production phase inaugurated by *Smiley Smile.*[43] Perhaps not coincidentally, it received the highest critical praise of any Beach Boys work since *Pet Sounds.*[44] The new production style on *Sunflower* is denser and more conventional than that of the *Smiley Smile* era, but it is not in any way a return to the Spectoresque style Brian had used in the early 1960s. Rather, it is an attempt to update the Beach Boys for the 1970s, an attempt encouraged by their new manager, Jack Rieley. Under Rieley's management, the group put out the albums *Surf's Up, Carl and the Passions—So Tough,* and *Holland,* the first of which took its title from another *Smile*-era composition resurrected for the album.[45] These three albums contain a mixture of middle-of-the-road music entirely consonant with pop style during the early 1970s with a few oddities that proved that the desire to push beyond conventional boundaries was not dead. *Surf's Up,* for example, contains two newly composed Brian Wilson songs, "A Day in the Life of a Tree" and "'Till I Die," that use unusual compositional procedures for rock. The former begins with an extraordinarily long pedal point under hymnlike chord changes on a Hammond organ. *Holland* includes a half-sung, half-spoken "fairy tale" written and composed by Brian. This piece was so unusual that it could not be included on the main disk of the album and was put instead on a separate seven-and-half-inch disk.

The conclusive and ironic end to any experimental compositional activity was forced upon the Beach Boys by their first number-one product since "Good Vibrations": *Endless Summer.*[46] But *Endless Summer* was a compilation album of successful singles, all of which were composed before *Pet Sounds.* The message that the success of this album sent to the group only reinforced their concert experience: it was the old surf and hot-rod material that audiences wanted to hear. From this point on, Beach Boys albums lost all sense of experimentation and innovation; milking the formula that gave them their initial success became the focus of their new music. In some senses, 1974 is the year in which the Beach Boys ceased to be a rock 'n' roll band and became an oldies act.

3

Sometimes failure and success occupy the same side of the coin, and sometimes this condition works ironically to the advantage of art. Clearly, Brian Wilson's successes put him in the express lane toward catastrophic failure; remember that lighthearted *Smile* was the proximate cause for crushing depression. But that album was also the dysfunctional parent to a series of sensitive if emotionally injured children. *Smiley Smile* and its siblings have long been bullied by legions of critics and loved by only a few. The critics have only seen their failure as rock music; the friends, however, have seen their success as genuine artistic expressions and as brave breaks with conventions—conventions whose borders the Beach Boys previously had worked hard to define. But the group then went into the great void beyond. Very few interested in rock music took notice at the time, and most classically oriented musicians did not even know that such an expedition was being undertaken. What influence could these innovations then have? The short answer is, not much. *Smiley Smile, Wild Honey, Friends*, and *20/20* sound like few other rock albums; they are sui generis. One could perhaps point out the affinities between the Beach Boys' late-1960s experiments and an album like Todd Rundgren's *A Wizard/A True Star* (1973), which mimics aspects of Brian's compositional style in its abrupt transitions, mixture of various pop styles, and unusual production effects.[47] But it must be remembered that the commercial failure of the Beach Boys' experiments was hardly motivation for imitation.

In the end, we must conclude that the Beach Boys' late-1960s experiments were not reproducible. They succeed on their own terms—that is, as ingenious artistic experiments—only because of the talent and musicianship of the people involved. They fail, however, because few understand how to listen to them: definitely not rock music, and not high-toned enough to be considered classical music. Some might say that they fail also because they were the product of failure: the *Smile* debacle. In this light, they are poor substitutes for what could have been, for the maturing of the fun-loving Beach Boys into the serious Studio Men. But this is uncharitable; it is not art or skill or vision that was lost with *Smile*, only ambition and mania and confidence. Reluctantly leaving these on the beach when the setting of Brian's sun drove them away, the Beach Boys tried to carry on inside and at night without them. Yet they ended up dreaming of high art while in a nightmare of commercial failure. When the *Endless Summer* dawned, they awoke from both, took down their surfboards, and groggily returned to the beach, knowing that they would never leave it again.

Notes

I would like to acknowledge here my friend Dan (now the Reverend Daniel) Meyer, in whose delightful company I first heard the strange and fascinating sounds from *Smiley Smile* and *Friends*, and at whose house we later tried to play these albums during a party, only to have some disgruntled guest commandeer the stereo in the name of rock 'n' roll.

1. Jim Miller, ed., *Rolling Stone Illustrated History of Rock 'n' Roll*, rev. and updated ed. (New York: Random House, 1980), 162–63.

2. Greg Shaw writes that "the Beach Boys and Jan and Dean established surfing as the biggest overnight sensation since the twist" (*Rolling Stone Illustrated History of Rock 'n' Roll*, 107). Brian Wilson biographer David Leaf portrays Jan and Dean as followers and not as genuine instigators of the surfing fad; see his *The Beach Boys* (enlarged edition of *The Beach Boys and the California Myth*) (Philadelphia: Courage Books, 1985), 36. Dick Dale and his band the Del-Tones are usually credited with creating surf music, largely because many of their early gigs were for surfers' parties on the beach.

3. This popular vocal style, exemplified in groups such as the Hi-Lo's and the Four Fresh-

men, was a constant musical staple in the Wilson household during Brian's formative years. Murry Wilson, Brian's father, was a pop composer and arranger manqué who encouraged and participated in his sons' early musical interests. David Leaf gives a thorough report about music in the Wilson household during the 1950s in *The Beach Boys*, 14–19. Sometimes described by the label "vocal jazz," this style that Brian was exposed to is perhaps better characterized by reference to its roots in the collegiate men's glee clubs of the late nineteenth century. (The Yale Whiff'n'Poofs are one of the best known examples.)

4. "Their Hearts Were Full of Spring" was a particular Beach Boys favorite; it was recorded at least three times. The first version is on the album *Little Deuce Coupe* (Capitol 1998 [1963]), where it appears under the name "A Young Man Is Gone." Released on an album that marked the beginning of the "hot-rod" period, the music had lyrics Brian thought were unsuitable, and he penned new ones telling of a young man's death (a reference to James Dean?) in a car crash. The second version appears on *Beach Boys Concert* (Capitol 2198 [1964]) and was recorded in 1964, though without Brian on the top part. The recording from which example 2.1 was transcribed was made in 1967 during a rehearsal for a live concert in Hawaii; it is included as a bonus track on the CD reissue of *Smiley Smile/Wild Honey* (Capitol CDP 7 93696 2 [1990]).

5. Brian Wilson's penchant for complex modulatory structures in surf music is perhaps best exemplified in "Drag City," a song he cowrote with Jan Berry and Roger Christian that was recorded by Jan and Dean. Again, taken separately, the verse and refrain are fairly ordinary; but the modulatory link between them is thrilling. The verse progresses I–II–V–I in G major. In connecting to the refrain, the final I of the verse moves to ♭II (A♭) which pivots to become ♭VII (!) for the B♭-major refrain set in twelve-bar blues form. A♭ later appears as a key area after a typical ascending half-step modulation.

6. In his 1991 autobiography (*Wouldn't It Be Nice* [New York:HarperCollins Publishers, 1991] written with Todd Gold), Brian attributes much of the motivation for his artistic progress to an intense competitive drive, especially with the Beatles (pp. 89–90) and Phil Spector, and to marijuana use (pp. 111–13), and incipient mental illness (*passim*—the autobiography is fashionably confessional about these matters).

7. The Beach Boys, *The Beach Boys Today!* Capitol 2269 (1965), and *Summer Days (and Summer Nights!!)*, Capitol 2354 (1965).

8. Walter Everett discovers a powerful relationship of text and music here. Brian's wish that "they all could be California girls" is, of course, impossible to realize; the inability of I–II to reach V, then, underscores this impossibility.

9. The Beach Boys, *Pet Sounds*, Capitol 2458 (1966); rereleased on CD as Capitol CDP 7 48421 2 (1990) with three additional tracks not contained on the original album and extensive liner notes by David Leaf.

10. Brian Wilson reports that the album title, which on one level is highly personal— [Brian's] Pet [i.e., favorite] Sounds—was actually inspired by bandmate Mike Love's derisive opinion of the music: "Who's gonna hear this shit? The ears of a dog?" Wilson and Gold, *Wouldn't It Be Nice*, 140.

11. Brian cites Spector as the source for much of his experiments in instrumentation. See Leaf, *The Beach Boys*, 73. Brian also benefited by using many of the same studio musicians that Spector used—the famous "Wrecking Crew." See Hal Blaine with David Goggin, *Hal Blaine and the Wrecking Crew* (Emeryville, Calif.: Mix Books, 1990), 76–78.

12. Leaf, *The Beach Boys*, 82.

13. The chord in question is enharmonically equivalent to a VII^7 in B major (a half-diminished seventh). The voice leading of the chord, however, argues for the custom-made notation shown in example 2.6a, in which G♯, understood as $\hat{7}$ of A, is counterpoised with B♭ as ♭$\hat{2}$. I treat this kind of mixed-function harmonic structure in detail in my recent book, *Har-*

monic Function in Chromatic Music: A Renewed Dualist Theory and an Account of Its Prece-dents (Chicago: University of Chicago Press, 1994).

14. An additional complication affects the tonal center of the verse. The introduction to the song begins with the harmonic progression of the refrain—that is, with the descending tetrachord from A major. One would seem justified, then, in hearing the song in A, save for a crucial D in the horn melody over the initial A-major triad. Tonal ambiguity thus appears in the very first measure of the song.

15. The Beach Boys, *Beach Boys' Party!* Capitol 2398 (1965).

16. Precedents for *Party* can be discerned on other Beach Boys albums. For example, on *The Beach Boys Today!* the track "Bull Session with Big Daddy" is nothing more than a mini-mally organized interview with the Beach Boys conducted by the editor of a Capitol Records fan magazine, Earl Leaf. The group is in no mood for serious discussion, and most of the track consists of the participants joking around and trying to figure out how to distribute food from a take-out order. On *Summer Days*, the song "Bugged at My Old Man" is a hilari-ous twelve-bar blues in which Brian vents frustration at his father. The rest of the group occa-sionally chimes in with Greek-chorus comments, minimally tuned. The song is recorded sim-ply without any production touch-up.

17. Just before the "real" version of "I Get Around" fades out completely, one of the singers (Brian himself?) can be heard to affect the satirical tone later used throughout the *Party* version.

18. "Good Vibrations" was originally released as a single (Capitol 5676 [1966]) and later included on the album *Smiley Smile* (Brother T-9001 [1967]). The CD rerelease *Smiley Smile/Wild Honey* combines *Smiley Smile* with *Wild Honey* (originally Capitol T-2859 [1967]), includes six alternate tracks that never appeared on either album (including "Their Hearts Were Full of Spring," discussed earlier), and features extensive liner notes by David Leaf.

19. Leaf, *The Beach Boys*, 78.

20. Wilson and Gold, *Wouldn't It Be Nice*, 131.

21. Actually, there *is* an introduction to the song: a one-beat cry/sigh/moan by the lead singer, Carl Wilson. Significantly, this motive recurs—though buried deep within the record-ing mix—at each transposition level in the refrain.

22. The stark effect of the splice is mitigated by allowing the last chords of episode 1 to decay during the beginning of episode 2.

23. This bonus track can be found on the *Smiley Smile/Wild Honey* CD cited above.

24. The lyrics of the early version are quite different from those in the released version, which were credited to Brian and Mike Love. The lyrics in the rough version may have been written by Tony Asher. See Wilson and Gold, *Wouldn't It Be Nice*, 138.

25. See Leaf, *The Beach Boys*, 90, for Brian's original conception of "Good Vibrations" as a rhythm and blues song. Leaf (*The Beach Boys*, 94) also reports that other rough versions of "Good Vibrations" exist.

26. Wilson and Gold, *Wouldn't It Be Nice*, 145.

27. *Smile*—its purpose, contents, and concept—has been the focus of intense investiga-tion. Leaf, *The Beach Boys*, covers the album in chaps. 8 and 9. A crucial if eccentric docu-mentary source is Domenic Priore, *Look! Listen! Vibrate! Smile!* (Surfin' Colours Productions [privately printed], n.d.), which contains many newspaper clippings, reprints from maga-zines, and some original essays by knowledgeable observers such as Leaf, Priore, and Brad Elliot. Despite all the research, it is still difficult to pin down exactly what *Smile* was to be about. David Anderle, a record company executive close to Brian during this time, explains:

> Brian was so creative at this time [late 1966] it was impossible to try to tie things up . . . we were talking about doing humor albums . . . there was the *Smile* talk . . . there was "The Elements" talk. There were film ideas and TV ideas and health food ideas and

entire recordings of just water sounds, all part of an atmosphere of "anything goes." All the various projects that never happened that were part of all that . . . very intensely creative period of time. Every day, something was happening . . . the humor concept was separate from *Smile*, originally. (Leaf, *The Beach Boys*, 97. The quotation is Leaf's transcription of an oral interview.)

28. The Beatles, *Sgt. Pepper's Lonely Hearts Club Band*, Capitol 2653 (1967). Brian's sense of competition with the Beatles was noted earlier. Paul McCartney has acknowledged the Beach Boys' influence, especially during the making of *Sgt. Pepper's*. See David Leaf's transcription of a telephone interview with McCartney in the liner notes to the CD rerelease of *Pet Sounds*.

29. Leaf, *The Beach Boys*, 99–100. Brian himself has said that "I couldn't pull the songs together." Wilson and Gold, *Wouldn't It Be Nice*, 161.

30. "Heroes and Villains" was released as a single (Brother 1001 [1967]) slightly in advance of the *Smiley Smile* album, on which it also appeared.

31. The Beach Boys, *Surfin' U.S.A.*, Capitol 1890 (1963).

32. See Miller, *Rolling Stone Illustrated History of Rock 'n' Roll*, 168.

33. The Beach Boys had earlier played with this repetitive compositional form in "You're Welcome," the B side of the "Heroes and Villains" single. The insistent repetition in that song is mitigated by the extraordinary long fade-in, giving an impression of development absent in "Whistle In."

34. An occasional glockenspiel note can also be heard at the beginning of the verses. The basic instrumental idea described here—organ, honky-tonk piano, and electronic bass—is the Beach Boys' standard set-up through much of the post–*Pet Sounds* music. Note the lack of percussion and, especially, guitars.

35. A listener can spend a lot of time trying to untangle various conversational threads in this background. The clearest utterance, sung/spoken by Brian, is a vaguely chilling remonstrance: "Don't think you're God."

36. It is interesting to note in this regard that the Beach Boys recognized this problem early and attempted to counter it by forming their own recording company in association with Capitol, called "Brother Records." Brother would give them more financial independence from Capitol so that they could indulge their interests with less interference. The collapse of *Smile* also took down Brother, though it was revived when the Beach Boys signed with Warner Brothers in 1970. By that time recording companies had been forced to grant their artists greater independence. Brother was thus acceptable to Warner Brothers, whereas Capitol had found the idea subversive only a few years earlier.

37. Leaf, liner notes to *Smiley Smile/Wild Honey*, 10.

38. One exception is "Darlin'," which Brian had originally conceived and written in 1963 for another group, but which he rearranged for *Wild Honey* (See Leaf, liner notes, 11). Because of its genesis, however, "Darlin'," could not very well be recorded in the new production style, so it was given a more polished production effort.

39. The Beach Boys, *Friends*, Capitol 2895 (1968).

40. Miller, *Rolling Stone Illustrated History of Rock 'n' Roll*, 166.

41. The Beach Boys, *20/20*, Capitol 133 (1969).

42. Leaf, *The Beach Boys*, 100.

43. The Beach Boys, *Sunflower*, Warner Reprise 6382 (1970).

44. See Irwin Stambler, *Encyclopedia of Pop, Rock, and Soul* (New York: St. Martin's Press, 1977), 44.

45. The Beach Boys, *Surf's Up*, Reprise 6453 (1971); *Carl and the Passions—So Tough*, Reprise 2083 (1972); and *Holland*, Reprise 2118 (1973).

46. The Beach Boys, *Endless Summer*, Capitol 11307 (1974).

47. Todd Rundgren, *A Wizard/A True Star*, Bearsville 598 (1973). On *Faithful* (Bearsville 698 [1976]), an album that paid tribute to the musical innovations of a decade earlier, Rundgren artfully covered "Good Vibrations" along with songs by Bob Dylan, the Beatles, Jimi Hendrix, and the Yardbirds.

3

Blues Transformations in the Music of Cream

DAVE HEADLAM

In 1966, guitarist Eric Clapton joined with bass player Jack Bruce and drummer Ginger Baker to form the rock trio Cream. While Clapton tended toward a style of electric blues close to the Mississippi Delta and Chicago blues songs he venerated, with the combination of Bruce's elaborate bass lines and Baker's jazz-influenced drumming Cream quickly became the best known of the original "power trio" blues-based rock bands and prepared the ground for the later group Led Zeppelin to begin the transition from blues-based rock to heavy metal. Cream's assimilation and transformation of blues songs and styles is part of the widespread influence of American popular music—jazz, blues, rhythm and blues, and rock 'n' roll—on the development of British rock music in the late 1950s and 1960s. While this influence has been well documented in its biographical, historical, cultural, and sociological aspects, the purely musical features of the various transformations, such as Cream's recasting of blues songs into rock songs, have received less attention.[1] However, in view of the reception of rock music by audiences who knew little of its background or context but responded primarily to the music itself—the rhythm, volume, and timbres—it is clear that these features deserve serious consideration. In this article I will focus on some musical aspects of Cream's adaptations of blues songs into rock and also comment on some of the band's original but blues-based compositions. The conclusion outlines some of the problems inherent in a such a music-analytical approach and suggests some avenues for further study.

Background

The popularity of electric blues, rhythm and blues, and rock 'n' roll in the 1950s spread beyond the shores of the United States into many countries, but the music found a particularly receptive audience in Great Britain. British musicians had previously been influenced by American music styles, among them a New Orleans jazz style named "trad," and had created a hybrid folk music known as "skiffle." The latter was adapted and played by many groups, perhaps most famously by members of the Beatles.[2] In the later 1950s, the styles of popular performers such as Elvis Presley, Jerry Lee Lewis, Chuck Berry, and Buddy Holly influenced many British musicians in the direction of rock 'n' roll.[3] Unlike the majority of their white American counterparts, however, musicians and audiences in Britain became intensely interested in black American performers and sought out not only rock 'n' roll but the antecedent blues and rhythm-and-blues styles.[4] In London, Chicago electric blues of the 1940s to early '60s and the instrumentation of electric guitars, harmonicas, and loud rhythm sections were particularly popular.[5] Musicians such as Willie Dixon, Howlin' Wolf, Sonny Boy Williamson II, Little Walter, and Muddy Waters became famous through their imported records and personal appearances.[6] Many of these performers, and even the earlier solo country blues players who preceded the Chicago blues styles, toured in England; among them were Leadbelly in 1949, Big Bill Broonzy in the early 1950s, Muddy Waters in 1958, Sonny Boy Williamson II in 1963, and Howlin' Wolf in 1964.[7] Muddy Waters also toured England in the early 1960s, where his amplified blues, described as "Screaming Guitars and Howling Pianos" in the papers, reportedly "shocked" audiences. When Waters returned two years later, however, he found that every band had become loud.[8]

The pioneers of native British blues bands, who played jazz at first but gravitated toward rhythm and blues, were Chris Barber, Graham Bond, Cyril Davies, Alexis Korner, and John Mayall. These musicians formed groups such as the Blues Incorporated (1961–67), Cyril Davies and the All-Stars (1963–64), the Graham Bond Organization (1963), and the Bluesbreakers (1963). In short order, players from these bands formed or inspired a second wave of groups, most of which began playing covers or adapted versions of blues, rhythm and blues, and rock 'n' roll songs, but gradually transformed the music into rock music in successive albums appearing in the mid to late 1960s. Among the many such groups were the Kinks (1962), the Rolling Stones (1962), the Animals (1963), Manfred Mann (1963), the Spencer Davis group (1963), the Yardbirds (1963), Pretty Things (1964), the Who (1964), Cream (1966), the Jeff Beck Group (1967), Fleetwood Mac (1967), Ten Years After (1967), Free (1968), and Led Zeppelin (1969).[9] A notable addition to this list is the American Jimi Hendrix, who came to Britain in 1966 at the behest of Animal Chas Chandler and formed a trio, the Jimi Hendrix Experience, fusing blues, rock 'n' roll, rhythm and blues, and the pyschedelic lyrics, drugs, and instrumental effects with which many British groups, among them Pink Floyd and the Beatles, had been experimenting.[10] Hendrix also jammed with Cream and was an important influence on Clapton.[11]

The success of the Beatles and the "Mersey Beat" groups—the label given to Liverpool-based "British invasion" bands—started a wave of popularity for British rock bands in the United States in 1964. The London-based groups that played Chicago blues songs in rock settings, most notably the Rolling Stones, also became well known and, in effect, introduced Americans to their own music in an altered form.[12] The original blues singers, relatively unknown to American audiences, suddenly became popular in revivals of the 1960s; they were sought out, some not having performed for years, for concerts and recordings, in some cases to open for the British acts that covered their music.[13] Many of the original black artists had renewed careers—ironically, with almost exclusively white audiences—because of the immense popularity of the white British rock musicians.[14]

The development of rock music, from its African American blues, rhythm and blues, and rock 'n' roll basis through its English restyling and back to the United States and the rest of the world, encompasses many social, historical, cultural, and musical factors. Cream and Clapton in particular are most strongly associated with the tendency of musicians to reach back beyond rock 'n' roll to country and electric blues for inspiration and musical and textual material. Both the resiliency and adaptability of this music are apparent on Clapton's recent release *From the Cradle* (Reprise Records, 1994), which aligns his present superstardom with his roots: songs by familiar names such as Elmore James, Muddy Waters, and Willie Dixon in carefully reconstructed styles. Thirty years earlier, Clapton's group Cream occupied a central place in the transformation of blues songs into rock. This transformation has many aspects, but primary for this study are those features I consider to be purely musical; these are the changes in instrumentation, harmony, timbre, and above all rhythm and tempo that yielded a music to which listeners—many of whom had never heard of the original songs or artists nor had any relation to their history or culture—responded in unprecedented numbers.

Cream

The three members of Cream had each previously played in blues and trad bands: drummer Ginger Baker in Alexis Korner's Blues Incorporated and the Graham Bond Organization, bass and harmonica player and lead vocalist Jack Bruce in Blues Incorporated, the Graham Bond Organization, the Bluesbreakers, and Manfred Mann (1966), and guitarist Eric Clapton in the Roosters (1963), Casey Jones and the Engineers (1963), the Yardbirds (1963–65), and the Bluesbreakers (1965–66).[15] With these three skilled and innovative players forming a trio—a somewhat unusual rock-band ensemble at the time—Cream became known primarily for its instrumental virtuosity, combining Clapton's blues-based single-string lead guitar style with Bruce's pioneering enhanced role for the electric bass guitar and Baker's jazz-influenced drumming.[16] Their concerts consisted largely of extended jams on blues-based material.[17] Cream enjoyed immense success but lasted for only three years, from 1966 to 1968; the farewell concert took place on 26 November 1968 at the Royal Albert Hall in London.

Songs

Cream's first album, *Fresh Cream* (1966), set a pattern for the band. One side comprises new songs, composed mostly by Jack Bruce and various collaborators, and the other side contains reworked blues songs. This duality is less apparent on the second album, *Disraeli Gears* (1967), but is emphasized in the third release, *Wheels of Fire* (1968), a double album including one studio record of mostly new songs and one live record of mostly extended improvisations on blues songs. These three albums were followed by a compilation of live cuts and studio recordings on *Goodbye Cream* (1969), and many albums with various versions and combinations of early, live, and studio songs have appeared since.

A list of blues songs covered by Cream and released on albums is given in figure 3.1.[18] As is often the case with covers or rock songs based on earlier blues songs, the credits on albums must be viewed with caution, as the credit may be to a specific recorded performance, such as "Sittin' on Top of the World" by Howlin' Wolf, and it is often difficult if not impossible to acknowledge an original author. For instance, "Rollin' and Tumblin'" is attributed in the album liner notes to Muddy Waters, but the song is part of a family of songs with similar musical and textual characteristics that may have first been recorded by Hambone Willie Newbern but probably extends back to the early part of this century and even beyond.[19] In figure 3.1, the song titles are given, listed under the first album release, as well as the names associated with the songs or alternate titles or versions of the songs as composers, arrangers, or performers in various sources (most notably Sheldon Harris, *Blues Who's Who*), and, where applicable, the name of the artist to whom the song is attributed on the album. The wide-ranging repertoire includes songs from the early Mississippi Delta blues by Robert Johnson and Skip James, songs from Chicago electric blues by Muddy Waters and Howlin' Wolf, and even a rock 'n' roll song by Chuck Berry.

Robert Johnson and "Cross Road Blues"

Clapton has said that he identified strongly with the songs of Robert Johnson (1911–38), who is generally considered to represent the culmination of the Mississippi Delta blues style.[20] Johnson recorded twenty-nine songs, twelve of which exist in alternate takes, for a total of forty-one recordings on the Vocalion label of the American Record Company (ARC) in November 1936 in San Antonio and in June 1937 in Dallas, Texas. Columbia issued a first volume of songs on *Robert Johnson: King of the Delta Blues Singers* in 1961, then a second volume in 1970. In 1990, Columbia released a complete Johnson collection in the *Roots 'n' Blues* series, with all twenty-nine songs in the forty-one takes.[21] Johnson's enormous influence has come to light in several recent studies that trace a path from Johnson through Muddy Waters and Elmore James to Eric Clapton and Keith Richards and retrospectively find in Johnson's songs the roots of rock music.[22]

Of Johnson's recorded songs, "Cross Road Blues," "Terraplane Blues," "Milkcow's Calf Blues," and "Stones in My Passway" are similar enough in melody, form, and guitar accompanimental figures that they may be regarded as members of a family

Figure 3.1. Blues Songs covered on Cream albums (only first instance given)

Fresh Cream, Atco 206 (1966)
"Cat's Squirrel" (also "Mississippi Blues"): Charles Isaiah ("Doc") Ross
"I'm So Glad": Nehemiah ("Skip") James
"From Four Till Late": Robert Johnson
"Rollin' and Tumblin'": attributed to Muddy Waters
"Spoonful": Charlie Patton, "A Spoonful of Blues" (1929); attributed to Willie Dixon
    (U.K. version only)

Disraeli Gears, Atco 232 (1967)
"Outside Woman Blues": Blind Joe Reynolds

Wheels of Fire, Atco 700 (1968)
"Sittin' on Top of the World": Armenter ("Bo") Chatmon and Walter Jacobs Vinson of
    the Mississippi Sheiks, recorded by Howlin' Wolf
"Crossroads": Robert Johnson, "Cross Road Blues"
"Traintime": John ("Forest City Joe") Pugh; attributed to John Group
"Born under a Bad Sign": Booker T. Jones and William Bell

Top of the Milk, Atco 4534 (1968)
"Steppin' Out'": James Bracken
"Big Black Woman Blues": Tommy Johnson, "Big Fat Mama Blues"

Early Cream, Springboard 4037 (1977)
"Louise": Howlin' Wolf; attributed to Whiting/Robin
"Five Long Years": Ike Turner
"The First Time I Met the Blues" ("The First Time I Met You"): Eurreal ("Little Brother")
    Montgomery
"Stormy Monday": John Lee Hooker
"Too Much Monkey Business": Chuck Berry

---

of songs comprising variations on a basic pattern.[23] This interrelation reflects the tradition in which blues songs were copied and varied, in a continual reworking of basic musical and textual material, in an oral tradition stretching back into the nineteenth century. The advent of recordings meant that songs could be documented in a fixed form, but it also allows us to see how Johnson varied his material, as the differences between the alternate takes of his songs we have left today indicate. In the two cuts of "Cross Road Blues," for instance, the first version recorded has additional verses and is faster and more raucous, closer to "Terraplane Blues," than the slower, more measured second version.[24] The discussion below concerns the second recorded version.

As with many of Johnson's songs, "Cross Road Blues" may be interpreted within the context of the textual and harmonic structure of the model twelve-bar blues form (fig 3.2).[25] In this form, the text is organized in a three-line AAB structure. Each line occupies four bars, with bars divided into four internal beats, and each begins on a different harmony—I, IV, then V—but all end on I. The textual form is thus complemented by a maximum of harmonic differentiation at the onset of the three lines, with the successive I, IV, then V chords also creating a large-scale harmonic progres-

Figure 3.2. Model 12-bar pattern compared with form of Johnson's "Cross Road Blues"

Model			
text	A	A	B
harmonies	I	IV I	V (IV) I
4-beat bars (intro)	1 2 3 4	5 6 7 8	9 10 11 12
Johnson			
verse 1 (*1 *2 3 4)	1 2 *3 4 5 6	7 8 *9 10 11	12 13 14 15
verse 2	1 2 3 +4 5	6 7 8 9 +10	11 12 13 14
verse 3	1 2 3 4 5	6 7 8 9 10	11 *12 13 14
verse 4	1 2 3 4 5	6 7 8 9 10	*11 *12 13 14

(* = bar with three beats, + = bar with five beats)

sion confirming the key. Within each line, the vocal phrase generally takes two bars (mm. 1–2, 5–6, and 9–10), leaving the remaining two bars (mm. 3–4, 7–8, 11–12) for instrumental commentary or development on the vocal melody, often in a call-and-response style. Over this two-bar alternation the harmonic rhythm accelerates through the form, lasting initially four bars (I), then two bars (IV–I), and finally one bar (V–IV; in variants of the twelve-bar form the IV chord may be either omitted or only implied), until measures 11–12, which symmetrically reverse the process by expanding back to two bars (I), followed by a four-bar duration (a formally differentiated I) overlapping into the beginning of the next verse.

In comparison with the model twelve-bar form, which, as is clear from its appearance in several of his other songs, was known to Johnson, the setting of "Cross Road Blues" has varying numbers of bars and even beats.[26] In the interpretation of the verse structures given in figure 3.2, where the model twelve-bar form is shown for comparison, the verses have fifteen, then fourteen bars, with three-beat and five-beat bars appearing among the conventional four-beat bars (marked with * and +, respectively, in fig. 3.2).[27] On the level of beats, divisions change between triple and duple (and can be notated with beats in durations of a dotted quarter or quarter; the transcription of the introduction and verse 1 in ex. 3.1 is notated in quarter beats following Scott Ainslie and Dave Whitehall, *Robert Johnson*); this lower-level fluidity reflects the changing higher-level metric groupings.

An important factor in the rhythmic flow is the vocal line, which constantly changes registers and grouping emphases within phrases. Although the vocal line in successive verses has a similar underlying shape and is upbeat oriented, except for the striking downbeat beginning of the text of the second verse ("standing at the crossroad"), the placement of words in relation to the meter varies. For instance, the important word "crossroad" appears on a downbeat at the outset of the first verse (ex. 3.1, m. 5), but subsequently in the first verse, then the second verse, it shifts to the second beat (ex. 3.1, m. 11, fig. 3.2, verse 2, m. 1), then to the last eighth of a bar, crossing over the bar line (verse 2, mm. 5–6). Other vocal shifts occur in the fourth verse, where the phrase "You can run" is similarly shifted in relation to the metric arrivals (upbeat to m. 1, m. 6 downbeat), and the opening bars of the recitative-like B sections in each verse are, as described below, quite ambiguous metrically. In gen-

Example 3.1. Johnson's "Cross Road Blues," introduction and verse 1

Example 3.1. (*continued*)

eral, Johnson's vocals are extraordinary for their melodic range and for the pervasive slides and bends, falsetto notes, and effects such as moans and cries. The overall impression is varied and proselike, with Johnson inflecting the successive text phrases differently in almost each case.

In addition to the vocal inflections, the grouping articulations at bar lines result from several factors, principally (but not exclusively) changes of harmony, from the IV chord beginning the A' section and a subsequent motion to I within the section, and from the V chord beginning the B section and subsequent motion to I within the section; bass-note attacks between and within harmonies; and motivic groupings and repetition of figures. The changes of harmony are, as noted, integral to the overall form. With regard to the effect of bass notes, Johnson's complex guitar part contains three layers: a bass accompaniment on the lower strings, a midrange chordal layer, and a high-register soloistic-motivic part, which is alternately chordal or single line. The constant registral shifts that keep each of the layers alive throughout the song also help to keep the rhythm fluid, but bass notes played either singly or with supporting midrange chords tend to define the meter, acting as stronger impulses creating downbeats. In verse 1, for instance (ex. 3.1), the bass attacks beginning measures 9, 10, and 11 reassert a four-beat grouping after the three-beat measure 8. A bass attack supported by a motivic grouping reestablishes a four-beat grouping in measure 15 after the three-beat measure 14. This important motive, which recurs in measures 19–20 of verse 1 (ex. 3.1), is expanded in verse 2 to five beats (m. 4 of verse 2, see fig. 3.2). In general, bass-note attacks and motivic groupings determine the subtle metric groupings throughout.

Particularly striking in "Cross Road Blues" is Johnson's setting of the third line of text in verses 2 and 4, bars 11–12 in both. This location in the blues form is often a point of harmonic clarity and direction, as a clear statement of a dominant harmony to motivate a return to tonic, part of the "turnaround" back to the tonic harmony. In "Cross Road Blues," however, both metric and harmonic ambiguity characterize this point in the verses. The groupings either include a three-beat bar or are ambiguous; for instance, the passage identified as bars 11 and 12 in the second verse, accompanying the text "Didn't nobody seem to know me, ev'rybody pass me by" (ex. 3.2) defies even a single beat-based reading (my interpretation of four-beat bars 11 and 12 in ex. 3.2 is an approximation, merely maintaining the surrounding four-beat groups). Harmonically, Johnson supports the text with only a single guitar line, featuring a "snap" pizzicato on the tonic note A on the half-beat. This pizzicato attack could define a new downbeat, leaving surrounding 7/8 and 9/8 bars, or it could be interpreted as a syncopated attack spanning two bars (as shown in ex. 3.2). Either way, it initiates an oscillating figure leading back to the clear downbeat statement of tonic harmony in the following bar. In what may be interpreted as a particularly intense instance of text painting, the emphasis on this tonic note seems to contradict any dominant chord function ("Didn't nobody seem to know me") and its rhythmic placement negates the preceding metric units ("ev'rybody pass me by"). In the similar location in verses 1 and 3, the dominant chord and bar lines are more sharply articulated, but with only one bar of V (mm. 12 and 11, respectively), followed by the tonic harmony.

An important factor linking Johnson's songs into family groups is the guitar accompaniment, which is itself dependent on the tuning and related technique. Of the twenty-nine songs, about half feature the guitar in an open or "Spanish" tuning with a major triad on the open strings; in "Cross Road blues" the strings are tuned E–A–E–A–C♯–A (beginning from the lowest string).[28] The triad in the open strings allows for the use of a slide (a metal bar or, originally, a bottle neck) which can press from one to six strings on the same fret. The slide permits a greater variety of melodic nuance than is possible when playing with fingers only, allowing the guitar to imitate the voice more closely through slides and tremolos and lending the strings a sustain and a slight distortion that foreshadows the characteristic distorted sound of the electric guitar with an overdriven amplifier in the later Chicago blues and eventually rock music. The portamento-type guitar figures, which reflect the vocal line in Johnson's highly ornamented style, are evident in the slurs, grace notes, and glissando line marks shown in example 3.1.

Example 3.2. Johnson's "Cross Road Blues," end of verse 2

Anchoring the nuances of the slide guitar and voice are harmony notes on the lower strings, primarily those of the tonic and subdominant chords, both as seventh chords: A–C♯–E–G and D–F♯–A–C. In contrast to the clearly stated I and IV chords, the "Cross Road Blues" family of songs has an unusual setting of the expected dominant chord: in verses one (m. 12) and three (m. 11) it is strongly implied by the notes E–D–G, with the flatted seventh scale degree G instead of a raised G♯; but in verses two (ex. 3.2) and four, a focal tonic note appears, initiating a characteristic descent 1–7–6–5 (A–G–F♯–E) in a turnaround with only a faint outline of a preceding dominant. Throughout, the melody notes tend to gravitate around and between the I and IV harmony notes, with a strong tendency toward what is notated as a flatted third scale degree, notated variously as C or B♯ but is actually a highly flexible and characteristic melodic area of frequencies arrived at by bends and other pitch inflections.

The tendency for melody notes to operate within the tertian seventh-chord spans of the harmony is evident in the introductory figure (ex. 3.1, m. 3), where the note A is repeated against a descending line of G–F♯–F–E. This chromatic melody-based figure is more elaborate in other songs, and many commentators have noted the use of altered "diminished chords" or other more complex harmonies in these openings, in Johnson's and others' recordings.[29] The progression shown in ex. 3.3 from the introductory bars to "Kind Hearted Woman Blues" is typical: a succession of diminished triads results from a harmonized chromatic filling-in of the tonic seventh-chord spans C♯–C–B–A, G–G♭–F–(E), and E–E♭–D–(C♯) (mm. 1–3). The progression is followed by a reiteration of the tonic-to-dominant figure familar from "Cross Road Blues"—G–F♯–F–E in the bass against the reiterated tonic note

Example 3.3. Introduction to Johnson's "Kind Hearted Woman Blues"

A (mm. 3–4). These two chromatic figures are more defined examples of melodic tendencies toward filling-in of seventh-chord tertian spans found throughout Johnson's songs.

Eric Clapton and "Crossroads"

Clapton recorded several versions of Johnson's "Cross Road Blues" as "Crossroads," with the one-time recording group Powerhouse (1966), with Cream (in a live version, released on *Wheels of Fire*), with Blind Faith (live version on a bootleg album, 1969) and with Derek and the Dominos (1970). Clapton's own comments on his version of the song are illuminating: he looked for a riff or an essential melodic idea to extract from the original, which would act as the basis for a simplified transformation: "It became, then, a question of finding something that had a riff, a form that could be interpreted, simply, in a band format. In 'Crossroads' there was a very definite riff. He [Johnson] was playing it full-chorded with the slide as well. I just took it on a single string or two strings and embellished it. Out of all of the songs it was the easiest for me to see as a rock and roll vehicle."[30] The guitar and vocal parts in the first verse of Creams's "Crossroads" from *Wheels of Fire* are given in example 3.4a along with Johnson's original motivic figure for comparison with Clapton's pared-down derived motive or riff in example 3.4b.[31] Both are based on the neighboring figure A–G–A with a descent including the flatted third C/B♯. The Cream version of the figure is in a straight eighth-note rhythm with a syncopation on the fourth eighth note that deemphasizes the third beat, followed by a neighboring sixteenth-note G–A that pushes ahead, leading through the following two eighth notes into the downbeat of the next bar. In the arrangement, the motivic figure consistently follows the vocals of the A, A', and B sections of the text in the characteristic blues fashion (mm. 3–4, 7–8, and 11–12). New to Cream's version is the continual recurrence of the riff in the bass guitar part throughout the verse, which combines

Example 3.4a. Cream's "Crossroads," verse 1

Example 3.4b. Comparison of motives from Johnson and Cream versions of "Cross Road Blues" and "Crossroads"

with the drums to create and continually emphasize continuity in the regular metric drive.

This procedure of extracting or arranging motivic figures or riffs from blues songs and using them repeatedly within a simplified and regularized harmonic and metric framework is characteristic of Cream and other rock bands. The practice continued in the later band Led Zeppelin and beyond, when such riffs, now newly composed, became a staple of heavy metal.[32] The development of riff-based blues-rock, in which the complex rhythmic and melodic patterns of the earlier country and electric blues solo styles are simplified and evened out in a rock group setting, is an essential aspect of the transformation from blues to rock music.[33]

Along with a simplified riff, the form of Cream's "Crossroads" is trimmed into a standard twelve-bar pattern, with clear I, IV, and V harmonies (ex. 3.4a). In each verse, the vocals are accompanied by duple shuffle patterns in the guitar (muted, as shown in ex. 3.4a), with the riff in a two-bar "answer," in a standardized adaptation of the blues call-and-response style heard in the Johnson version. The intervallic "5–6"-motion shuffle patterns in the guitar, characteristic of rock 'n' roll and rock music in general, also stem from Johnson's influence—particularly the songs "Ramblin' on My Mind" and "When You Got a Good Friend"—although not as obviously in "Cross Road Blues" (the pattern is somewhat in evidence in mm. 1–3 of verse 2). The technique is related to boogie-woogie piano style and has been called "walking the basses."[34]

Aside from the adapted use of the shuffle pattern, Clapton's guitar playing in his "Crossroads" is quite unlike Johnson's technique and reflects more the soloistic style of other influences, such as B. B. King and Albert King. The three levels found in Johnson's song are split between the three players in Cream, with Clapton taking the top and middle layers, usually alternately, bass player Bruce taking the bottom and middle layers, and drummer Baker filling in the bottom and middle registral spans. Clapton plays in a regular tuning and adds extended solos (between the second and third and the third and fourth verses), with uses of bent notes, tremolo vibrato, and slides and distortion from an adapted repertoire of stylized figures characteristic of electric guitar blues.[35] His vocals, while retaining some contour features of the Johnson version, are also reduced and regularized in relation to the meter.

Other obvious changes in the transformation from Johnson's "Cross Road Blues" to Cream's "Crossroads" are the faster tempo, the amplified volume, and, as noted, the added drums and bass.[36] In the verses, bass player Bruce reiterates the basic riff and adds running lines in a constant and complex counterpoint to Clapton's upper layer in the solo section, and drummer Baker similarly fills in the textural and registral space with varied attacks and timbres from the drum set in the solo section. As is evident in "Crossroads," but even more so in other Cream songs, both Bruce and Baker were innovators, developing and exploring their enhanced roles within the new, improvisatory trio rock format. Bruce simultaneously plays rhythmic and harmonic roles; an accompanimental role, filling in the texture and providing running lines against the lead guitar, and occasionally even a solo role. On the drums, Baker fills in textural and rhythmic spaces in a manner characteristic of jazz trios, where the drums become more elaborate when the soloist improvises and the instrumental texture thins out.

Arguably, the most significant aspect of Cream's adaptation, and perhaps of the transformation from blues to rock in general, is in the basic rhythm. In Johnson's solo blues style as realized in his "Cross Road Blues," meter itself is a compositional and performance device which comes in and out of focus in response to the fluid rhythms and changing accents in the lower-level beats. The irregular groupings extend to smaller beat divisions, with an interplay between triplet "swing" and duple divisions of the beat (as shown in ex. 3.1). In Cream's rock version, an unwavering duple meter is a maintained in a duple 4/4 rock beat with straight eighth notes.[37] The added drums and bass emphasize and stabilize the meter, with beats stressed equally; offbeats, especially within the repeating riffs, are thereby strongly syncopated in relation to the driving, accented beat.

Listening to Johnson's "Cross Road Blues" and then to Cream's "Crossroads" is an extraordinary musical experience, even aside from the historical context of the parallel Faustian reputation that links Johnson and Clapton. Johnson's irregular rhythms and variation in the support for a firm metric beat suggest a more personal, idiosyncratic vision, particularly in the ambiguous setting of the "clincher" third line of each verse of the text, where the rhythmic and harmonic momentum is dissipated rather than reinforced (ex. 3.2). By contrast, Cream's "Crossroads" is driving and powerful, with a relentless reinforcement, then turnaround, of harmonies that assimilates the third line of text within the inexorable forward motion and progression of the meter, suggesting the communal, overdriven state of society that surrounded Cream in the 1960s.

Before leaving "Crossroads," however, it must be noted that Johnson himself allowed for alternative interpretations of the song in his own two versions and in the other songs that share the basic tonal and formal materials of "Cross Road Blues." One such song, "Terraplane Blues"—Johnson's most popular release—in particular, is regular throughout in both form and meter, maintaining the twelve-bar structure and building up momentum through the consistent reinforcement of the four-beat measures. The fourth verse of the song even reduces the accompaniment to a characteristic recurring four-note upbeat riff (notes A–B♯–C♯–E) of the kind described by Clapton as essential for his vision of "Crossroads" as a "rock and roll vehicle." As numerous writers have observed, Johnson's many different playing styles both summarized those of his predecessors and anticipated those of his descendents.

Muddy Waters and "Rollin' and Tumblin'"

While Clapton adapted "Crossroads" directly from the 1930s Johnson recording, Delta blues had already undergone a transformation into Chicago electric blues in the 1940s and '50s.[38] Possibly the most influential musician in this regard was Muddy Waters. Waters, who was recorded in Mississippi by the musicologist Alan Lomax in 1941, went to Chicago in 1943 and became instrumental in changing acoustic country blues into an electrified group setting, along with musicians such as Willie Dixon, Howlin' Wolf, and Sonny Boy Williamson II.[39] From early smaller ensembles, with electric guitar, harmonica, and drums, Chicago electric blues tended in the 1950s toward larger groups with guitars, amplified vocals, harmonica, saxophones, and rhythm sections that included piano, acoustic bass, and drums. The heyday of the music was about 1945–55; after 1955 record labels became more interested in rock 'n' roll, though the style was revived in the late 1960s in connection with the rise of British rock adaptations of the songs by the Rolling Stones, Cream, and other groups.

Waters began recording for the Chess record label in 1947 with an ensemble of piano, saxophone, and bass but soon changed to a more pared-down sound, playing electric guitar accompanied by string bass (with "Big Crawford"). In 1950 Waters recorded a version of the song "Rollin' and Tumblin'," but earlier he had recorded two other versions, with added musicians "Baby Face" Leroy Foster (1923–58) on vocals and drums and Little Walter playing harmonica. Of these two earlier versions, "Rollin' and Tumblin' Part 1" is largely instrumental with untexted vocals, and "Part 2" is in a style closer to that of his later recording, with the text giving shape to the verse but maintaining an improvisatory quality in the song.

"Rollin' and Tumblin'" is one of a family of songs that share a distinctive formal shape. The family includes Robert Johnson's songs "Travelling Riverside Blues" and "If I Had Possession over Judgment Day"; the latter contains the line "And I rolled and I tumbled and I cried the whole night long."[40] The form is interpreted in the context of a twelve-bar blues model in figure 3.3. The I chord that would normally appear in measures 1–4 is altered to IV–I, paralleling the pattern in measures 5–8, and the I chord sections (corresponding to mm. 3–4, 7–8, and 11–12 of the model) are irregular in length, lasting for different numbers of bars. The most characteristic feature, however, is the added two beats (generally notated as a 2/4 bar) to accommodate the upbeat beginning of each line of the text (my transcription of the introductory instrumental verse of Waters's recording of "Rollin and Tumblin' Part 2" is given in ex. 3.5).

In addition to the added two beats beginning each phrase of the verse, the repeating motive over the I chord (guitar part, mm. 3–4, 9–11, and 15–17 in ex. 3.5) is

---

Figure 3.3. Schematic of Waters' "Rollin' and Tumblin'" form (length of I chord varies)

text	A		A		B	
harmonies	IV I		IV I		V IV I	
bars	(+2) 1 2 3 4 (+2)		5 6 7 8 (+2)		9 10 11 12 (+2)	

(+2 = added two beats)

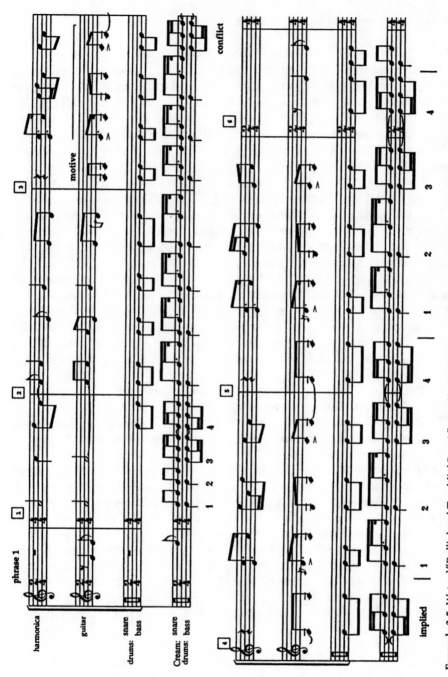

Example 3.5. Waters' "Rollin' and Tumblin' Part 2," opening instrumental verse with drums from Cream version added

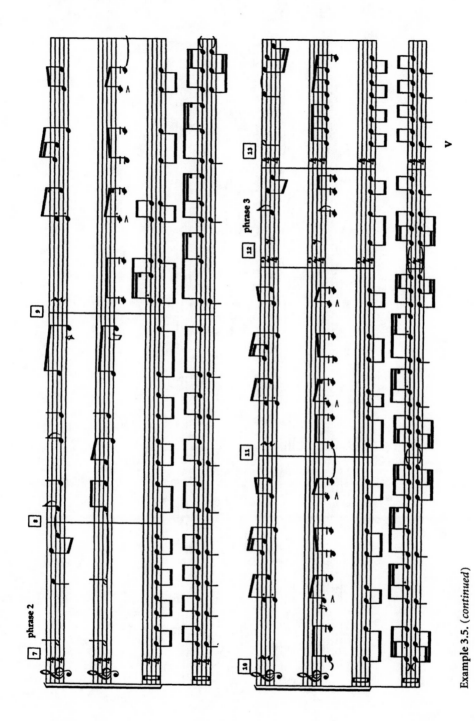

Example 3.5. (continued)

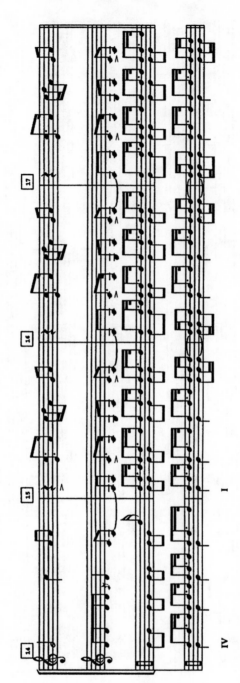

Example 3.5. (*continued*)

also characteristic of the family and can be heard in embryonic form in the Johnson songs and with a successively clearer and more defined role in the Waters and then Cream recordings. It is syncopated in the metric context, creating an offbeat emphasis on beats two and four. An added bass drum part in the Waters version shown in example 3.5 beats straight eighth notes, and intermittent snare brushes highlight the syncopation of the motive on the I chords in measures 9 and 15–17. When comparing this version to Waters's later recording, it is noteworthy that the bass part in the latter includes slaps and other articulative sounds that recall the added drum part.

Cream's "Rollin' and Tumblin'"

Unlike "Crossroads," where Cream substantially altered the original, the band's version of "Rollin' and Tumblin'" is a close recreation and elaboration of the Waters-Foster-Little Walter versions. Cream's "Rollin' and Tumblin'" appears on their initial album (1966), and an extended live version was released later on *Live Cream* (1969). The trio of harmonica, guitar, and drums and most of the melodic content is maintained, but in a more highly charged electrified and distorted setting, which reflects in an exaggerated way the distortion from the electric guitar and poor recording quality of the originals. The common element linking Cream's two settings is the emphasis on the repeated motive already present in Waters's version (ex. 3.5). Unlike "Crossroads," where Cream's signature riff needed to be culled from elements of the original version, the riff in "Rollin' and Tumblin'" was already fully formed. Such riffs are characteristic of many Chicago electric blues songs, and rock players like Clapton were clearly influenced by these songs as they placed ever greater emphasis on these riffs.

The syncopation of the repeated riff in Cream's "Rollin' and Tumblin'" is emphasized by the drums, which have a greatly enhanced role in Cream's version. The drums do not, however, reinforce the metric framework, as in "Crossroads," but add a metric conflict that emphasizes the offbeats of the motive, then effect a complete metric shift that transforms the metric setting of the motive. The Cream drum part is added below the corresponding bars of the Waters version in example 3.5. In the first full bar this drum part has a tied two-beat figure on beats 3 and 4, reinforcing the meter by grouping beats 3 and 4 together in a larger two-beat upbeat that recalls the syncopated metric structure of the riff in "Crossroads." When the motivic riff arrives two bars later, however, the tied two-beat drum figure shifts to beats 4 and 1, giving the impression of a downbeat on the notated second beat, which matches the emphasis on beats 2 and 4 in the motive. The conflict between the syncopated drum part and riff and the four-beat meter lends a fluidity to the rhythm somewhat characteristic of the original version.

The full implication of the conflict becomes apparent, however, in the middle solo section of Cream's three-part ABA arrangement of the song. The initial A section, which corresponds to the verse form of the original, is brought to a full stop; then a B solo section based entirely on the riff ensues, but with the riff now shifted in relation to the meter so that it begins with an upbeat rather than an afterbeat (see

Example 3.6. "Rollin' and Tumblin'" motive as afterbeat and upbeat

ex. 3.6 and 3.7). This shift, implied in the previous conflict, completely changes the character of the riff. The drums reinforce the shifted meter, then continue with a syncopated bass drum pattern under the snare, as the solo builds in intensity. After the solo, the original metric arrangement returns, based on the original verse form, with the conflicting syncopation of the motive supported by the drums as before (as in ex. 3.5).

Rhythmically, the elaborate solo improvisatory section and metric shift and large formal ABA shape in the Cream version of "Rollin' and Tumblin'" marks a fourth stage in an evolutionary progression in the song: (1) the original subtle intimation of a syncopated motivic motion in the family of songs characterized by the text "Rollin' and Tumblin'"; (2) the more defined but still rhythmically fluid use of the

Example 3.7. Cream's solo section in "Rollin' and Tumblin'" with motive shifted to upbeat position

motive with supporting bass slaps in the Muddy Waters version; (3) the added but intermittent snare brushes and bass drum supporting the syncopated motive, and the extended instrumental version in the more elaborate renditions recorded by Waters with Leroy Foster and Little Walter; and (4) Cream's high-energy, amplified, distorted version with its formal differentiation by the sole emphasis on the riff in a middle B section and the metric conflict and shift provided by the drum parts in relation to the riff in the A and B sections, respectively.

Unlike "Crossroads," where Cream transformed the original in instrumentation and rhythm, their version of "Rollin' and Tumblin'" is a conscious though exaggerated stylistic re-creation of its repeating riff, instrumental sound, vocal style, and rhythmic characteristics. Rather than simplify the original the Cream version actually takes the rhythmic implications of the syncopated riff to a new level of complexity. Cream's "Rollin' and Tumblin'" thus marks a different direction in blues adaptations than "Crossroads," one closer to the style and spirit of the original, but still taking advantage of the enhanced role of meter and strong syncopations characteristic of rock rhythm.

Howlin' Wolf and "Sittin' on Top of the World"

The song "Sittin' on Top of the World," in a version from 1957 by singer Howlin' Wolf, is an example of a later style of Chicago electric blues. The ensemble, typical of Wolf's Chess label recordings in the latter 1950s, includes piano, bass, drums, and two guitars, with Wolf on harmonica and vocals.[41] Although they work together in a group, each instrument plays in a soloistic style throughout, somewhat reminiscent of early jazz bands. The drums are notable in this regard, adding offbeats and flourishes in a soloistic manner matching those of the other instruments. The guitars both fill in the middle of the texture with chords and add answering gestures to the vocal phrases in a typical blues style (see my transcription of the opening bars in ex. 3.8, which omits the drums).[42] The harmonica plays the introductory verse, takes a solo in the third verse, and returns to end the song. The piano has the most interesting part, a running commentary in the upper register using boogie-woogie type patterns (given only in mm. 1–3 in ex. 3.8). While the other parts are in a lazy triplet division, the piano part moves between duple, triple, and other division gestures in a manic counterpoint.

The form of the song is based on an eight-bar blues pattern extended to an irregular nine bars by an extension in measures 8–9 (fig. 3.4). The turnaround in the eighth and ninth bars, using the harmonies I–IV–I–V, accompanies a motivic figure played on the guitar (ex. 3.8). The chord progression has the distinctive feature of a minor IV chord in measure 4, part of a linear voice-leading motion of $F^4-E\flat^4-D^4-D\flat^4-C^4$ ($\hat{1}-\flat\hat{7}-\hat{6}-\flat\hat{6}-\hat{5}$) in the upper line of the guitar (mm. 1–5), over harmonies I–V/IV–IV–iv (minor IV)–I.

Example 3.8. Howlin' Wolf's "Sittin' on Top of the World," opening instrumental verse

Figure 3.4. Extended form of Wolf's "Sittin' on Top of the World"

mm.	1	2	3	4	5	6	7	8	9
	I	V/IV	IV–iv	I	V	I	I–IV	I–V

Cream's "Sittin' on Top of the World"

The Cream studio version of "Sittin' on Top of the World," from the album *Wheels of Fire*, is in a slower tempo and has an equal, heavy emphasis on the beat in rock style. A transcription of the guitar and bass parts and vocals of the introduction and beginning of the first verse is given in example 3.9; the drums closely follow the bass guitar rhythms.[43] The three-part texture consists of combined drums, bass, and rhythm guitar, with an overdubbed solo guitar (with a processed sound) adding a running commentary throughout the introduction and in the verses, answering the vocals in the blues call-and-response pattern. This solo guitar part substitutes for the guitar and harmonica responses in the Wolf version but only to a small extent for the continuous piano elaborations; that boogie element is largely abandoned in Cream's adaptation.

The rhythm in Cream's version is altered dramatically from the shuffle triplet of the original to a martial rhythmic figure in triplets played with equal weight. The straight rhythm persists in the slightly slower triplet eighths of the verses. In the solo section, however, the accompaniment changes to an abrupt syncopated gesture articulating only the first two of the previous six sixteenth attacks per beat. This altered rhythm persists into the final verse, emphasized by an increasingly elaborate drum part, as part of an overall dramatic increase in rhythmic complexity and tension in the latter part of the song, imposing an overall dramatic progression on the form of the Wolf version. The original nine-bar form of the verses is retained, with a more pronounced and defined motive in the eighth and ninth bars (see ex. 3.9). The motive is set in octaves between the guitar parts, with counterpoint created (m. 8) by note alterations and flourishes in the upper part. Perhaps reflecting the jazzlike style of the original, the opening I and IV chords are recast as more complex ninth chords, and the V chord (m. 6) is an elaborated V#9. The extended harmonies are reflected in the chromatic neighboring figure in the accompaniment, which compensates somewhat for the lack of a characteristic aspect of the Wolf version—the minor IV and descending chromatic voice-leading line (F–Eb–D–Db–C).

In Cream's arrangement of the song, the change in texture from the larger ensemble to the prototypical rock trio setting is quite drastic. In the live version, the lack of the rhythm guitar part for much of the song leaves a spare texture that is far removed from the original. Unlike in "Crossroads," there is no characteristic riff that the song is organized around; the unifying role is taken by the martial rhythm in the drums and the distinctive end motive of the nine-bar verse. The more complex harmonies of the accompaniment are somewhat at odds with the strongly blues-oriented solo guitar lines in the studio version; the simpler bass and guitar texture of the live version offers a closer stylistic match. The song points up one of the principal characteristics of Cream's albums: the dichotomy between its fixed "studio" style and its live "improvisatory" style. Wolf's original version is itself too complex and too

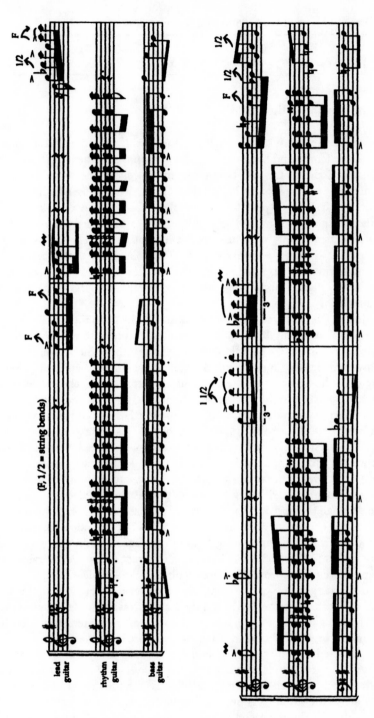

Example 3.9. Cream's "Sittin' on Top of the World," opening instrumental verse

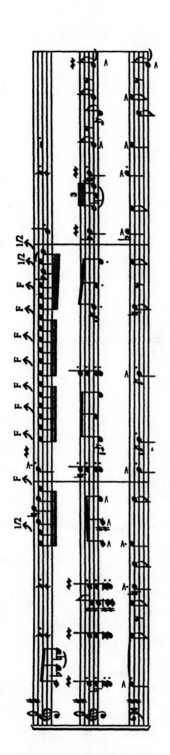

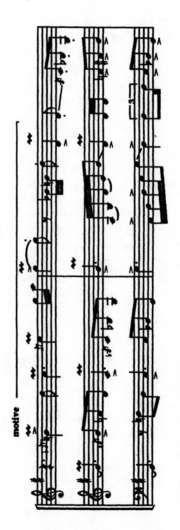

Example 3.9. (*continued*)

Example 3.10a. Cream's "Sunshine of Your Love" motive

transformed from its blues origins for Cream to adapt it to its live style of rock trio format as easily as the previous two songs discussed above; it seems to require the studio treatment, yet it is also a blues-based song more characteristic of its live style. Thus "Sittin' on Top of the World" combines in one song the duality of Cream and many of the blues-based rock bands, formed as improvisatory groups focused around stylistic re-creation but forced to confront and assimilate the recording style of ensembles like the Beatles, with their newly composed songs and use of studio technology.

Original Songs

In addition to reworking previous material, Bruce, Baker, and Clapton wrote new blues-influenced songs.[44] These songs can be placed into four categories. The first type is twelve- or sixteen-bar blues with slight variations, as in "Strange Brew" and "Politician" (twelve bar) and "Sleepy Time Time" (sixteen bar). The classic twelve-bar blues form is evident in "Strange Brew," after Albert King's version of "Oh Pretty Woman," which first appeared, with different words, as "Hey Lawdy Mama" by Cream. The second type is a song with single chords and repeated motivic figures like A–G♯–E and B–D–E; Cream's song "NSU" stems from similar riff usages in songs like "Cats Squirrel," "Spoonful," and "Traintime," with an added semitonal transposition using two of these motivic figures a semitone apart: C–E♭–F and C♯–E–F♯. A third type of new composition by Cream is based on the V–IV–I–V end and turnaround of a blues; an example is "Take It Back."

The fourth type of Cream composition is blues derived, with a repeating motivic figure. The tune "Sunshine of Your Love" has a riff based on the minor blues pentatonic scale with the characteristic added ♭5 scale degree (ex. 3.10a).[45] In the verse and chorus structure, the verse begins like a twelve-bar blues form (I–IV–I), but its initial eight bars are followed by an eight-bar chorus that consists of a prolonged V chord, with supporting harmonies, in the local key of V, of: C/♭III and G/♭VII (ex. 3.10b). In the sections prolonging V, the thirds of the melody incorporate C♯, which clashes against the accompanying ♭III C chord as a harmonic extension of the traditional melodic ♭3̂/3̂ dichotomy of blues.

While a distinctive feature of "Sunshine" is the drum part, in which Baker con-

Example 3.10b. Chorus from Cream's "Sunshine of Your Love"

centrates on the lower tom sounds and uses an articulation and sound reminiscent of the jazz drumming in the Woody Herman or Benny Goodman bands, the most memorable and forward-looking feature is the recurring newly-composed riff. "Sunshine of Your Love," Cream's best-known song, is a culmination of the British adaptation of blues into rock and also the direct precursor of Led Zeppelin and heavy metal, where this type of blues-based motivic riff and harmonic motions like A–C–G or E–G–A (as in "Whole Lotta Love") serve as the basis for a seemingly endless number of songs.

Conclusion

Writers on the subject of analysis of rock music note that beyond the usual problems of trying to somehow explain music in words, popular music, existing primarily in recorded form, is dependent to an even greater degree than art music on the circumstances of its production, particularly the qualities of sound not easily discussed in music-theoretical or musicological terms, such as the timbre of Clapton's guitar on "Sittin' on Top of the World" or of Howlin' Wolf's voice on his version of the song. As in ethnomusicology, transcription itself is seen as not only problematic but at times as even a political act, serving as part of a broader cooption for the purposes of legitimation and control. Thus, the typical approach based on transcription found in music theory journals or even guitar magazines tends to be regarded with great suspicion and may even be rejected.[46] Aside from the transcription-heavy articles in guitar magazines, there is only a small body of analytical writings on rock music worthy of the name.

Writings on rock and other popular musics tend to consist of arguments from every conceivable point of view—sociological, economic, historical, psychological, technical, and so on—except the music analytic. When considering the problems of explaining the rock music referred to in this article, however, it is important to note that, with the exception of a relatively small group of devotees, audiences who responded to Cream's music in the 1960s had not listened to the original blues versions of most of the songs and were not even aware that there were earlier versions. The only context for most of the audience was supplied by the musicians themselves, particularly those like Clapton, who learned the songs through hours of study from recordings—painstakingly internalizing the notes and rhythms—and then transformed the originals by filtering them through their own musical experience and presenting them using the music technology of the day. This musical connection with the audience and the times is a significant one, and yet, until recently, the elusive question of just what the connection was between the blues originals, the rock reworkings as transmitted by the musicians, and the largely white audience's favorable response has been answered almost exclusively by discussions of race, social history, lyrics, or economics—rarely in terms of musical features of rhythm, harmony, melody, or style.

Critics of a purely musical approach may protest that what is left is an impoverished discussion of notes and rhythms in a vacuum. There is no need to leave out the social histories and cultural studies, however, merely a need to allot musical analysis its proper place. The story of Cream's adaptation of blues songs is a complex one, with the musical aspect of the story playing an integral part—a part as necessary for us to consider as any other aspect if a convincing and thorough understanding of this stylistic transformation is to begin to take shape. I regard my efforts in this chapter as merely one step along the way; I am hampered, of course, by the lack of precise terms and concepts as well as by the lack of a methodology for a systematic discussion of essential elements of rock music, elements such as the qualities of the sound itself: the volume and loudness, timbral effects of distortion and overdriven amplifiers, and the vocal quality. But I also consider this study an argument in favor of music analysis in a field that has long been dominated by the extramusical.

Given these caveats, my comparative discussions of three songs by Cream in relation to their forerunners suggest a few avenues for future study; I will briefly outline four of them here. First, in examining Johnson's "Cross Road Blues"—and, in fact, throughout my analyses above—I have tended to privilege harmony. The standard explanation of blues harmony views it in terms of scales; this is, I believe, misleading when discussing accompanied blues songs, since it undermines the strong harmonic basis of the instruments usually employed (guitar or piano). A melodic approach based on relationships around the chord tones as boundary pillars seems truer to the musical structure of such songs—particularly the melodic-harmonic dichotomy in Johnson's guitar technique—and regarding the harmonic tertian spans (between root and third, third and fifth, and fifth and seventh) as continuous tonal fields for melodic inflection obviates the need to tie melodic interpretation down to any specific notational representation or for arguments about the veracity of notating the third scale degree as systematically flatted or sharpened. The standard blues figure given in example 3.3 above is the most fixed version of this melodic traversing of harmonic spans, while the constant glissandi and moans in Robert Johnson's vocals represent perhaps the least fixed version. Future discussions of blues and rock music need to resolve or at least consider the harmonic versus melodic explanation for musical events.

Second, central to Cream's transformations of blues songs is the creation of fixed signature riffs out of accompanimental motives and the concomitant evening out of rhythms and forms into consistent and continuous meters. The riffs, essential features of rock songs like Cream's "Crossroads," are seemingly transferred from a melodic to a harmonic basis—a process already evident in many Chicago electric blues songs. Thus, rather than figures embedded in an existing harmonic context, they begin to define that context, and, in some Cream songs, but to an ever greater extent in the music of Led Zeppelin and later bands, the riffs themselves become virtually the entire basis for the songs. In these cases, the pronounced metric settings of these riffs, which emphasize built-in syncopations invariably occurring within expanded upbeats to the following downbeat, are an integral aspect of the structure of the music. A thorough study and cataloging of the different aspects of the transformations of these riffs from blues to rock songs would be extremely useful for stylistic definition.

Third, discussions of rhythm in rock music in relation to riffs, forms, and other levels of durations and proportions are often hampered by a confusion between rhythm and meter and how these arise from the grouping structures of harmonies, melodies, bass notes, phrasing, and other musical features. In regard to country blues, the problem is compounded by a confusion of perspective: is it more useful to regard, for instance, Robert Johnson's songs as beginning from a regular metrical basis, as many writers do, with the surface described as "irregular"? Or is an irregular (or, better, not necessarily regular) rhythmic approach more appropriate, with any regular surface meter regarded as a compositional and performance by-product of the grouping structures? Johnson's varied style and oeuvre suggests that not only may either approach be relevant for different songs, as in "From Four till Late" (regular, metric starting point) and "Hellhound on My Trail" (irregular, rhythmic starting point), but that both may be relevant even within the same song, as in "Cross Road Blues," if an adequate discussion of Johnson's complex assimilation of his musical heritage is to be achieved. Cream's regularizing approach strongly suggests that consistent meter is a primary structural determinant in their versions, but their awareness of the distinctions between rhythmic and metric patterns is clear in their version of "Rollin and Tumblin'," where they compound the syncopation of the original, taking this rhythmic feature through a stronger metric conflict and finally a metric shift. Any musical interpretations that fail to take these distinctions into account risk generalizations that miss the essential rhythmic dynamic.

Finally, writers on rock music need to define a systematic yet managable basis for describing the properties, both technical and aesthetic, of the sounds themselves. A distinctive feature of rock music compared to its blues basis is the increased variety of and focus on timbre. Current discussion of sounds in rock and other popular musics tends to be technical or subjective. Some connection between the two is desirable as a way of explaining the formal, rhythmic, and motivic functions of sound and timbre and their role in listeners' perceptions of the music.

These four areas—harmonic versus melodic distinctions, the role of riffs, rhythmic versus metric interpretations, and meaningful definitions of sounds themselves—are only some of the problems encountered in analyzing blues and rock music. In this article I have touched on each of them to varying degrees in my discussions of Cream's reworkings of earlier songs, but a much more detailed and systematic accounting would be necessary for any kind of conclusive study to emerge. While daunting, such a study is eminently worthwhile; my own preliminary work has led me to a far deeper appreciation and understanding of both the source songs and Cream's transformed versions. In the end, this is my only truly defensible justification for advocating a greater role for musical analysis in the study of rock music.

Notes

1. For discussion of British rock adaptations of American blues, see Michael Bane, *White Boy Singin' the Blues* (New York: Penguin Books, 1982); Bob Brunning, *Blues: The British Connection* (Pool: Blandford Press, 1986); Nik Cohn, *Rock from the Beginning* (New York: Pocket Books, 1970; reprint of Stein and Day, 1969); Bob Groom, *The Blues Revival* (London: Studio Vista, 1971); David Hatch and Stephen Millward, *From Blues to Rock: An Analytical History of Pop Music* (Manchester: Manchester University Press, 1987); and Richard Middleton, *Pop Music and the Blues* (London: Victor Gollancz, 1972).

2. That the seminal skiffle song "Rock Island Line," released by Lonnie Donegan (Decca F 19647, 1956), also appeared on the album *New Orleans Joys* by the Chris Barber Band and is based on a song by the American blues singer Leadbelly (Huddie Ledbetter, 1889–1949) is illustrative of the many-faceted influences of American music in postwar Britain.

3. See Cohn, *Rock From the Beginning*, 142–47; Groom, *The Blues Revival*, 7–24; Hatch and Millward, *From Blues to Rock*, 96–107; and Middleton, *Pop Music and the Blues*, 162–74.

4. See Bane, *White Boy Singin' the Blues*, 149–61; Groom, *The Blues Revival*, 98–105; and Hatch and Millward, *From Blues to Rock*, 94–107.

5. For Chicago Blues, see Michael Rowe, *Chicago Blues* (New York: Da Capo Press, 1981); reprint of *Chicago Breakdown* (London: Eddison Press, 1973).

6. Brunning, *Blues*, chap. 1. Many musicians found blues records in specialty record shops, such as the Swing Shop in Streatham (Brunning, *Blues*, 152) or in mail-order catalogs from American record companies. One such company, Arhoolie, was founded by Chris Strachwitz, who bought old Bluebird, Decca, and Vocalion records and sold them in mail-order magazines to English fans from 1959; other labels were Blue Goose, Adelphi, and Country. For a more detailed discussion, see *Guitar Player* 6/5 (July/Aug. 1972): 16.

7. Other musicians visiting England included John Lee Hooker, Champion Jack Dupree, Little Walter, Buddy Guy, Memphis Slim, Sonny Terry, and Brownie McGhee. See Brunning, *Blues*, 166–98; and Groom, *The Blues Revival*, 7–24 and 98–105.

8. See Brunning, *Blues*, 12; *Guitar Player* 17/8 (Aug. 1983): 41; Hatch and Millward, *From Blues to Rock*, 103.

9. See Brunning, *Blues*; Hatch and Millward, *From Blues to Rock*, 94–107; Cohn, *Rock From the Beginning*, 164–87; and Middleton, *Pop Music and Blues*, 187–209. Although the British groups were by far the most popular, many American white bands in the 1960s were also playing the same repertoire of blues songs in transformed settings: Paul Butterfield and the Butterfield Blues Band with Michael Bloomfield and Elvin Bishop (1963), Captain Beefheart (1964), the Sparrow (later Steppenwolf, 1964), the Blues Project (1965), the Doors (1965), the Grateful Dead (1965), Jefferson Airplane (1965), Canned Heat (1966), the Steve Miller Band (1966), Santana (1967), Bob Dylan, John Hammond Jr., and Janis Joplin. See Bane, *White Boy Singin' the Blues*, 182–96, 197–204, and 213–27; Mary Ellison, *Extensions of the Blues* (London: John Calder, 1989), 51–106; and Hatch and Millward, *From Blues to Rock*, 107–15.

10. Bane, *White Boy Singin' the Blues*, 199–201; and Middleton, *Pop Music and the Blues*, 227–51.

11. Harry Shapiro, *Eric Clapton: Lost in the Blues* (New York: Da Capo Press, 1992), 74.

12. Charles Keil (*Urban Blues* [Chicago: University of Chicago Press, 1966]) has compared Willie Dixon's recording of "Little Red Rooster," which sold 20,000 copies, to the Rolling Stones' version, a close cover, which sold 500,000 copies. Keil posits that the Stones' success stemmed from retaining the black blues style but combining it with the contemporary image of punk nonconformity.

13. See Groom, *The Blues Revival*. Freddie King has credited Leon Russell, Clapton, John Mayall, Johnny Winter, Michael Bloomfield, Paul Butterfield, and John Hammond for the blues revival.

14. Much writing on this period notes that black audiences avoided blues and blues-based rock, instead moving on to soul music in the 1960s.

15. For Cream, see Hatch and Millward, *From Blues to Rock*, 104–6; Frank Kofsky, "The Cream: An Interview with Eric Clapton," in *Rock Giants*, ed. Pauline Rivelli and Robert Levin (New York: World Publishing Company, 1967); and Richard Middleton, *Pop Music and the Blues*, 247–49. For Bruce, see Chris Jisi, "Jack Bruce and Billy Sheehan: The Face of the Bass," *Guitar World* 10/4 (April 1989): 34. For Clapton, see Brunning, *Blues*, 30–49; Ray Coleman, *Clapton!* (New York: Warner Books, 1985); Robert Palmer, "Eric Clapton," *Rolling Stone*, 20 June 1985; reprinted in 15 Oct. 1992:126–28; and Shapiro, *Eric Clapton*. See also Clapton features in *Guitar for the Practising Musician*, "Blues Classics Vol. I" (Summer 1989): 50; *Guitar Player* 10/8 (Aug. 1976) and 19/7 (1986); *Guitar World* 10/12 (Dec. 1989); and *Masters of Rock* 8/1 (Spring 1992). Clapton himself wrote an essay, "Discovering Robert Johnson," which appears in the booklet that accompanies *Robert Johnson: The Complete Recordings*, Columbia C2K-46222 (1990), 22–23.

16. The rock trio format was relatively new; other trios were Rory Gallagher's band Taste (1965) (see Brunning, *Blues*, 236), the Jimi Hendrix Experience (1967), and, in the United States, Blue Cheer (1966).

17. Bruce claimed that Cream only started doing its extended improvisations after hearing the long concert evenings provided by groups like the Grateful Dead on the West Coast in 1967. See "Jack Bruce," *Guitar World* 10/4 (Apr. 1989): 34. Clapton had had experience with extended improvisations in the Yardbirds; see Shapiro, *Eric Clapton*, 44.

18. While I have tried to be comprehensive in the list given in figure 3.1, it is undoubtedly incomplete; nonetheless it at least gives some idea of the extent of Cream's reworkings of

blues songs. For sources on the blues songs in figure 3.1, see Sheldon Harris, *Blues Who's Who: A Biographical Dictionary of Blues Singers* (New York: Da Capo Press; reprint, New Rochelle, N.Y.: Arlington House, 1979); and Shapiro, *Eric Clapton*.

19. For the "Rollin' and Tumblin'" family, see Peter Guralnick, *Searching for Robert Johnson* (New York: Dutton, 1989), 58; and Hatch and Millward, *From Blues to Rock*, 198.

20. See Clapton, "Discovering Robert Johnson," 22–23. For sources on Robert Johnson, see Samuel Charters, *Robert Johnson* (New York: Oak Publications, 1973); Werner Gissing, *Mississippi Delta Blues: Formen und Texte von Robert Johnson (1911–38)*, vol. 8 of *Beiträge zur Jazzforschung* (Graz: Akademische Druck- und Verlagsanstalt, 1986); Groom, *The Blues Revival*; Guralnick, *Searching for Robert Johnson*; and Stephen LaVere, *Robert Johnson*, booklet to *The Complete Recordings of Robert Johnson*, 5–21. Johnson in turn followed in the tradition of Willie Brown, Son House, Lonnie Johnson, Tommy Johnson, and Charley Patton.

21. According to Bob Groom (*The Blues Revival*), an Origin release in 1966 of a limited edition with the Johnson songs and takes that did not appear on the first Columbia album prompted the issuing of the second Columbia album. The extent of Johnson's influence is reflected by the appearance of the first Columbia album on the cover of Bob Dylan's third album, *Bringing It All Back Home* (Columbia 9128 [1965]).

22. Although Johnson has become known mostly for his country blues songs, it is worth noting that his generation was the first to be strongly influenced by radio and recordings, and he played a wide variety of songs and styles. Guralnick (*Searching for Robert Johnson*, 23) notes Johnson's affection for Bing Crosby (!), and that he traveled widely, going as far north as Windsor, Ontario.

23. This discussion and analysis are based on the transcriptions of Johnson's songs as they appear in Scott Ainslie and Dave Whitehall, transcribers, *Robert Johnson: At The Crossroads, the Authentic Guitar Transcriptions* (Milwaukee: Hal Leonard, 1992). Gissing divides the twenty-nine songs into five families (*Mississippi Delta Blues*, 150–52). For sources on country blues, see Ainslie and Whitehall, *Robert Johnson*; William Ferris, *Blues from the Delta* (Garden City, N.Y.: Anchor Press, 1978); Hatch and Millward, *From Blues to Rock*, 44–67; Middleton, *Pop Music and the Blues*, 13–70; Paul Oliver, *The Story of the Blues* (Barrie & Rockcliff: Cresset Press, 1969), "Blues," in the *New Grove Gospel, Blues, and Jazz* (New York: Norton, 1986); and Samuel Charters, *The Blues Makers* (New York: Da Capo, 1991), which is a revised reprint of Charters's two earlier books, *The Bluesmen* (New York: Oak Publications, 1967) and *Sweet as the Showers of Rain* (*The Blues Men*, vol. 2) (New York: Oak Publications, 1977).

24. Compare Guralnick (*Searching for Robert Johnson*, 57) who notes that Johnson had his songs worked out ahead of time and generally set, without a great deal of variation. "Cross Road Blues" was recorded in San Antonio on Friday, 27 Nov. 1936.

25. Peter Van der Merwe (*Origins of the Popular Style: The Antecedents of Twentieth-Century Popular Music* [Oxford: Clarendon Press, 1989], 216) notes that W. C. Handy published songs in the twelve-bar form beginning in 1912. Hatch and Millward (*From Blues to Rock*, 185) note the twelve-bar form in Johnson's song "From Four till Late."

26. Writers on blues are split on whether the comparison to the twelve-bar form is a valid one. Scott Ainslie and Dave Whitehall note that with his use of changing rhythmic groups in "Cross Road Blues," Johnson "seemed determined to keep the listener off-balance" (*Robert Johnson*, 52), thus assuming a background regularity against which Johnson consciously worked. The comparison seems valid, but the main point is the changing rhythmic and metric groups, not whether Johnson intentionally varied a strictly even metric norm.

27. In determining the proportions given in figure 3.2, as well as the transcriptions given in examples 3.1 and 3.2, I began from the transcription of Johnson's "Cross Road Blues" in Ainslie and Whitehall, *Robert Johnson*.

28. Ainslie and Whitehall notate their transcription in A but assert that Johnson used a capo to yield the key of B major.

29. See, for instance, Hatch and Millward, *From Blues to Rock*, 62–63.

30. Clapton, "Rediscovering Robert Johnson," 22–23.

31. The transcription is from Fred Sokolow, transcriber, *Eric Clapton: Crossroads*, vol. 1 (Milwaukee: Hal Leonard, 1989). In "Crossroads," Clapton substituted the fourth verse from Johnson's "Travelling Riverside Blues" for the third verse from "Cross Road Blues," as the text to this third verse is difficult to decipher. In addition to Clapton's version, "Cross Road Blues" has been covered by many other musicians, including Stephen Stills, John Hammond Jr., Lynyrd Skynyrd, Ry Cooder, Rory Block, and the Turtle Island String Quartet.

32. For a detailed discussion of Led Zeppelin's adaptation of existing songs, see my "Does the Song Remain the Same? Questions of Authorship and Identification in the Music of Led Zeppelin," in *Concert Music, Rock, and Jazz Since 1945: Essays and Analytical Studies*, ed. Elizabeth West Marvin and Richard Hermann (Rochester, N.Y.: University of Rochester Press, 1995), 313–63.

33. As I discuss below, the process had already occurred in the music of the Chicago electric blues musicians such as Muddy Waters, and rock 'n' roll songs by figures such as Chuck Berry are often based on a recurring guitar riff; but in "Crossroads" Cream adapted their version directly from the original "Cross Road Blues." This type of musical reworking is, of course, not only found in blues, but has occurred throughout, for instance, the history of jazz and other musics.

34. See Guralnick, *Searching for Robert Johnson*, 37 and 58; and Hatch and Millward, *From Blues to Rock*, 186–90.

35. Clapton's guitar style is analyzed in Dave Whitehall, "Steady Rollin' Man: An Analysis and Overview of the Eric Clapton Style," *Guitar World* 10/12 (Dec. 1989): 128–29. In addition to Johnson, Clapton admits to influences from Big Bill Broonzy, Blind Lemon Jefferson, Buddy Guy, Elmore James, B. B. King, Freddy King, Otis Rush, Hubert Sumlin, and Muddy Waters; see *Guitar Player* 17/8 (Aug. 1983): 41.

36. See Hatch and Millward, *From Blues to Rock*, 101, who are of the opinion that the faster tempo of blues adaptations was a "common error among British bands."

37. The change in rhythm and meter is characteristic of many aspects of rock music in relation to its antecedents. For instance, Keith Richards has described how early rock 'n' roll drummers were still swinging with acoustic bass, as in Chuck Berry's "Sweet Little Rock and Roller," but with the 1960s, straight rock eighths emerged, as in Eddie Cochran's reworking entitled "Sweet Little Rock." See *Guitar Player* 23/11 (Nov. 1989).

38. See Rowe, *Chicago Blues*.

39. For Waters, see Jas Obrecht, "Muddy Waters," in *Blues Guitar: The Men Who Made the Music* (San Francisco: GPI Books, 1990).

40. Guralnick (*Searching for Robert Johnson*, 58) notes a first recording of a song with the same text by Hambone Willie Newbern. Hatch and Millward (*From Blues to Rock*, 23–24, 198) call the family "Minglewood Blues/Rollin' and Tumblin'" and note a recording of "Forty Four Blues" by Gus Cannon's Jug Stompers in 1928 as "Minglewood Blues." The Waters-Leroy-Little Walter versions were rereleased on *Chicago Blues: The Early '50s*, Blues Classics 8 (1965). Howlin' Wolf also performed a brief version of "Rollin' and Tumblin'" accompanying himself only on guitar, in a 1968 revival of an earlier version of the song (*Howlin' Wolf: Unissued and Alternate Recordings, 1948–68*, Blue Night Records BN 073–1667 [1979]).

41. The song has Howlin' Wolf on vocal and harmonica, Hosea Lee Kennard on piano, Jody Williams and Hubert Sumlin on guitars, and Earl Phillips on drums; no bass player is listed, but the bass part may have been played by Willie Dixon. The most distinctive feature is, of course, Wolf's voice, which, as Peter Guralnick noted, was "inimitable, cutting with a sand-

paper rasp and overwhelming ferocity but retaining at the same time a curious delicacy of shading, a sense of dynamics and subtlety of approach" ("Howlin' Wolf," liner notes for *Howlin' Wolf: His Greatest Sides Volume 1*, Sugar Hill Records Ltd. [1983]). An in-depth analysis of not only Wolf but Johnson and Waters would have to take the "grain" of their voices into account in a systematic way.

42. The arrangement has two guitars, but it is difficult to separate the two. The notated guitar part in the transcription is compiled from the two parts, which are divided into one guitar with the riffs and brief figures and the other playing the chords on the recording.

43. The transcription of the Cream arrangement is from Any Aledort, transcriber, "Sittin' on Top of the World," *Guitar for the Practicing Musician* 7/7 (May 1990): 49–64. Cream's live version of the song is freer rhythmically, with a thinner texture of alternating solo and rhythm guitar against a running bass in shuffle patterns, and drums with only hints of the martial rhythm in the studio version.

44. Cream's newly composed songs, mostly by Bruce, use English folk song sources, harmonic and melodic patterns after Beatles songs, and psychedelic songs with effects. For instance, a bizarre pychedelic track from the third album is called "Pressed Rat and Warthog"; in the song trumpets sound and the voice intones a sort of children's story text. The songs "White Room" and "Tales of Brave Ulysses" are based (as is the Bob Dylan song "All along the Watchtower," also recorded by Jimi Hendrix) on the prototypical rock progression I–♭VII –♭VI.

45. The transcription in examples 3.10a and 3.10b is from Sokolow, *Eric Clapton: Crossroads.*

46. See, for instance, Susan McClary and Robert Walser, "Start Making Sense! Musicology Wrestles with Rock," in *On Record: Pop, Rock, and the Written Word* (New York: Pantheon Books, 1990), 277–92; Richard Middleton, *Pop Music and the Blues*, and *Studying Popular Music* (Milton Keynes: Open University Press, 1990); Philip Tagg, "Analysing Popular Music: Theory, Method, and Practice," *Popular Music* 2 (1982): 37–67; and Robert Walser, *Running with the Devil: Power, Gender, and Madness in Heavy Metal Music* (Hanover: Wesleyan University Press, 1993).

4

"Joanie" Get Angry

k. d. lang's Feminist Revision

LORI BURNS

1

Joanie Sommers's 1962 hit single "Johnny Get Angry" positions women within a patriarchal society.[1] Defining her role in terms of male dominance, the singer invites her male partner to demonstrate his authority, saying "Johnny get angry, Johnny get mad / Give me the biggest lecture I ever had . . . show me that you care, really care for me." Contemporary singer k. d. lang takes this incitation to anger to its logical conclusion: physical abuse. Her 1985 performance (recorded on videotape[2]) casts a feminist eye upon the earlier song and the social values that it represents. Indeed, lang's interpretation is intended to problematize the issue of violence against women. She manipulates the original song setting to emphasize the inherent imbalance of power between the female and male roles. This chapter analyzes text/music relations in the original song in order to consider how the "feminine" and the "masculine" are constructed within the musical discourse of the song. It then explores how lang develops the original material to reflect the social tension it contains.

The Song Text

I will begin with a brief overview of the text, which is reproduced in figure 4.1. There are three verses, each of which is followed by a statement of the refrain. Figure 4.1 also indicates the overall musical division of the song into instrumental breaks and vocal sections. The Sommers and lang versions both begin with an instrumental introduction; each version also has an instrumental break following the second refrain. Figure 4.1 assigns lyrics to the kazoos in the Sommers break and to the guitar in the lang break. Even though the words are not actually sung, the instruments represent the given text by playing the melodic material that is associated with it: in the Sommers version, the kazoos take the melody of the complete refrain; in the lang version, the guitar plays the melody associated with the first two lines of the verse, followed by the last two lines of the refrain. Figure 4.1 also indicates the textual content of the coda section. Following the third refrain, Sommers repeats fragments from the last line of the refrain, fading out without a clear cadence. Lang's coda features an extensive vocalise, also on fragments of text from the last line of the refrain, followed by a guitar solo on the last two lines of the refrain, leading to a true cadential ending.

Throughout the song text, a woman addresses her male partner, whom she identifies as "Johnny." Since the woman never reveals her own name, I will refer to her as "Johnny's girlfriend."[3] In the first two verses, Johnny's girlfriend describes a scene or confrontation with Johnny. In each of these verses, the first two lines describe a test of his feelings for her, the third line focuses on his reaction to the test, and in the fourth line she expresses her frustration with this reaction. In verse 1, she tells him that their relationship is over just to test his feelings, but when he responds by simply hanging his head, she is disappointed. Her exclamation leads her into the refrain, where she vents her frustration and identifies the response she was looking for: she wants him to be angry, to lecture her. She also identifies the type of man she wants—a "cave man," suggesting someone primitive and physically overwhelming. In the last line of the refrain she implores him to "show me that you care, really care for me." Thus, verbal and physical domination are equated with a demonstration of commitment. The internal repetition in the phrase "care, really care" emphasizes her appeal.

In verse 2, Johnny is put to the test again; she recounts how he allows another man to cut in when they are dancing together. When Johnny doesn't complain about Freddie's interruption, she is disappointed by his behavior—"meek," as opposed to the desired image of the cave man evoked in her refrain. The verse leads into the refrain, where Johnny is once again urged to anger, to action. The refrain explicitly equates male action with male anger. Thus, in this song, males are either passive or angry, and Johnny's girlfriend makes it clear which type of man she wants.

The third verse is written from a different perspective. Rather than chastising him, Johnny's girlfriend tries to appeal to his manhood, to convince him that he should be in command of their relationship. She accomplishes this by positioning herself as a weak little "girl" and by providing a larger social context, justifying her desires as being those of "every girl." She wants her relationship to be consistent with that of patriarchal society. This translates into being physically and socially dominated; she "wants someone who she can always look up to." She continues to appeal

Figure 4.1. Musical division and text of "Johnny Get Angry"

Instrumental Introduction

V1   Johnny I said we were through
        Just to see what you would do,
        You stood there and hung your head,
        Made me wish that I were dead! Oh,

R1   *Johnny get angry, Johnny get mad,*
        Give me the biggest lecture I ever had,
        I want a brave man, I want a cave man,
        Johnny show me that you care, really care for me.

V2   Ev'ry time you dance with me
        You let Freddie cut in constantly,
        When he does you never [don't] speak,
        Must you always be so meek? Oh,

R2   *Johnny get angry, Johnny get mad,*
        Give me the biggest lecture I ever had,
        I want a brave man, I want a cave man,
        Johnny show me that you care, really care for me.

Instrumental Break

Sommers (kazoos)   *Johnny get angry, Johnny get mad,*
                    Give me the biggest lecture I ever had,
                    I want a brave man, I want a cave man,
                    Johnny show me that you care, really care for me.

lang (guitar)   Ev'ry girl want someone who
               She can always look up to,
               I want a brave man, I want a cave man,
               Johnny show me that you care, really care for me.

V3   Ev'ry girl wants someone who
        She can always look up to,
        You know I love you of course,
        Let me know that you're the boss! Oh,

R3   *Johnny get angry, Johnny get mad,*
        Give me the biggest lecture I ever had,
        I want a brave man, I want a cave man,
        Johnny show me that you care, really care for me. Johnny,

Coda

Sommers   *Care for me Johnny,*
                 Johnny, Johnny, Johnny, Johnny,
                 Johnny . . . [voice and inst. fade out; no cadence]

lang   voice: *Johnny,*
                  Johnny,
                  Johnny, Johnny, Johnny, Show me that you care,
        guitar: *I want a brave man, I want a cave man*
                  Johnny, show me that you care, really care for me. [cadence]

to him in the third line, when she actually expresses her love for him. In the final line, she clarifies her view of the ideal relationship: she wants him to be the boss, she wants him to dominate her.

The text of this song reflects the social attitudes of the 1950s and early '60s, a time when women stereotypically were subordinate to men. Given that the song was written and produced by men, it should not come as a surprise that the song upholds this view of male-female relationships. Joanie Sommers's role in the production of "Johnny Get Angry" is that of an actor, someone who can articulate the feminine, who can appeal to the masculine, who will accept the role of "Johnny's girlfriend." This song belongs to a generation of "girlfriend songs" from the 1950s and '60s, songs about teen romance performed by "girl groups" such as the Shirelles, the Crystals, and the Shangri-Las.[4] In these songs, the young girls worship the boys as heroes and willingly accept a submissive role. Indeed, Ruth Scovill writes that during this period, "the majority of lyrics defended male superiority and female subservience. Rock music of the fifties was based on a relatively naive sexism of follow-the-status-quo-and-you-will-live-happily-ever-after. Songs did not realistically express the experiences of being a woman or present choices or strong role models for women. . . . Most popular songs have been written by men, and so portray a male viewpoint."[5] Some of the songs, like "Johnny," even went so far as to suggest the physical control of the girlfriend by the boyfriend; an extreme example in this context is the Crystals' "He Hit Me (And It Felt like a Kiss)," which was released in the early 1960s, but withdrawn.[6] Despite the bleak view of gender relations that is offered by such songs, it is important to observe here that there have been female artists who have fought against the stereotype. An important early song in this regard, for instance, is Lesley Gore's "You Don't Own Me" from 1964.[7]

Lang's Feminist Revision

Sommers's 1962 recording presents a particular image of women, an image that does not reflect the ways in which women have tried, at many stages in the history of the feminist movement, to redefine their role in society. Lang, in her 1985 performance, offers a feminist interpretation of the earlier song. As a self-proclaimed feminist, she has rejected gender stereotyping throughout her career. She says firmly: "My personal fight is not to fall into the social [formula] of what a woman should be. Although I don't necessarily hate an image like Dolly Parton's, because that's how she feels comfortable. I'm just saying . . . individuality in women is important. There's a strength there."[8] Lang has worked hard to create a positive role model for women and explains her popularity with female audiences as follows: "I'm offering women something that they don't have a lot of: a strong example, something that's geared more toward women's feelings."[9] In this context, her performance of "Johnny Get Angry," a song in which a woman invites abuse, might be considered unusual. When asked about her choice to sing "Johnny Get Angry," lang explains: "I guess I try to look at things in all dimensions. I try to deliver a song like "Johnny Get Angry" with layers, so that a member of the audience who has been abused can go, wow, she's talking to me, or a guy who's sitting there dreaming about slapping his wife can also feel something from it. I received a letter just the other day from a feminist saying, 'I'm really upset by you doing "Johnny Get Angry" because I can't figure out whether you're condemning or condoning it.' I would assume that a woman who looks and acts like me, well, it would be pretty obvious what I felt about it."[10]

But how might a feminist look at such a piece of music? Popular-music critic Simon Frith has written, "The question we should be asking is not what does popular music reveal about 'the people' but how does it construct them."[11] This leads me to explore two questions: What is the social statement that lang is trying to make with this song? And how does she construct the female role in relation to her male partner? With regard to women taking charge of woman's media images, the media critic Rosemary Betterton writes: "What is at stake is the power of images to produce and to define the feminine in specific ways. By investigating what controls the image and how its power operates, feminist criticism can begin to explore the ways in which women can produce and take possession of their own images."[12] Ultimately lang makes a powerful feminist statement simply by illuminating the frightening consequence of women being dominated by men. I believe she wants us to reflect on the following questions: Is there a fundamental difference between male authority and abuse? Is one the logical outcome of the other? And perhaps most problematic, what part do women play in the abusive relationship?

Lang claims that her goal is to look at a song in all its dimensions, to deliver it with "layers" of meaning. The medium of videotape instantly adds another layer, by giving her the opportunity to act out the story. In Sommers's performance, Johnny's girlfriend appears as the sole character. She addresses Johnny, so we believe that she is delivering the text to him, and our impression of him is only created through her reference. Lang, by contrast, manages to establish Johnny's presence. We understand through lang's performance that Johnny actually does strike his girlfriend. Lang wants to realize explicitly the implications of the song text: an invitation to abuse can result in abuse.

Lang acts as a commentator or interpreter throughout her performance by playing both the role of Johnny's girlfriend and the role of Johnny. Whereas Joanie Sommers gives a credible performance of the feminine role, lang appears to parody the masculine and feminine roles. It is hard to imagine that she could sing this song without some self-reflection or tongue-in-cheek interpretation. Joanie Sommers gives a charming performance of the song, maintaining a sweet (almost childlike) vocal quality and even emotional disposition throughout. She attempts to get what she wants from Johnny by exploiting the "little girl" aspect of femininity. In contrast, lang creates an emotionally charged drama, leading to a climactic crisis through her dramatic actions and her development of the original musical language. She suggests another possible interpretation of the woman's role in this song. Lang's woman is experienced and aggressive. In her hands, the song is not just about female submissiveness, or if it is, this is being presented through female aggression with a demand for being slapped down.

Lang's actions contribute to the impression that she is role playing. During the lengthy introduction she walks around the stage with her head bent down, striking herself repeatedly on the forehead. This action is puzzling: she might be playing the role of Johnny, or she might be playing the part of a commentator, an impersonator preparing to make a "face" of some sort. She emerges from this posture in order to sing the first line of the verse, and it is clear that she is now playing the role of Johnny's girlfriend, addressing Johnny. She sings these opening two lines rhythmically out of sync with the accompanying instruments. There are many possible interpretations of lang's rhythmic distortions, but in connection with her role playing, I am struck by one: the rhythmic syncopations contribute to the ironic or parodic effect of lang's performance. This is, after all, a cover performance of a song written over twenty years earlier; lang is not merely playing roles within the parameters of the song itself, she is also taking on social issues from a previous generation, causing us to reflect on both the humorous aspects and the serious consequences of those values.

Lang returns to her opening posture before the second verse as well: she hangs her head and strikes herself again on the forehead. When she emerges in time for the second verse she is now apparently imitating a man, presumably Johnny. She alters her physical expression by waving her arms in the air in a stiff, awkward manner. She also changes her vocal quality. She sings the first two lines out of sync again but now emphasizes the rhythmic distortion by singing in short, stuttering notes; that is, she interrupts the musical flow from one word to the next by shortening the value of certain notes and replaces the lost values with rests. The text delivery is thus made monosyllabic and nonlinear. This manner of delivery depicts Johnny as a man who is incapable of subtle expression. For the third verse, lang emphasizes the textual content of "every girl wants someone who she can always look up to" by leaning back and looking up at Johnny. These lines are once again delivered out of sync with the accompaniment.

It is in the refrain that Johnny's girlfriend actually tries to induce his anger, and it is here that lang demonstrates the possible outcome of such anger. At the end of the text "Johnny get angry, Johnny get mad," lang punches her fist into the air, accompanied by a cymbal crash. In the original song, this musical punctuation was heard as an "innocent" rising scale passage in the violins. As lang sings the line "I want a brave man" she flexes her bicep to demonstrate physical strength. Through this gesture, she appears to taunt Johnny, by parodying his movements. The punch into the air and the flexed muscles imitate his actions, either actual or potential.

Lang increases the intensity of the violence with each statement of the refrain: in the first refrain the cymbal crash accompanies a punch into the air; in the second refrain, she uses her whole arm to mimic a strike; and in the final refrain she does not imitate a strike but actually reacts to being struck. Until now, the punches and strikes have been without consequence, perhaps imaginary. At this point, however, she throws her head to one side and stumbles as if she has been hit in the face.

Lang also draws our attention to the last line of text in the refrain, "Johnny, show me that you care." As she begins this appeal with his name she changes her vocal quality to a low, unpitched register, returning to her singing voice as the line continues. In the second refrain, the utterance is now heard in a higher register and has the vocal quality of a scream. In the final refrain, it is a shriek in a very high register. With this shriek, she explicitly acts out the beating—she sustains the shriek for a long time while she falls backward to the floor. Following her collapse, she holds an uncomfortably long pause. (In the recorded live performance, the audience becomes restless and nervously responds to the drama while she maintains her position on the floor; one male audience member actually shouts, "Get rid of Johnny.")

What follows is an extended coda in which lang remains on the floor, still unable to rise but continuing to sing "Johnny, Johnny, Johnny." She begins in a very high register and gradually descends, bending each pitch toward the next in a manner that imitates weeping. The singer's last statement is a repetition of the text "Show me that you care." The striking dramatic effect of this coda is that although Johnny's girlfriend is still unable to rise from the floor, she repeats the very request that got her into this position in the first place.

Text-Music Relations and Gendered Discourse in "Johnny Get Angry"

Lang's contribution to the feminist revival of the song is not simply a matter of adding a visual element. She transforms the musical structure itself, creating a commentary on the opposing gender roles that resides in the purely musical domain. During the analysis that follows I will draw upon traditional music-theoretical concepts of harmonic and formal structure, although these concepts will be reinterpreted from a feminist perspective. Susan McClary has explored ways in which theoretical definitions of harmonic and thematic elements such as cadence types, the opposition of major and minor, and dissonance resolution have been classified according to gender. She is interested in exploring how the binary opposites of masculine and feminine are mapped onto strong and weak elements in musical language.[13] McClary also explores the representation of gender and sexuality in musical narrative; the analytic approach of Heinrich Schenker, for instance, is considered for its ability "to chart simultaneously the principal background mechanisms through which tonal compositions arouse desire and the surface strategies that postpone gratification."[14] In this song, the metaphors of desire and resolution, or tension and release, are realized in the singer's efforts to induce male anger and the consequences of that anger: violence. While the application of Schenkerian analysis to a popular song may raise methodological questions, I believe that the analytical results prove the validity of this approach. Tonal harmonic function carries with it a code of predictable idioms and relationships. This popular song works within and plays upon well-known harmonic conventions, and a graph of the melodic and harmonic events clearly demonstrates the moments when harmonic implications are denied or realized.

In my earlier overview of the text, I summarized the textual content of verses 1 and 2. In the first two lines of each verse, Johnny's girlfriend puts Johnny to the test:

Verse 1:

line 1	Johnny I said we were through
line 2	Just to see what you would do

Verse 2:

line 1	Ev'ry time you dance with me
line 2	You let Freddie cut in constantly

With these lines, she tries to elicit a response, a demonstration of feelings from Johnny; this is her opportunity to use her feminine appeal to invite him to action. The musical support for these lines of text plays upon a familiar harmonic convention: the harmony oscillates back and forth between D-major and B-minor harmony in a I–vi–I–vi progression that sets up but repeatedly avoids the expected continuation of IV–V–I. Example 4.1 reproduces the first nine measures of Sommers's recording. The bass line repeats a chromatic descent from D to B, followed by a chromatic return to D. As an accompaniment to this, starting in measure 3, the rhythm guitar moves back and forth between D-major and B-minor harmony. The horn enters in measure 5 with F♯, which is heard alternately as the third of D major and the fifth of B minor. In the upper register, the piano enters in measure 7 with a repeated pattern: a rhythmic motive that rocks back and forth between a C♯–D–F♯ cluster and B. This motive suggests a B-minor harmony.

When the voice enters, these instrumental parts continue as support for the first two lines of text. Example 4.2 analyzes the vocal melody and its harmonic support. As the harmony oscillates between D and B, the voice, beginning on F♯, outlines a B-minor triad (F♯–D–B). Thus, when Johnny's girlfriend is expressing herself, trying to taunt Johnny into a response, the harmonic support is a plaintive repetition pattern of I–vi–I–vi, with the motivic falling third figures both in the bass's D–B and in the voice is F♯–D. This progression is harmonically weak; that is, it does not clearly define the tonic D through the conventional idiom of V–I. As we shall see, that stronger tonal progression will be reserved for a different part of the text.

In lines 3 and 4 of verses 1 and 2, Johnny's girlfriend describes Johnny's reaction and then exclaims her own frustration with what amounts to his non-reaction:

Verse 1:

line 3   You stood there and hung your head,
line 4   Made me wish that I were dead! Oh

Verse 2:

line 3   When he does you never speak,
line 4   Must you always be so meek? Oh

Example 4.2 demonstrates how the harmonic support for lines 3 and 4 now continues to the expected cadential progression in D major. The chromatic motive (from D to B) in the bass guitar and the rocking motive in the piano are no longer present. The bass now falls to G (subdominant of D) for the first time and then moves to A (dominant of D). The dominant is prolonged through her exclamation of frustration, resolving to the tonic when she begins the refrain with "Johnny get angry."

In the musical underpinning of the verse, the submediant, B minor, is the harmony associated with Johnny's girlfriend. When Johnny himself enters the song, as she describes his reaction to her test, D major is defined in a strong dominant-tonic resolution. Once D is defined through its dominant, her harmony (B minor) is then subsumed as subsidiary to this dominant. In lines 3–4, B is heard in the bass as a passing note between the root of V and its first inversion. The harmony supported by the B is IV⁶. Then, as the first inversion is introduced, the voice clarifies the function of B as a melodic neighbor to A in a dominant 9–8 resolution. D major is con-

Example 4.1. "Johnny Get Angry" (Sommers), mm. 1–9 transcription

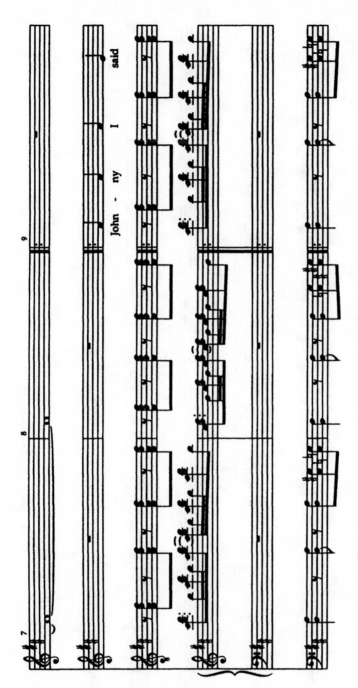

Example 4.1. (continued)

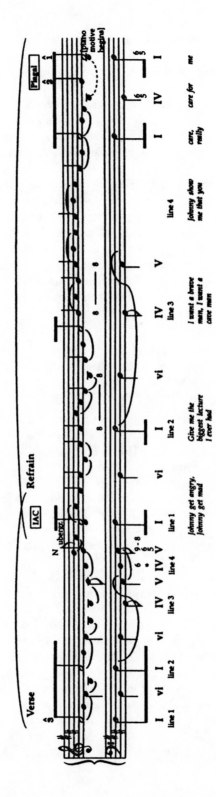

Example 4.2. Analytic sketch

firmed as the tonic when the dominant resolves at the beginning of the refrain in a phrase elision.

In her revision, lang develops two musical features of the original verse. First, lang sings lines 1 and 2 rhythmically out of sync with the accompanying instruments. That is, she enters off the beat and stays behind the beat for the first two lines, aligning rhythmically with the accompaniment at the beginning of line 3. As she moves into the refrain, the stronger rhythmic pulses and clearer tonal function appear as a striking contrast to the rhythmic syncopations and the weaker opening harmonic progression.

Second, lang alters the chord (marked by the asterisk in ex. 4.2) that passes between the dominant and its first inversion. She maintains the bass line here (A–B–C#), but substitutes the harmony of vi, B minor, as the passing chord between V and its first inversion. This simple substitution emphasizes the function of vi (the harmony associated with Johnny's girlfriend) as a subsidiary harmony to V (the harmony associated with Johnny) by articulating it explicitly as a passing chord.

The refrain of the song recasts the harmonic material of the verse to create a stronger harmonic progression in D. This is the moment in the text where Johnny's girlfriend reveals what she wants from Johnny:

Refrain:
line 1   Johnny get angry, Johnny get mad,
line 2   Give me the biggest lecture I ever had,
line 3   I want a brave man, I want a cave man,
line 4   Johnny, show me that you care, really care for me.

Example 4.2 indicates in Roman numerals the harmonic progression that supports the lines of text: lines 1 and 2 of the refrain recall the D major–B minor oscillation of the verse, analyzed as I–vi–I–vi. However, the vocal line no longer outlines the B-minor triad. It begins again on F#, the third of D major, but this time skips up to A. When B minor is introduced in the bass, the F# is held before it falls to D, the third of B. The outline of the vocal melody is therefore no longer a B-minor triad (F#–D–B) but rather a D-major triad (F#–A–F#–D). The voice does descend to B in line 2 of the refrain—not insignificantly—on the word "I"; that is, when Johnny's girlfriend refers to herself here, she descends to her pitch (B) and her harmony (B minor).

Line 3 of the refrain ("I want a brave man, I want a cave man") initiates the movement toward the dominant (from IV to V), recalling the harmonic progression of the verse. The resolution from V to I as she sings "Johnny, show me that you care" recalls the phrase elision at the end of the verse and the beginning of the refrain; the voice once again articulates the note B^4 as a neighbor to A^4 over dominant harmony, then falls to F# as the third of the tonic. Thus a melodic and harmonic connection is made between the lines of text "Oh, Johnny get angry" and "Johnny, show me that you care." The emotions of anger and affection are thereby linked; these ideas are singled out in the song to be supported by dominant-tonic progressions.

Lang significantly revises the dominant-tonic resolution at "Johnny, show me that you care." The original version and lang's expansion are given in example 4.3. In her presentation of the text, "Johnny, show me that you," lang expands the measure

a) Sommers

[*piano motive begins]

John - ny show me that you | care real-ly care for | me | | Verse 2

b) Lang

[*piano motive begins]

John- ny   Show me that you | care real-ly care | for | me | simile

Example 4.3. (a) Sommers. (b) lang

from its original 4/4 meter to 5/4. The expansion occurs in the first part of the mea-sure, where she develops three beats out of the original two. Lang imposes a full quarter rest on the downbeat, where the original had only an eighth-note rest. She then utters "Johnny" in the rhythm of two eighth notes, as compared to the quarter-eighth pattern of the original song. She inserts another full quarter rest before she continues with the line as it was sung in the original. The metric distortion of the original song interrupts the rhythmic flow of lang's version, highlighting this mea-sure as a critical moment in the drama.

The harmonic and melodic content of this measure is worthy of comment as well. In the Sommers version (ex. 4.3a), the text "Johnny, show me" is sung to the complete upper-neighbor motive A^4–B^4–A^4. Lang changes the melodic content of this measure in each of the three statements of the refrain. In the first statement of the refrain (ex. 4.3b), she utters the word "Johnny" without definite pitch and then enters with "show me" on B^4–A^4, thus emphasizing the B as an incomplete neigh-bor. In the second statement of the refrain, the exclamation is in a higher register and has a screamlike quality. In the final statement the exclamation has become a high-register shriek (at approximately G^5). She also, in this final statement, height-ens the rhythmic distortion with her unusually long pause as she falls to the floor. For lang, this is the dramatic and musical climax of the song. She thus highlights it as a significant moment in the musical discourse: the dominant harmony accompa-nies the violent act that throws Johnny's girlfriend to the floor. The resolution to the tonic takes place only after she has recovered enough to carry on. Indeed, even though she has been knocked down, Johnny's girlfriend still emerges with the reso-lution to tonic as support for the line "show me that you care."

An important feature of the vocal line, and one that is brought out by lang in her version, is the absence of the pitch E in the cadence at the end of the verse. The graph in example 4.2 shows a connection between the initial F♯ and the E in line 4 of the verse. The E is expected as the pitch that will arrive above the inverted dominant harmony in the bass. It is the logical continuation from the C♯ and D. However, the voice avoids this E, superposing instead the B–A gesture. The E is interesting precisely because the voice does not sing it; the logical tonal progression sets up certain expectations, and we are very much aware when these expectations are denied. It is significant that the avoided pitch is the cadential scale degree 2 supported by the dominant. The dominant is the harmonic event that triggers Johnny's actions; lang demonstrates this when she is knocked to the floor during the later dominant-tonic resolution at "Johnny, show me that you care."

The E supported by its dominant is also avoided in the cadential structure of the refrain. Here, the voice does articulate the logical melodic descent from F♯ through E to D, but this time the missing ingredient is the dominant harmony. A V–I resolution occurs at "Johnny, show me that you care," but this happens in the middle of the last line, leaving room for a final plagal cadential progression.

After the V–I resolution at "Johnny, show me that you care," the text continues with "really care for me," adding emphasis to her request. When she refers to herself here ("care for me"), she returns to the "weaker" harmonic language that was heard at the opening of the song. Example 4.2 shows how the bass articulates the plagal gesture D–G–D, while the soprano gradually moves down from F♯ (above D) through E (above G) to D. The E functions as an added sixth in the harmony of IV. The final tonic also includes an added sixth; as the voice ends with this cadence, the instruments return to the motivic material of the opening, including the piano motive that introduces C♯ on the downbeat as a displacement for the following B. Thus the final cadence is not allowed to be conclusive; the added sixth sonorities contradict clear resolution. The final D-major chord is "cluttered" or "weakened" by the B.[15] In the final gesture, the singer returns to "her" harmonic language, by reminding us of the earlier oscillation between D major and B minor. The plagal cadence with added sixths is a striking contrast to the clearer V–I progressions associated with Johnny.

Lang builds upon the weakness of this final plagal cadence. Although she leads into the plagal cadence of the original song, she disrupts its resolution through a rhythmic expansion of the vocal line. Example 4.3b shows how lang descends on the word "care" to the B[3] of the original line but then lingers there for a full half note, moving on to the expected vocal cadence E[4]–D[4] only after another quarter rest. By expanding the duration of the B[3] on "care" and then introducing a quarter rest before the continuation of the text, lang avoids the clear resolution of the "really care for me" plagal cadence. Although the bass moves in its cadential gesture D–G–D, the voice does not keep up but rather lingers over each word of the phrase so that by the time the voice cadences on "for me" the bass has already moved on in its chromatic descending pattern to B minor. Here lang takes an existing "weak" cadential gesture—a plagal cadence with added sixths—and weakens it further by taking closure away from D major and instead allowing B minor to complete the gesture (the overall harmonic cadence is thus I–IV–I–vi).

The final statement of the verse-refrain structure is further enhanced by its transposition up a semitone, a cliché in popular music but nonetheless a gesture that contributes to the unfolding of this particular musical-dramatic plot. In both performances, the transposition takes place in the instrumental bridge between the second refrain and the third verse.

Also distinguishing the final verse-refrain statement is the addition of the coda. Example 4.4a reproduces the vocal line from Sommers's coda. The voice is accompanied by the motivic bass line, which oscillates between I and vi (now E♭ and C), and the motivic piano pattern, which outlines the minor triad (now C minor). The vocal line emphasizes C and the harmony of vi. The final cadence at the end of the refrain was the added-sixth plagal cadence (in E♭), but during the coda, the vocal line outlines the harmony of C minor. First, Sommers embellishes the fifth of C with a G–F♯–G figure. Then she leaps up to C^5 and embellishes a descending C-minor triad as she reiterates, "Care for me, Johnny," repeating his name over several measures. This melodic material derives from the last line of the refrain, reproduced in example 4.4b. At the end of the refrain, however, C^5 is treated as a melodic neighbor note to B♭ in the context of E♭ major (B♭–C–B♭ functions as $\hat{5}$–$\hat{6}$–$\hat{5}$), and C^4 is harmonized as the third of the subdominant in the E♭-major plagal cadence. In the coda (ex. 4.4a), the same melodic material is reinterpreted to give emphasis to C. The pitch C^5 is no longer articulated as a complete upper neighbor to B♭, and C^4 is given C-minor harmonic support. The ending thus returns to the harmonic language of the song's opening in which the harmony oscillates between I and vi (D major to B minor, now E♭ major to C minor), and thus to the harmonic language that was associated with the desires of Johnny's girlfriend.

In her coda, lang once again expands upon the material from the original song. She begins it by further disrupting the final plagal cadence. Example 4.5 demonstrates how, in the final statement of this cadence (now in E♭) she moves from the cadential E♭ down to D, destroying the possible vocal closure on E♭. She then builds upon Sommers's original G–F♯–G gesture for several measures. She begins an octave higher on G^5 (recalling the register of her shriek) and steps down to C^5, bending each pitch toward the next in a manner that imitates weeping. From C^5 she leaps down to G^4. This general outline is repeated, then follows a series of low-register (although unpitched) utterances on the word "Johnny." Lang's last statement is a repetition of the text "Show me that you care" on the melodic pattern that Sommers outlined in her coda. This pattern, C–B♭–G–E♭–C, discussed earlier in connection with example 4.4b, recalls the last line of the refrain but emphasizes C minor ("her" harmony) rather than E♭ major.

The final word, so to speak, in lang's interpretation is given to the guitar. We hear a rhythmically "straight" version of the last two lines from the refrain, "I want a brave man, I want a cave man / Johnny, show me that you care, really care for me." Whereas the voice avoids a clear rhythmic presentation of the E♭-major plagal cadence, the final cadence is allowed here, although the added sixth in the final E♭ tonic is emphasized in the guitar melody; the guitar oscillates between E♭–C and F–C while E♭ is held in the bass. Through the guitar presentation we are reminded of the text that asks Johnny to demonstrate his affection through a display of power. It is interesting to consider the role of the male guitarist in this final presentation; his tone and style of presentation lend a lyrical quality to these lines of text. Perhaps the guitarist here represents Johnny after the beating, taking a gentler, more apologetic tone with his girlfriend. Such an ending evokes the cyclic nature of an abusive relationship.

Example 4.4. (a) Sommers's coda. (b) End of refrain

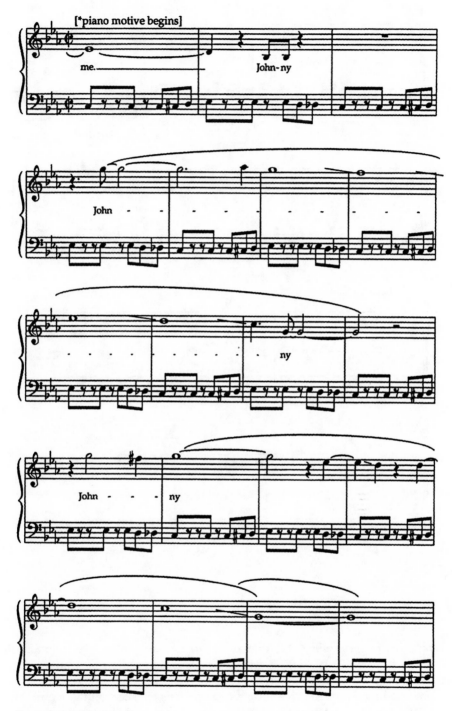

Example 4.5. lang's coda

Example 4.5. (*continued*)

Lang's Social Statement

Lang exaggerates the inherent features of the original song and carries them to their logical conclusion. By playing on the "weaker" versus the "stronger" features in the original song's musical discourse, she exposes the imbalance of power ascribed to women and men in patriarchal society. She wants us to reflect on the social situation: what is the woman's role in the cycle of abuse? In this particular song, the abused woman is represented by an ambiguous or "weaker" musical language as opposed to the "stronger" harmonic language of the man. Since the entire story is told by the woman, both gendered idioms are articulated by her; she therefore participates in the patriarchal stereotype of a weak female dominated by a strong male. However, she is not a passive victim, but literally goads him into violence. By encouraging the gendered roles, lang appears to assert that the woman is partly responsible for this social interaction. If she wants to be powerless in relation to a strong male, then she must be held accountable, to some extent, for the potential results. Lang is certainly not saying that the woman wants to be beaten—she weeps after the beating—nor is she saying that the woman is entirely responsible for her social situation—she is behaving as she has been taught to do—but lang is saying that the woman's desire for a femininity that is defined by male domination can lead to abuse. By realizing the potential results of this "femininity," she reminds women that it is dangerous to accept a passive role. Lang also explores, in her critical interpretation of the song, music's power to reflect and construct the gender roles of our culture.

Notes

Earlier versions of this chapter were presented at the British Music Analysis Conference in Southampton (Mar. 1993) and the conference on Feminist Theory and Music II in Rochester (June 1993). I wish to thank John Armstrong, David Lewin, and Susan McClary as well as the editors of this volume for their thoughtful comments on earlier drafts.

1. Joanie Sommers, "Johnny Get Angry," Warner 5275 (1962).

2. k. d. lang and the reclines, "Johnny Get Angry," performed live on the MuchMusic Big Ticket Special 1985); released on k. d. lang, *Harvest of Seven Years* (Warner Reprise Video, 1991).

3. I recognize that by doing so, I reduce her to a subordinate role, and that this is problematic. We will see that her role in the relationship is not merely subordinate; after all, she does taunt Johnny into a violent reaction.

4. See, for instance, the Shirelles, "Will You Love Me Tomorrow," Scepter 1211 (1960); the Crystals, "Then He Kissed Me," Philles 115 (1963); and the Shangri-Las, "Leader of the Pack," Red Bird 014 (1964).

5. Ruth Scovill, "Women's Music," in *Women's Culture: The Renaissance of the Seventies,* ed. Gayle Kimball (Metuchen and London: Scarecrow Press, 1981), 149.

6. The Crystals, "He Hit Me," label unknown (1962?). Written by Carole King and Gerry Goffin, this song is discussed briefly in Gillian G. Gaar, *She's a Rebel: The History of Women in Rock & Roll* (Seattle: Seal Press, 1992), 44–45, 118.

7. Leslie Gore, "You Don't Own Me," Mercury 72206 (1964). For extensive discussions of the role of women in rock music, see Simon Frith and Angela McRobbie, "Rock and Sexuality," *Screen Education* 29 (1978), reprinted in *On Record: Rock, Pop, and the Written Word,* ed. Simon Frith and Andrew Goodwin (New York: Pantheon Books, 1990), 371–89; Sheryl Garratt, "Teenage Dreams," *Signed, Sealed, and Delivered* (London: Pluto Press, 1984), reprinted in *On Record,* 399–409; Barbara Bradby, "Do-Talk and Don't-Talk: The Division of the Subject in Girl-Group Music," in *On Record,* 341–68; Ray Pratt, "Women's Voices, Images, and Silences," in *Rhythm and Resistance* (New York: Praeger Publishers, 1990), 143–74; Susan McClary, "Living to Tell: Madonna's Resurrection of the Fleshly," in *Feminine Endings: Music, Gender, and Sexuality* (Minneapolis: University of Minnesota Press, 1991), 148–66; S. Kay Hoke, "American Popular Music," in *Women and Music,* ed. Karin Pendle (Bloomington: Indi-

ana University Press, 1991), 258–81; Charlotte Greig, *Will You Still Love Me Tomorrow? Girl Groups from the 50s On . . .* (London: Virago Press, 1989); and Gaar, *She's a Rebel.*

8. k. d. lang, "Lesley Gore on k. d. lang," interview by Lesley Gore in *Ms.* 1/1 (July/Aug. 1990): 31.

9. k. d. lang, "Lang: Virgin Territory," interview by Brendan Lemon in *the Advocate,* 16 June 1992: 38.

10. lang, "Lesley Gore on k. d. lang," 31.

11. Simon Frith, "Towards an Aesthetic of Popular Music," in *Music and Society,* ed. Richard Leppert and Susan McClary (Cambridge: Cambridge University Press, 1987), 137.

12. Rosemary Betterton, *Looking On: Images of Femininity in the Visual Arts and Media* (London and New York: Pandora, 1987), 5.

13. McClary, *Feminine Endings,* 9–12.

14. McClary, *Feminine Endings,* 13.

15. Even though added-sixth sonorities are conventional in popular music, I wish to assert their contextual pertinence here.

5

Swallowed by a Song

Paul Simon's Crisis of Chromaticism

WALTER EVERETT

Grown men living in a kid's world!" So the trapped singer-songwriter Jonah Levin and his band are described by Levin's wife, Marion, in *One Trick Pony*, a film written by Paul Simon, who also stars as Levin. Rock 'n' roll is Jonah's life, and it is a field that, according to Simon, "really is not given to thinking—and *resents* thinking. Which I believe is the big error of rock 'n' roll. It's always aspired to be the music of the working class. And it's never been looked upon as a vocabulary for art and artistic thinking. . . . We have to be able to expand the vocabulary to express more complex thoughts."[1]

Ever since "The Sounds of Silence" topped the national singles charts in January 1966, Simon has been recognized for the merit of his poetic lyrics; but his musical materials have been given little analytical attention, even though his tonal language and rhythmic variety could at times attain a high degree of complexity, especially as they did during the 1970s. Following an introduction to Simon's compositional goals and methods, largely through his own words, this essay will explore examples of his tonal structures—particularly chromatic ones—that are quite atypical of rock music. A number of songs from the 1970s will be studied in varying degrees of detail, but closest analysis will be afforded two 1975 compositions, "Still Crazy after All These Years" and "I Do It for Your Love," and the 1980 song "Jonah."

Simon as a Thinking Rock 'n' Roller

Paul Simon has a respect for academia that must have been nurtured by his parents—both were teachers, his father (otherwise a string bassist in New York radio and television studio orchestras) having earned a Ph.D. in education. Simon came to world prominence as the writing member of the duo Simon and Garfunkel, folk singers with collegiate backgrounds; Simon's degree in English literature is from Queens College (both singers pursued graduate degrees, Simon in law and his partner in mathematics). Simon played guitar and usually sang the structural melody, Art Garfunkel singing the descant. The two produced articulate ballads of personal introspection and social concern in the mid to late 1960s that reflected their schooling. While he never pursued advanced instruction in music in an academic setting, Simon studied composition privately in 1974 with the New York jazz musicians Chuck Israels and David Sorin Collyer.[2] Simon has lectured numerous times on aspects of songwriting, including a semester-long course at New York University in the spring of 1970.[3]

Although he is largely untrained, Simon's comments on his own composition are quite insightful and will guide this analysis of his music. One quotation from a 1975 lecture supports a view of Simon as a thoughtful (if technically innocent) musician: "Instead of thinking in terms of chords, I think of voice-leading; that is, melody line and bass line, and where the bass line goes. If you do that, you'll have the right chord. [These voices] will give you some alternatives, and you can play those different alternatives to hear which one suits your ear. . . . Keep the bass line moving so you don't stay in one spot; if you have an interesting bass line and you roll it against the melody, the chords are going to come out right."[4]

This approach to composition is exemplified in "Night Game" (1975), sketched in example 5.1.[5] Only the barest bones of the verses are shown, but the sketch highlights the song's middle section, the bridge, in which a dizzying sequence of chromatic chords (listed below the analysis) supports a structural expansion of a dominant seventh. In line with Simon's comment above, it seems very much that chords here are in the service of voice leading. Given the arpeggiation of $V\natural/V$ (G–B–E), the bass line can even be heard to "roll" against the melody.[6]

The pitch materials of the vocal melody in the verse section of "Night Game" are restricted to the seven diatonic scale degrees of D major, but Simon sings pitch-classes F♮, C♮, D♯, A♯, and G♯ in the chromatic middle section to complete the aggregate. Of the title track from the same album, *Still Crazy after All These Years*, Simon says, "I didn't want to repeat the same notes in the second verse that I used in the first, so I wrote out all the notes of the song and all the notes that were missing in the scale, given that there are twelve notes from octave to octave. All those notes that weren't in the scale were the ones I wanted in for the next verse. The listener isn't aware that they are new notes, but the sound is pleasing to the ear. I change the key, and somehow it's fresh because you haven't heard those notes before."[7] While this discussion suggests a naive quality ("the listener isn't aware"), the manner of thinking strengthens the above argument that the chords in the middle section of "Night Game" were likely chosen to support a prior chromatic vocal line, a line that could only be alien to a naive listener.

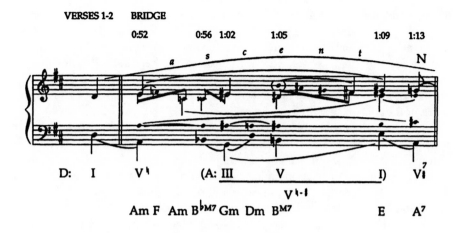

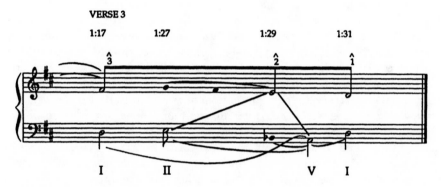

Example 5.1. "Night Game"

Another statement from the above-cited lecture would be grist for the implication-realization mill: "It's good contrast at this point [in "American Tune," 1973] to put in something that's texturally different from where I've been so far—to use something that startles the ear. All the chords I've played so far have been quite pure —majors, minors, sevenths—so I go to a C⁹. It's like a jazz chord, and sets me up to a different part of the song; it also changes my key. [A minor and then F are tonicized within the context of C.] I try not to let the listener know what's going on; every time I assume that the ear can predict what I am about to do, I try to change it."[8] The confounding of expectations is of great importance in Simon's compositions. An ability to bring this aesthetic alive enables his lyrics to communicate what is unstated; the critic Stephen Holden says of a 1973 album: "*Rhymin' Simon* shows, once and for all, that Simon is now *the* consummate master of the contemporary narrative song—one of a very few practicing singer/songwriters able to impart wisdom as much by implication as by direct statement."[9] In fact, Simon finds that the notion of musical implication guides his work right from the beginning of his compositional process: "I write from instinct, from inexplicable sparkle. I don't know why I'm writing what I'm writing. Usually, I sit and I let my hands wander on my guitar. And I sing anything. I play anything. And I wait till I come across a pleasing accident. Then I start to develop it. Once you take a piece of musical information, there are certain implications that it automatically contains—the implication of that phrase elongated, contracted, inverted or in another time signature. So you start with an impulse and go to what your ear likes."[10] The importance for Simon of the play of implications, both those realized and those thwarted, will be explored in much of the analysis below.

Simon is chiefly known for compositions of the 1960s and 1980s that are diatonic both on the surface and at structural levels, but much of his work of the 1970s is characterized by a sophisticated handling of innovative chromatic structures, enabling one to hear a career-spanning arch-shaped curve of tonal complexity in his work from 1964 through 1990. His early folk-based Simon and Garfunkel recordings (1964–1970)[11] are either strictly diatonic (tonal, as in "I Am a Rock," or modal, as the dorian "The Sounds of Silence") or—beginning with their third album (1966) —make use of one or two embellishing applied chords (as in "Homeward Bound" and the later "Mrs. Robinson" and "The Boxer"). Mode mixture appears on the 1968 album *Bookends* (in "Old Friends" and "Overs") and in the title track from *Bridge over Troubled Water* (1970), but it is not generally characteristic of Simon's writing. Neither tonicization nor modulation is in evidence in this body of work. Similarly, sixteen of the twenty-one songs on Simon's last two albums, *Graceland* (1986) and *Rhythm of the Saints* (1990) (both promotions of world musics), are completely diatonic within a single major-minor system, and four other songs on these albums shift abruptly between two tonal areas that are themselves prolonged without chromaticism; only one of these twenty-one songs ("Further to Fly") has any degree of chromaticism. Thus, Simon's chromatic music from the mid to late 1970s constitutes a kind of midpoint in an arch that stretches from the diatonic music of the Simon and Garfunkel years to the diatonicism of Simon's more recent music, not unlike the way that "Night Game" inserts a chromatic bridge between two diatonic verses. In 1983, Simon put his interest in the total chromatic (as discussed in relation to "Night Game") into a context that directly relates to the "arch of complexity": "I have gone through different phases in my music writing. There was a time when I used a little exercise—incorporating all of the twelve notes in the chromatic scale—to get me going. I used this technique for a while, but I don't any longer because I am going back to simpler melodies. Originally I moved away from the simple songs because I thought they were *too* simple."[12]

An experimental composition, "So Long, Frank Lloyd Wright," on his last album before the break with Garfunkel (1970) points to an early interest in chromaticism that subsequently matured through the 1970s, gaining in intensity with the tonally adventurous 1973 recording *There Goes Rhymin' Simon* and peaking in the 1975 album *Still Crazy after All These Years* and the soundtrack for the 1980 film *One-Trick Pony*. All twenty songs of these latter two jazz-influenced collections evidence some interest in chromatic voice leading, and those with the deepest chromatic structures will be discussed in detail.

The six-year span between the chromatic *One-Trick Pony* and the diatonic *Graceland* is divided by a single new album, *Hearts and Bones* (1983); significantly, this album is largely diatonic, though it does include two songs based on chromatic structures: "When Numbers Get Serious" and "Rene and Georgette Magritte with Their Dog after the War." One wonders why Simon reverted to simpler tonal structures. *Still Crazy* was enormously popular, but sales and critical reviews of *Pony* and *Hearts and Bones* were progressively disappointing.[13] Just as important to Simon as the issue of commercial appeal, perhaps, is another guiding aesthetic principle: it could be that Simon tired of the artificial ("learned") aspect of his most complex music. He has always shown a reverence for what to him is real, "honest" music, as in the indigenous folk musics of America, Peru, the Caribbean, South Africa, and Brazil; elements of this music have surfaced in all periods of his work. Simon supports this interpretation in discussing his reggae-flavored "Was a Sunny Day" (1973): "I like the Jamaican music because it is about their real lives: It's unpretentious and they don't have in the back of their head that this is their hook that's going to sell a million anything. They're not sophisticated and they're not phonies."[14] Even the tonally involved "Rene and Georgette Magritte" has at its core evocative choral quotations of three examples of 1950s doo-wop music, and as "street" music, doo-wop also represents folk culture. So it might well be posited that early in the 1980s, Simon's musicianship had grown to a point of crisis between the goals of complex artistic statement and direct, natural expression. Put another way, Simon had apparently lost a great number of his superficial listeners with the large proportion of his material that required more inquisitive ears for appreciation.[15] Perhaps the balance between these two aims (a wide and a deep audience) is most focused in his interest in jazz—a popular, indigenous medium that usually admits of more complexity than does rock. Among Simon's uses of jazz musicians are the following: members of Dave Brubeck's group appear on "The 59th Street Bridge Song" (1966); Stephane Grappelli graces Simon's eponymous first LP (1972); *Rhymin' Simon* features an authentic Dixieland-era New Orleans band as well as arrangements by Quincy Jones; the LPs of 1975 and 1980 are steeped in sophisticated New York "cocktail lounge" jazz; and Al DiMeola appears on *Hearts and Bones*. The question of Simon's waning interest in chromaticism, and the return to diatonicism that it seemingly provoked, will again be addressed in this essay's conclusion, but first we must study the nature of the composer's chromatic crisis.

Simon's Chromaticism and Spirals

As mentioned earlier, neither tonicization nor modulation is in evidence in Simon's diatonic work with Garfunkel. While the statement is true in the normally understood senses of the terms, there are two procedures that might call for qualification. For one, the ending of "At the Zoo" (1967) features an alternation of relative major and minor; in this song a single tonal center might be called into question since there is no functional relationship between the otherwise-prolonged major "I" and its minor "VI"; any sense of a I–VI–I neighbor function is overpowered by a strong passing chord that tonicizes VI. This is a technique that reappears in a few other of Simon's songs: it is the basis of the endings of "Kodachrome" (1973) and "My Little Town" (1975), as well as the entirety of "Think Too Much (b)" (1983).[16] Secondly, the coda of "Baby Driver" (1969) employs what is sometimes referred to among musicians as the "truck driver's modulation," a sudden shift from one tonal center to another—usually a half step above—that is not functionally related to the first.[17] The metaphor is particularly apt for "Baby Driver," which concludes with the sounds of formula racing cars added to the mix. The relationship is recreated, interestingly, between verses in several songs on the later release, *Rhythm of the Saints*.[18] Both of these procedures do raise the issue of opposing tonal centers, but they pale in tonal interest when compared with the complexities of Simon's later solo works.

Another of Simon's statements, made in 1983 during the recording of *Hearts and Bones*, will serve as the springboard for a discussion of his most innovative achievements in chromatic writing: "One of the most satisfying achievements—if you can make it work—is when a song follows a circular route and ends up back where it should have been at the beginning, but one plane higher, like a spiral. You cover ground and when you return home it's familiar, but you should have covered enough ground so that when you return to the beginning it's not the same in feel, title or melody."[19] The image of a spiral is one that clarifies a favorite tonal technique of Simon's, whereby tonal centricity is challenged by a modulation in a bridge passage; there is always a return to the verse structure, but there may or may not be a return to tonic. Usually, the reason for any lack of return to tonic lies in the narrative intent, which has also been described in cyclic terms: "all of Simon's songs have a cyclic narrative structure: they unravel through a succession of episodes but always return to their point of departure, whether or not anything is actually resolved."[20] The same statement is true of Simon's tonal relationships. In some cases, the musical return to a higher plane is portrayed by a modulation to a higher key, in others by an unusual method of returning to the original tonic. I shall first examine those songs in progressive key centers.

The voice-leading basis of "So Long, Frank Lloyd Wright" is sketched in example 5.2. The verse structure, highly chromatic on the surface (appropriate to the bossanova style), begins with an auxiliary cadence that progresses VI♯–IV–V–I. The bridge (at "Architects may come and architects may go") moves from VI to a tonicized IV, which then proceeds as a pivot chord by acting as V of the VI♯ that begins the third verse, effecting a modulation up a half step from F♯ to G, a bit more artfully than with the traditional truck-driver method. Here, such a drastic motion satisfies the chromatic nature of the surface, which had not previously been reflected at deeper levels. It might be thought that this structural integrity with a face of tonal abandon was intended as an homage to the architect whose cantilevered masterpieces could seem to defy gravity. Actually, the reference to Wright is a red herring; Simon is actually saying goodbye to Artie (an architecture major as an undergraduate), who—as revealed in the final verse—harmonized many nights "till dawn" with Simon through their teenage years. With this inside knowledge, the sentimental listener may hear the chromatic parting as a complex and difficult one.[21]

In a similar vein, the bridge section of "Silent Eyes" (1975) allows the verse structure, heard twice in G♯ minor, to appear in a new key, A minor, in its third appearance. Likewise, "You're Kind" (also 1975) presents two verses in A major before the bridge prolongs IV–V♯ of B, announcing the tonal center of the third verse and coda.[22]

Simon creates an unassuming little wonder in "One Man's Ceiling Is Another

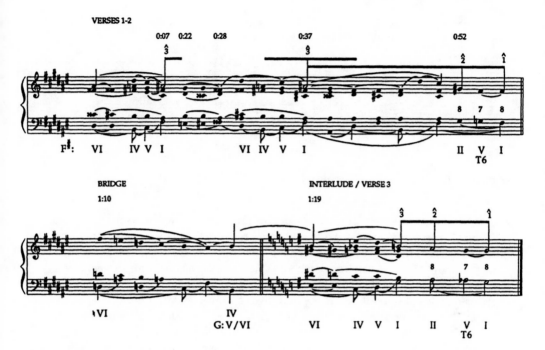

Example 5.2. "So Long, Frank Lloyd Wright"

Man's Floor" (1973), a funky Randy Newman–like honky-tonk bayou blues.[23] In this song, the modulating spiral is fastened end to end to form a toroid, rather than a cylindrical, helix. Example 5.3 shows that the song's three verses appear in successively lower fifths: in C, in F, and in B♭ (cf. 0:52, 1:32, and 2:32); the fifths are divided so as to produce a large progression in descending thirds from IV all the way back to I. The modulating link in each case depends upon two factors, both of which confound the listener's normal expectations: an unusual pivot-chord modulation within each verse and an unusual harmony that ends each verse. Example 5.4 indicates (a) the bass structure for each verse, (b) a standard blues harmonic pattern, and (c) the actual harmonic values of "Ceiling."[24] Shown are both the pivot-chord modulation at measure 9 and the unusual ending on the submediant; in a reversal of the usual tonal procedure, one consequent phrase (mm. 9–12) that ends with a perfect authentic cadence is followed by a repeated consequent (mm. 13–16) that ends with a deceptive cadence. As suggested in example 5.3, the submediant is tonicized only in the bridge that follows the second verse; because VI had already been achieved at the end of that verse, the bridge plays no part in the modulatory scheme, unlike the songs previously discussed. The three verses bring the song back to its point of origin, repeated in the coda: a dorian-flavored descending scale in G minor. G is referred to as tonic in example 5.3, because of the song's stable beginning and ending. But there is no leading tone, and G is hardly tonicized; any feeling of tonal structure resides more in the spiral shape of the modulating process than in the centricity of any particular pitch class.

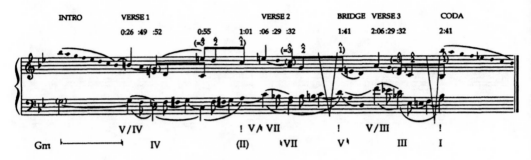

Example 5.3. "One Man's Ceiling Is Another Man's Floor"

What makes this song particularly interesting is the witty text-painting role of the tonal process. The poetic text describes fights between tenants of adjacent floors that result from their failure to observe the "apartment house rules," which presumably promote courtesy between neighbors. No occupant of one floor can get along with that of another; even "the elevator man don't work here no more." The conflict between flights is symbolized by the odd pivot modulation and unresolved deceptive cadence that contrast a number of tonal centers that successively produce an octave relationship, G to G. (The competing contentions in the text of the song's refrain—the title—can be heard as a metaphor for the function of the pivot chord.) The octave also portrays the contrast between two floor levels in the opening and closing scales (shown in example 5.5, an octave scale doubled in octaves) and, most, significantly, in Simon's vocal refrain to the first verse, which pits the two contending consequent phrases (describing the $\hat{3}$–$\hat{2}$–$\hat{1}$ upper-voice closure; cf. 0:52 with 0:55 in ex. 5.3) in contrasting registers an octave apart. The number of ways that the octave functions in "Ceiling" is a testament to Simon's ability to develop the implications of his musical materials, all in service of the narrative intent.

"Still Crazy"

A structure that progresses from one tonal center to another portrays psychological disintegration in the title track from *Still Crazy after All These Years*. Example 5.6, a foreground sketch of the entire song, shows that the first two verses are in G major, and the third begins there (at 2:39) but moves through a chromatic modulation (at 2:50) to A major, at which level the song closes. A lack of musical integration is already an issue in the electric piano's introduction (see ex. 5.7), which moves from A to G (in an auxiliary cadence) and simultaneously shifts from the upper voice (e^1–$d\sharp^1$–e^1) to an inner voice (b–c^1–b); the shift is realized by a melodic sequence of the opening three measures, which constitutes an attempt to integrate the two voices into a single line. This attempt at integration is characteristic of the introduction as a whole: it foreshadows both the opening vocal line and a move from A to G that appear in the bridge-interlude; it highlights (in mm. 3–5) a rendering of the transitional bass pitches C–B–A from the interlude (in a different ordering and metrical function); it predicts the upper-voice neighbor relationship of bridge-

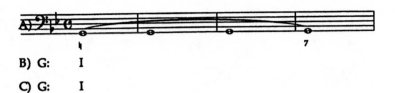

Example 5.4. "One Man's Ceiling Is Another Man's Floor"

interlude-verse 3 (see ex. 5.6); and it borrows the motive of measures 7–8 from the final cadence (at 3:07–3:08). The attempt at integrating the tonal progressions from A to G in the bridge-interlude and from G to A in the third verse yield an expanded fifth progression (marked "X-5 prg" in ex. 5.6), comprising the distance from e^2 to g^1 in the former and a contracted fifth progression in the latter (spanning d^2–a^1); in each case the third scale degree in the structural descent changes identity: $c\#^2$ "becomes" b^1 at 2:34 and then b^1 "becomes" $c\#^2$ at 2:50.

Chuck Israels, one of Simon's teachers at the time this song was composed, has praised his own jazz partner, Bill Evans, for an original approach to the turnaround (the time-marking vamp that follows the structural close of one chorus and prepares the beginning of the next). Distinct among jazzers, "Evans' view of the turnaround was that it belonged to the following chorus, rather than to the one just ending. In practice this meant that a new idea introduced at the turnaround could be carried over into the next chorus."[25] In "Still Crazy," Simon applies this motivic pro-

Example 5.5. "One Man's Ceiling Is Another Man's Floor"

cedure to his tonal structure. The second verse ends on a G⁹ harmony (see ex. 5.6, 1:20); the consonance of the vocal closure on Î of G is undermined by the stubborn second scale degree in the strings and keyboard, which then transfers up an octave for the beginning of the bridge on II. The turnaround at the verse's cadence predicts the shift of tonal center to A, and the return to the tonic at 2:37 redeems the cadence with its pure (ninthless) octave.

   The relationship between these two cadences, analogous to interruption form, is a brilliant frame for the nondiatonous bridge-interlude, the portion of the song in which the vocal persona comes to terms with his inner character. In the song's first verse, the protagonist describes a chance evening meeting with an "old lover." When

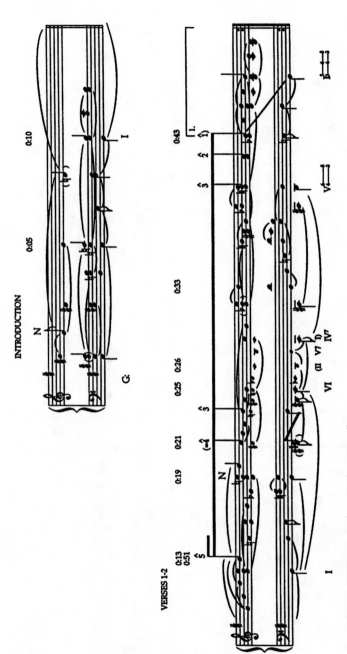

Example 5.6. "Still Crazy after All These Years"

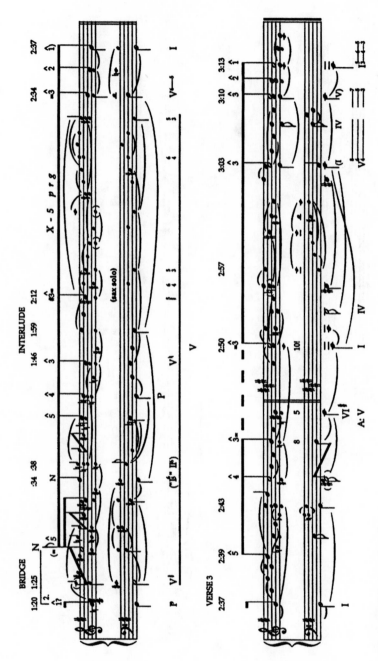

Example 5.6. (continued)

Example 5.7. "Still Crazy after All These Years"

he sings that he "just smiled," he hints that he was thinking or feeling more than he had communicated, that the surface is a deceptive cover for unarticulated ideas. Following this opening verse, the listener might guess that the refrain, "still crazy after all these years," would refer to an infatuation (crazy in love) on the protagonist's part, but this is not the ultimate meaning of the text. In the second verse, the singer (apparently unknowingly) reveals antisocial and paranoid tendences; in the line "I ain't no fool for love songs that whisper in my ears, 'still crazy after all these years,'" the lonely singer shows that he perceives the emotional yearnings of his heart as if they were menacing and accusatory auditory hallucinations. The nonconsonant cadence, predicting a shift of tonal center, reveals that the singer's cover is blown, and that all sides of his personality are about to be examined, just as he returns home alone.

The bridge unfolds some time after the parting, at "four in the morning." By saying that he's "crapped out," he may mean that he's exhausted, or that he didn't "get lucky." But he is unambigous in that he knows he is very lonely and, long after the witching hour, is far from a stable state of mind.[26] He resolves not to worry over his emotional problem, secure in the belief that "it's all gonna fade." The listener does not know whether it is the singer's loneliness, his waking consciousness, or his existence itself that is going to fade; this vague statement leads to an interlude (featuring a saxophone solo) on V/V, with the character of a fantasy, hinting that we are witnessing a melange of shifting realms of thought, whether in the singer's conscious or dreaming state. A shift from minor to major mode at the introduction of the sax (at 2:12) does seem to indicate a change from a pessimistic to an optimistic outlook, or maybe this is the point at which the singer succumbs to sleep. Various levels of thought are portrayed by a nesting of neighbors: G is used at 2:29 as a neighboring

IV of D, which is itself a neighboring IV of A. In a similarly progressive pattern, this A resolves through successive fifth motions to G, the original tonic, at 2:37.

These cycles return the singer to the present time, the day after the encounter, for the final verse. He expresses antisocial, perhaps violent, instability with the line "I fear I'll do some damage one fine day," and then immediately adopts a defiantly arrogant tone with "but I would not be convicted by a jury of my peers" (he will, he reasons, be judged criminally insane: "still crazy after all these years"). This appearance of braggadocio is set with the defiant chromatic modulation to A major, and the (false) new stability is emphasized by the fact that the A major harmony at 2:50 functions as I, unlike the II of IV that had appeared at analogous places in verses 1 and 2 (as at 0:26). The independence from the original tonic of the final tonal center aptly symbolizes the singer's unpredictable mental and emotional state, ultimately one of an unwarranted swaggering self-confidence that seems oblivious to its lack of moorings, both psychological and tonal.

Returning to Tonic; Tritones

While the songs discussed above employ progressive tonal structures, many of Simon's songs exemplifying a spiral structure do so with tonicizations of remote areas in the bridge with the original tonic regained in the final verse. Several examples of this are heard in *One-Trick Pony*. The film describes the simultaneous dissolutions of band and marriage that mirror each other in the eyes of guitarist Jonah Levin, an artist with fourteen years' experience on the circuit, ever hopeful for the big break that will lead to stardom. Jonah is having a hard time keeping his band together while playing small clubs in northern Ohio and western New York, when it looks as if the key to success finally appears in the person of record company executive (weasel) Walter Fox, who arranges a record deal with Levin. After the band records the basic tracks and vocals for Jonah's strongest song, "Ace in the Hole," producer Steve Kunelian (played by Lou Reed) proceeds to drown out the work of Levin's soloists by overdubbing strings, sax, and chorus so inappropriate to Levin's artistic intent—but, to Kunelian's and Fox's minds, the guarantee of a surefire commercial success—that the singer's integrity can be redeemed only by the destruction of the master tape, and with that, the destruction of all hopes for a continued musical career. The song "Jonah" tells the singer's story. The opening two verses first describe the routine of playing gigs and then Jonah's reason for holding on tightly to dreams of success. The chorus, "They say Jonah, he was swallowed by a whale, but I say there's no truth to that tale; I know Jonah, he was swallowed by a song," lays bare the symbol that characterizes Levin, who is trapped (so his wife has been saying for some time, and so he finally comes to realize himself) by his complex relationship with music. In the film, Jonah is reborn through the destruction of his recording; in this song, rebirth is suggested in the last verse, which recounts the disappearance from the "biz" of many would-be musicians who have somehow been able to escape their musical whales.

Example 5.8 shows "Jonah" to be unusually rich in chromatic function, including a fourth progression (0:32 to 0:43) that contains a tonicizing motion from I to III of

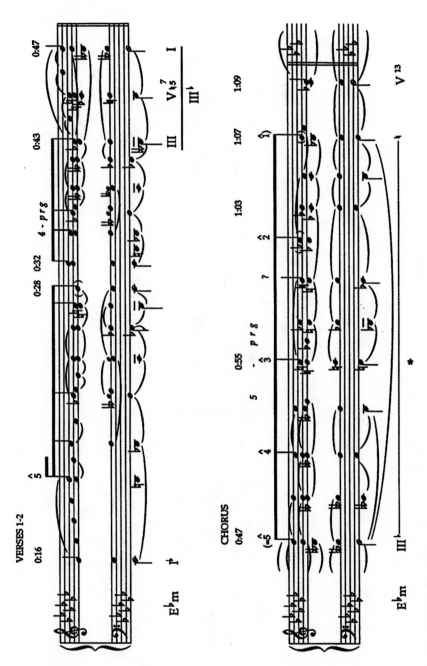

Example 5.8. "Jonah"

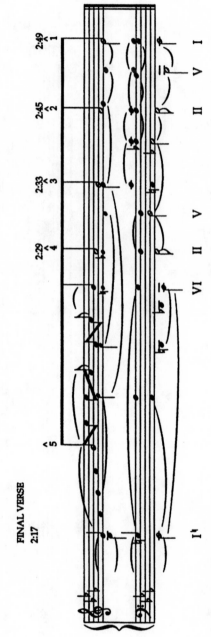

Example 5.8. (continued)

III♭ and a fifth progression (0:47 to 1:07) that seems to include a diminished third, c♭²–a♮¹, articulated at the point (0:55) at which Simon declares a lack of truth, the point at which the singer resolves to tell the listener that Jonah was swallowed not by a whale but by a song. Point 0:55, marked in example 5.8 with an asterisk, is the crux of the song's chromatic language; it will be referred to as the "Jonah chord." Example 5.9 shows the voice-leading model for the song's chorus. As sketched here, the G♭-minor passage supports a diatonic fifth progression in parallel tenths against the bass; a 10–7 sequence in the outer voices (Simon is again rolling his bass line against the melody) provides a harmonic progression via descending fifths that moves to the leading tone, F♮, to which the dominant's root, D♭, is added before cadencing on G♭. The model is completely diatonic except for two concessions to the surface: the concluding Picardy third and the d♭♭¹ (see asterisk), the model for the Jonah chord.[27] Example 5.8 indicates a structural change in the Jonah chord at the surface: G♭ is replaced by the tone a half step lower; this tone is spelled as an F, rather than as a G♭♭, to preserve the new series of descending fifths in the bass that begins on this F and ends on the prolonged G♭. The F supports A rather than the model's B♭♭, although this upper-voice tone can still be heard as the third scale degree of the fifth progression at a level beneath the surface.[28] The question mark appearing above the line in the example alludes to the ambiguity raised by the consonant status and hypermetrical strength of G♮ (following the fishy a♮, the listener is led to wonder whether G♮ might be part of the line), a tone that is not even enharmonically related to the model's upper voice. The second scale degree, A♭, is elided for the seventh G♭ at 1:03, furthering the confusion between the diatonic and chromatic scale degrees. The surface preserves a 10–7 sequence (which becomes chromatic at the sounding of the Jonah chord), but the bass fifth motions are given a completely new character by the slip (from the model's G♭ to the song's F) at the Jonah chord, which proceeds in a few "extra" fifths to the root (not to the leading tone, as in the model) of the dominant. The gulp is audible at the Jonah chord, at which point the model is swallowed by the song; both Jonah and the listener are swallowed by A♮, and both are further threatened by the following G♮.

The story of redemption told in the last verse is musically portrayed by the return to a fresh-sounding tonic; the mode has changed from the opening E♭ minor to a closing E♭ major.[29] Despite similarities between all verses in the deep middleground, the final verse is composed out with a foreground very different from that of the previous verses. This is a unique approach for Simon but one that exemplifies his above-stated goal of spiraling back to a verse with a new melody. Notably, the final verse is largely diatonic, the song having freed itself from its chromatic crises. (The important exception to diatonicism is the passing tone in the bass at 2:33; as a visual reminder of the Jonah chord, this tone is spelled A♮ rather than B♭♭.[30])

In several songs, Simon contrasts tonal centers a tritone apart. The pessimistic song "Everything Put Together Falls Apart," called by one writer the "focal point" of Simon's "depressing" first solo album, features the tonicization of B♭ within the context of E major in each of three verses, in unstable passages that are dominated by changing meter and irregular phrase lengths and relationships.[31] Another tritone relationship obtains in the unusual appearance of a ♭V triad in "Long Long Day" (1980). Example 5.10 shows how this chord functions in the capacity of a neighbor-

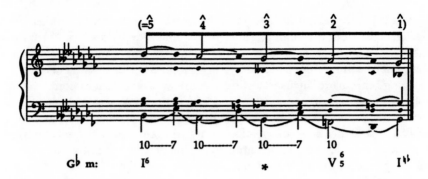

Example 5.9. "Jonah"

ing subdominant to a retransitional Neapolitan. More common for Simon is a design in which the tonal center of the bridge is a tritone distant from that of the verse. In "Tenderness" (1973), the verses are in C major and the bridge is in F# minor. The return to C major is achieved through an unusually colorful jazz pivot chord, whereby a thirteenth chord on the Neapolitan of F# minor is reheard as V^{13} of the opening harmony of the verse, which is V$^{9}_{\flat 5}$ of IV.[32]

The title song from *One-Trick Pony* uses the jazz technique of tritone substitution in its retransition. Example 5.11 sketches the song's bridge section and indicates its tonal relationship to the preceding and the following verses. The harmony at 1:39 is articulated as a B$\flat^7$ chord but it functions as V^7 of A minor; its tritone, A$\flat$–D, is an enharmonic substitute for G#–D, the diminished fifth within E^7. This chord is prepared dramatically with measured acceleration in the crash cymbal and electric bass, as can be seen in example 5.12, which presents the essential parts of the bridge, beginning at 2:47. Note how the drummer (Steve Gadd) follows two breve-length crashes with four whole-note-length crashes (marking breve-length intervals with dynamic accents); the next eight bars (mm. 149–56) feature half-note-long cymbal crashes, and the tension is further heightened by loud quarter-note values in the bass and—at the climax—the cymbal. The "wrong note," B$\flat$, is emphasized in the bass (played by Tony Levin) with a two-measure trill.

The poetic text of the bridge (see ex. 5.12) compares the smooth moves of a "one-trick pony" to the "herky-jerky motion" that burdens the singer. The popular press has interpreted this image of the pony as a representation of Jonah, who is constantly asked to perform his one hit.[33] But this interpretation seems off the

Example 5.10. "Long Long Day"

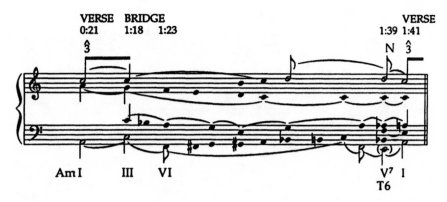

Example 5.11. "One-Trick Pony"

mark. In the film, Levin's band works as a warm-up act for the B-52s, who are shown performing "Rock Lobster" as Levin and company return to the green room.[34] The instrumentation of the new-wave classic "Rock Lobster" is restricted to a very simple diatonic guitar ostinato and drums; the lead vocal is not pitch specific and the two backing singers provide occasional organum. Yet the B-52s enjoy headline status while Jonah's far more adventurous compositions fall on deaf ears. As shown in examples 5.11 and 5.12, the bridge of the film's title song is based upon a rising chromatic scale in the bass that prolongs F (first heard as IV of III, finally heard as V of the V^7 substitute). To hear this "easy" music of the B-52s as that of the envied one-trick pony, and Levin's complex song as the result of pulling from a "bag of tricks" of learned artifice a chromaticism of "extra moves" and an expressive but "herky-jerky" rhythm, would seem to be a more sensitive and correct interpretation of the film's title than that given by mainstream critics. This phrase in example 5.12, then, is heard to represent—as clearly as does the chorus of "Jonah," but with a different poetic image—the crisis of chromaticism from which Paul Simon extricates himself only by his resumption of interest in tonally non-demanding world musics.

"I Do It for Your Love": Surface Chords and Timbre

"I Do It for Your Love" is a soft, pretty song in ternary form at a moderate tempo with jazz chords and an unobtrusive instrumentation; the composition's essential lines are as transcribed in example 5.13. The song's text comprises tender thoughts upon the dissolution of a marriage (it was composed as Simon's own marriage to Peggy Harper was ending). The following analysis will uncover the expression of the poetic theme of detachment in the interrelationships between the song's formal structure, its vocabulary of chromatic harmony and voice-leading oddities, and its instrumentation.

The tonal literature abounds with works that exhibit strong, multifaceted interrelationships between their respective harmonic contents and their formal structures: the forms are essentially composed out by harmonies. With "I Do It for Your

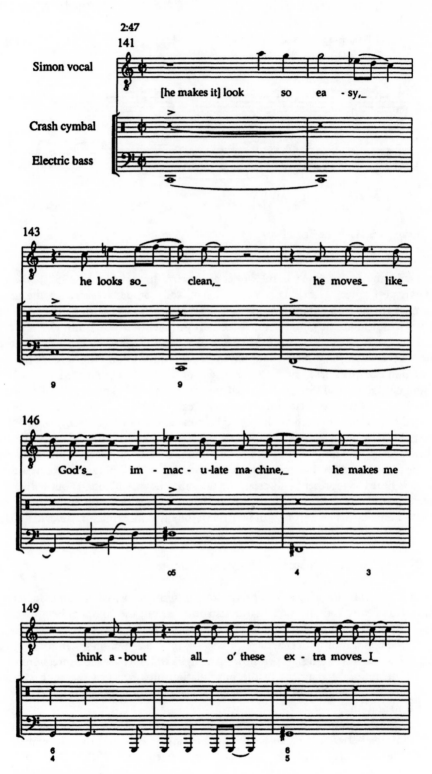

Example 5.12. "One-Trick Pony"

Example 5.12. (*continued*)

Love," the listener is faced with a structural continuum, closely related to the harmonic series, that progresses from formal arrangement through harmony to timbre. The three nodes on this theoretical continuum relate in various ways to express the poem's basic theme, that of detachment. I shall first take up the relationship between surface chords and timbre; the song's form and harmonic structure will be discussed as related to structural voice leading below.

The reduced score represents most of the inner-voice content (played by the "rhythm" instruments) with figured-bass notation. Many extended tertian sonorities (a stylistic borrowing from jazz) are employed. The root of nearly every chord

Example 5.13. "I Do It for Your Love"

has its seventh, and some have ninths and elevenths; some of these added tones are anticipations (such as the guitar's e^1 in m. 2), some suspensions (such as the same e^1 in m. 4); some resolve (such as the guitar's c^2 in m. 5), and some are apparently left hanging (such as the electric piano's e^2 in m. 8).

The upper register is particularly inhabited by nontriad tones, most spectacularly by the a^3 repeated by the triangle (mm. 15–23, 47–50, and 57–58). This pitch sounds as an inverted pedal above the fray of harmonic tension and resolution; it is occasionally (but only coincidentally) a triad member when A and D function as roots. Pitch-class A has another high-register nonharmonic appearance, as the first note of the descant vocal line that accompanies the beginnings of the second and third verses (mm. 17 and 47). This voice is very far removed from any typical harmonic function, sounding as a "quint" doubling of the lead vocal part, which itself features nontriadic tones.

Another notable pitch in the upper register is the b^2 heard both in the oboe in the introduction (m. 5) and in harmonics at the top of the guitar's fingerboard in the

Example 5.13. (*continued*)

first two verses (mm. 14 and 22). While pitch-class B is a member of the E-minor chord of measures 14 and 22, the B-minor triad that is arpeggiated in both the oboe and guitar figures has a timbral integrity that sets it at odds with the underlying E-minor harmony (all members of which triad sound throughout); the F♯ seems to feel no obligation to resolve, and does not (in its own instrumental timbre).[35]

The triangle, oboe, and guitar's harmonics discussed above, all nonresolving nonharmonic tones that are highlighted registrally and timbrally, represent ethereal sounds divorced from the harmonic structure. They act as unnaturally amplified upper partials—and in the case of the B-minor "triads" and the "quint" doublings, partials of partials—high up in the harmonic series; they are distantly related to their fundamentals (the chord roots), but the emphasis of these tones tends to

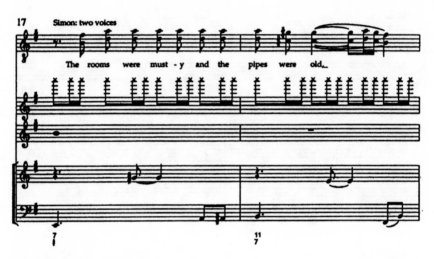

Example 5.13. (*continued*)

reduce the unifying, earthbound effect of harmonic function. This is a high-in-the-series version of a similar detachment shown in the relationship between the song's chord roots; although unifying fifth motions are prominent in the bass (as in mm. 1, 3, and 4; and 6, 7, and 8; in both passages, the bass falls from E to A to D), the tonic chord itself is never heard before the song's final three measures.

Several aspects of the poetic text are related to the dichotomy of unity and detachment that is expressed timbrally. Perhaps most obviously, the first verse refers to specific colors to set a mood of depression: "we were married on a rainy day; the sky was yellow and the grass was grey." (A lack of passion in this wedding remembrance is further conveyed by two other images: the line "we signed the papers and we drove away" conveys the matter-of-factness of a writer's grip and the smell of car

Example 5.13. (*continued*)

exhaust, instead of a more tender image of, for instance, a couple holding hands.) A warmer color, orange, appears as a cold fighter in the second verse (m. 21), and its complement, blue, is suggested in the final verse's reference to the two hemispheres of the globe (mm. 49–50). In the bridge (labelled "B" in ex. 5.14), orange and blue are wed in the bleeding of dyes in a rug (mm. 30–31), presumably caused by the rainstorm through which the rug is carried. This image of bleeding is a symbol of both dissolution and of pain, and it artfully blends together a color from the marriage's happy months (that of orange juice), and another color that invokes the unhappy "blues" of the two hemispheres that grow to be poles apart. The opening sound of two words chosen in measure 31, "bled" and "blue" (the similar sound of

Example 5.13. (*continued*)

which is amplified by a repeated syncopation on a repeated pitch) recreates through
assonant onomatopoeia the aural image of the "blat" of the raindrops that cause the
bleeding, a metaphor that strengthens the directness of the singer's reference in the
ensuing verse to the splashing of tears.[36] The colors orange and blue, each borrowed
from a different verse, are united through dissolution in the interposed B section by
a wetting that weds the rain of the first verse to the tears of the last.

The image of the bleeding rug is one that is universally comprehensible, even
though it may represent to the listener a bit of a riddle at first. The fact that this puzzle is emotionally evocative yet not mawkish would be significant to the composer;
Simon once told an interviewer that the quality he most admired in John Lennon's

Example 5.13. (*continued*)

mature Beatles songs was their ability to tell "little stories that are enigmatic but very powerful." Asked if that was his goal in composition, he replied: "Yes. That, plus I try to open up my heart as much as I can and keep a real keen eye out that I don't get sentimental. . . . And when you hit it right, you produce an emotional response in the listener that can be cathartic. And when you're wrong, you're soppy, sentimental. Or you can go the other way and try to be more enigmatic. When it works, that's good. It mystifies, like a good puzzle or a magic trick. When you miss, it's pretentious. I find it very painful to miss on either side."[37] With the bleeding rug, Simon seems to have found an image that puzzles without being ambiguous or pretentious and is emotionally communicative without pandering.

The poetic images of "I Do It for Your Love" are unusually colorful for rock songs, largely because some of the individual words (such as "the Northern and the

Example 5.13. (*continued*)

Southern hemispheres") carry much more specific meanings than do most words in
rock poetry. Of his use of the word "alien" in "Song about the Moon" (1983), Simon
says, "now, because you rarely hear the word 'alien' in a song, your ears have to tune
in, which is good. . . . I think most songs should be written in the vernacular. . . . I
will sometimes break the vernacular by using a word that normally wouldn't appear
in a song."[38]

In addition to the qualities of the poetic images, a timbral polarity is created by
Simon's arrangements of phonemes, both vowels and consonants. In the first verse,
high partials are stressed as formants in a relatively large number of vowels (twelve

Example 5.13. (*continued*)

of twenty-nine, including the end rhymes "day," "grey," and "away") and consonants (featuring a high concentration of the "s" sound in "sky was ... grass was ... signed the papers"); the presence of the whistled high partials is amplified by a closely miked vocal recording technique. The proportion of "high" to "low" vowel sounds begins to change in the second verse (where only seven of twenty-eight are high, and the end rhymes are low as well: "old," "cold," "hold"). High partials are still emphasized in the second verse by the timbres of "sh" ("shared") and the combination of soft "g" with "j" ("orange juice"), all of which suggest shivering. The refrain, "I do it for your love," emphasizes low vowels with a warm chest tone in the low register and is double tracked for emphasis. The bridge contains the warmest vowel sounds (only three of twenty-eight vowels feature high formants), and backing vocals sustain the low "ooh" throughout. These contrasts may be heard to represent the dispassionate (head-tone) memories of a wedding day, the warmer memories of a shared illness, and the most emotionally meaningful memory (obliquely personal as it is), that of the bleeding rug.

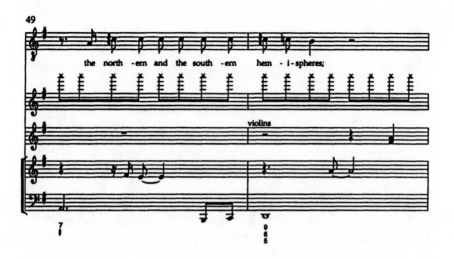

Example 5.13. (*continued*)

"I Do It for Your Love": Structural Voice Leading and Harmony

Heinrich Schenker has discussed the "inauthentic interval," a deceptive vertical entity that arises from the coincidental rhythmic interplay between voices in foreground diminution.[39] As is true of most rock music (as a manifestation of spontaneous heterophonic group composition), "I Do It for Your Love" contains a number of juicy inauthentic intervals, particularly involving the electric piano. See, for instance, the different rates of descent in the voice and piano in measures 12–13, or the "parallel ninths" between the voice and piano in measure 15. When this piano figure, g^2–$f\sharp^2$–e^2, was introduced in measures 6, 7, and 8, the g^2–e^2 third seemed to belong to the chords of measures 6 and 7 but not to that of measure 8, into which it was suspended. The analytical sketch (ex. 5.14) suggests that one might hear the repeated figure in measures 6–8 as a ghostly remnant of an extinct initial tonic har-

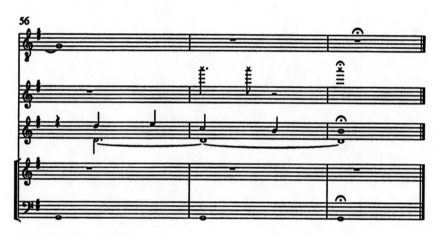

Example 5.13. (*continued*)

mony; the e² itself would then be a passing tone that "resolves" with the vocal entry
(just as the oboe's f♯² of mm. 6–7 resolves in the piano's e²). This figure achieves
motivic significance by virtue of its appearances in the guitar (mm. 14 and 22), in
accordion/vocal solos performed by one Sivuca in measures 44 and 52–54 (m. 52
features inauthentic "parallel seconds"), and its reverberation in the structurally
important e♯²–f♯²–e♯² vocal figure in measures 20–32.

If "I Do It for Your Love" is notable for its healthy dose of carefree nonharmonic
tones, it is equally remarkable for its peculiarly "missing" but implied structural
tones that are called for, but do not appear, in the voice-leading structure. This is
true not only of the "missing" opening tonic chord (due to the auxiliary cadence)
but also of the third and second scale degrees in three of the four structural
descents. It is quite curious that the structural third scale degree, B (which should be

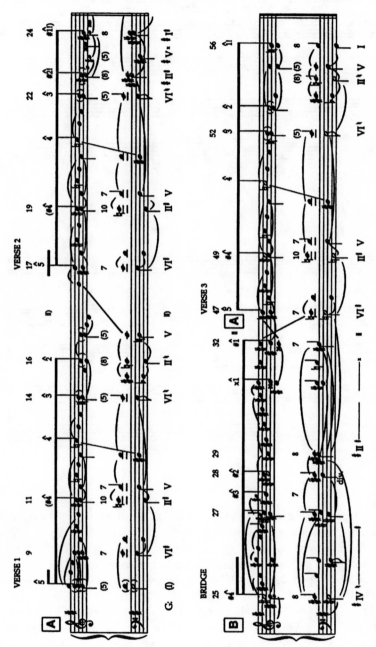

Example 5.14. "I Do It for Your Love"

sung in mm. 14 and 22), is offered by the guitar harmonics, and that the second scale degree, A (missing in m. 15), appears in the triangle—two timbres that sound unrelated to the foreground harmony. These tones seem unified with the background but divorced from the foreground. The transcription reveals that all implied tones are present in the texture but not in the vocal part. This distance between the surface and the structure, despite weak ties through ethereal timbres, is yet another example of the dual theme of unity and detachment.

The fundamental quality of the pitch structure in this song lies in its chromatically produced tritones. In the verses (marked "A," mm. 9–24), at least every other measure features a diminished fifth or augmented fourth (as part of fully diminished seventh or dominant seventh sonorities) involving the voice part. The melody has a strong lydian quality, especially on the surface, where the c♯2 of measures 10–11 is afforded a consonant support (major tenth) that is not given the diatonic c♮ of measure 13 (counterpointed in the foreground by a diminished seventh). This procedure poses the diatonic tone as a "chromatic" passing tone, a characteristic that was heard to transform the bridge of "Jonah." This c♯2 (an augmented fourth above the first scale degree) is corroborated as a structural tone when prolonged as the head tone for a descending linear progression in the bridge (mm. 25–32). This prolongation in the bridge of a structurally dissonant tonal area is called for by the verse's structural upper line in measures 17–24, which descends the diminished fifth from primary tone d2 to inner-voice g♯1 (note the exclamation points in ex. 5.14); this raised first scale degree is applied as the fifth of ♯IV, the area tonicized in the opening of the middle section. Clearly, the formal structure of this song is based upon unstable harmonic relationships that confound any listener's expectations.

The bridge, beginning a tritone away from the tonic, deserves closer attention. Poetically, it represents the singer's introspective moments addressing what had happened between the early events of his marriage (first two verses) and its dissolution (last verse). Befitting the expression of his innermost thoughts (with low, warm chest vowels, as discussed above), Simon uses a device common to introspective middle sections in vocal works by Mozart and Schubert. His vocal line here projects structural inner voices (which represent inner, close-to-the-soul images) that soar above the structural upper line (the usual embodiment of a singer's rational discourse), in a great emotional discharge.[40] This can be heard by comparing measures 25–32 in the score and the graph. The differences in many aspects between a song's verse and its bridge, and their value in expressing a poetic message, have been discussed by Simon in terms that are quite relevant to "I Do It for Your Love":

> If I have an unusual, unpredictable harmonic structure, I might find relief by changing the time signature, or using a simpler harmonic structure in the bridge, but in another key.
>
> All of these elements [melody, rhythm, harmony] have lyrical implications. The lyrics and the music have to work synergistically for the song to be good; if the song makes a radical change harmonically, there has to be a change lyrically as well. It can be, ironically, opposed to the initial change, but there has to be some recognition that something else is happening; it's a marriage, not just two elements wandering off any which way they like.[41]

This goal will be exemplified as I turn to the song's moment of most radical harmonic change, the retransition, and its role in portraying the poetic shift.

I have already discussed the painful image of the bleeding rug, measures 30–32. It is at this moment, the climax of the bridge, that the composer chooses to develop most fully the effect of the tritone. While all of the verse's augmented fourths and diminished fifths had resolved according to tonal norms, a series of tritones here "bleed" into each other as do the dyes of the rug. In measure 31, for instance, the diminished fifth F♯ over B♯ slides down to the augmented fourth E♯ over B♮; because the harmony of measure 31 spells a French augmented-sixth chord, a second tritone sounds simultaneously with E♯/B; that is, G♯ over D♯ is an augmented fourth that "bleeds" into the diminished fifth G♯ over C♯ in measure 32. For a motivically integrated retransition, Simon uses tritone substitution in keeping G♯ and C♯ (respelled as D♮) as common tones in returning from A♯7 (m. 32) to the tritone-distant E7 chord that begins the final verse (m. 47).[42] The singer's return to the verse puts his inner-voice emotional discharge into the past and brings him back to the rational structural upper voice with "the sting of reason" (note the high head-tone partials in both vowels and consonants in this phrase), a sting made more poignant by the maintenance of G♯, completely eliding the root of tonic harmony (G major). Tonic harmony—and for that matter, a structural diatonic first scale degree in the upper line—is expressed for the first time only in the song's very last chord, concluding a nearly diatonic descent in the upper voice; the lydian raised-fourth scale degree, of course, precludes a purely diatonic structure.

The ultimate arrival of tonic also completes a structural arpeggiation of the diminished seventh chord expressed by the roots of ♯IV (m. 25), ♯II (m. 29), VI♯ (m. 47), and I (m. 56). All three of the harmonies VI, ♯IV, and ♯II appear in both major and minor forms,[43] a further testament to the song's development of chromatic relationships. The ♯IV and ♯II are also closely related by similar descents from c♯1 in the tenor register (see graph) in measures 25–27 and 29–32 and by the integration in the projected inner voice of the motion from g♯2 (mm. 25–26) through f♯2 (m. 26) to e♮2 (m. 27). Most likely, it is only after hearing both the structural motion from ♯IV to ♯II in the B section and the tritone-based retransition that the listener is convinced that the opening dominant-seventh harmony on E is of structural value as part of the arpeggiation of the fully diminished seventh formation, ♯IV–♯II–VI–I. Perhaps the unfolding of this chord represents the singer's uncertainty as to which direction he will face next, as he reviews the various moods brought about by his reflections on his marriage. The consonant, seemingly stable ending on the tonic is offset somewhat by the fact that the singer never clearly expresses what "it" is that he does for love.

The song's conclusion uses timbral associations with the earlier solo (mm. 33–46) to confirm the notion that the singer indulges in flights of fantasy as well as adopting a harsh view of reality. As he remarks coldly and matter-of-factly that "love emerges and it disappears" (mm. 51–52), he is accompanied by both the warm ("romantic") sound of violins and the warm "ooh" vowel of Sivuca's mezzo-register vocal remembrance of the G–F♯–E motive.[44] Both timbres appear elsewhere only in measures 33–46 (where Sivuca's vocal solo doubles her accordion line at the unison). If these timbres are to represent Simon's warm memories of early love, the solo passage (which is a half-time version of the second verse's voice-leading structure, featuring asymmetrical beat divisions and new syncopations) can be heard as a Felliniesque fantasy suggested by the cathartic memories displayed in the bridge. Putting previous discussion in this context, the song's formal structure progresses from the catharsis of the bridge through a wordless solo of dreamlike remembrance in another "time," to a rehearing of the bridge, which leads back to the reawakening to reality, brought on suddenly by "the sting of reason, the splash of tears," and the shift of a tritone.

The analysis provided above suggests that "I Do It for Your Love" can be heard as a remarkable portrayal of emotional distance through the musical analogue of the distance between structure and surface by the uses of (1) jazz procedures that give nonchord tones the freedom to not resolve and give important structural tones the freedom to not sound, (2) the relation of upper partials in the harmonic series to intervallic dissonances and to particular combinations of phonemes, (3) emotional connotations given certain timbres, (4) structural roles played by the tritone in the lydian scale and in formal-harmonic relationships, with the technique of tritone substitution forming the backbone of a structural arpeggiation of a diminished seventh chord, all in a tonal context, and (5) the outpouring of inner-voice turmoil in an emotionally charged contrasting middle section that returns with a shock to a rational hearing of the upper voice in the last verse, which finally realizes its goal in the tonic.

Simon Spirals Back to Diatonicism

Ever since Paul Simon suffered a sports injury to his left index finger in late 1972, he has at times had great difficulty in playing (and composing at) the guitar. This and a number of other pressures mounted in the late 1970s. In 1979 he settled out of court with CBS, his exclusive label since 1964, after a bitter dispute. Simon's first record for his new label (the *One-Trick Pony* soundtrack for Warners) received a disappointing reception. Given the film's treatment of the critical difficulties that face a musician because of the noncommercial complexity of his composition, the poor reception of the film and album must have dealt a very personal blow. The composer sought analysis for a writer's block that developed shortly after the failure of *Pony*. The analyst, Ron Gorney, coaxed Simon back to work with reminders of his importance to his audience. Perhaps these reminders brought Simon back from the personal world of chromaticism to the more universal position for more direct (for Simon, more honest) diatonic means of communication. And so, the complex voice leading, the innovative chromatic techniques, the ties of the poetic text to musical structure (including the spiral formal effect, the great differences in musical materials between the verse and the bridge, and even the conscious advantage taken of the twelve-note aggregate) that had reached a crisis point in the albums of 1975 and 1980, all apparently came to represent facets of one compositional challenge that had been, for the composer, sufficiently overcome. In 1976, Simon was quoted as saying,

So much of what I hear on the radio is *boring*. . . . I think part of the reason is because it's not real. It may be real—maybe—if you're eighteen, but not if you're thirty. People thirty years old wonder why they're not getting off on popular music the way they once did, and it's because nobody's singing for them. When you reach a certain age you're not naive anymore. Everything I write can't be a philosophical truth, but it certainly isn't innocent—because I'm not.

Music is forever; music should grow and mature with you, following you right on up until you die.[45]

But perhaps its tonal complexity ebbs after you are swallowed and released.

Discography of Paul Simon Compositions Discussed in This Essay

Simon and Garfunkel

"The Sounds of Silence" / "We've Got a Groovy Thing Goin'" (Columbia 43396), single released November 1965.

The Sounds of Silence (Columbia 9269), February 1966:
  1. "The Sounds of Silence"
  11. "I Am a Rock"

"I Am a Rock" / "Flowers Never Bend with the Rainfall" (Columbia 43617), May 1966.

"Homeward Bound" / "Leaves That are Green" (Columbia 43511), June 1966.

Parsley, Sage, Rosemary, and Thyme (Columbia 9363), October 1966:
  4. "Homeward Bound"
  6. "The 59th Street Bridge Song (Feelin' Groovy)"

"At the Zoo" / "The 59th Street Bridge Song (Feelin' Groovy)" (Columbia 44046), March 1967.

"Mrs. Robinson" / "Old Friends/Bookends" (Columbia 44511), April 1968.

Bookends (Columbia 9529), May 1968:
  4. "Overs"
  6. "Old Friends"
  10. "Mrs. Robinson"
  12. "At the Zoo"

"The Boxer" / "Baby Driver" (Columbia 44785), April 1969.

Bridge Over Troubled Water (Columbia 9914), February 1970:
  1. "Bridge over Troubled Water"
  5. "So Long, Frank Lloyd Wright"
  6. "The Boxer"
  7. "Baby Driver"

Paul Simon

Paul Simon (Columbia 30750), February 1972:
   3. "Everything Put Together Falls Apart"

There Goes Rhymin' Simon (Columbia 32280), June 1973:
   1. "Kodachrome"
   2. "Tenderness"
   5. "One Man's Ceiling Is Another Man's Floor"
   6. "American Tune"
   7. "Was a Sunny Day"

Still Crazy after All These Years (Columbia 33540), October 1975:
   1. "Still Crazy after All These Years"
   2. "My Little Town"
   3. "I Do It for Your Love"
   4. "50 Ways to Leave Your Lover"
   5. "Night Game"
   9. "You're Kind"
   10. "Silent Eyes"

"Still Crazy after All These Years" / "I Do It for Your Love" (recorded live in London, December 1975) (Columbia 10332), April 1976.

One-Trick Pony (Warner Bros. 3472), September 1980:
   3. "One-Trick Pony"
   6. "Ace in the Hole"
   8. "Jonah"
   10. "Long Long Day"

Hearts and Bones (Warner Bros. 23942), November 1983:
   1. "Allergies"
   3. "When Numbers Get Serious"
   4. "Think Too Much (b)"
   5. "Song about the Moon"
   8. "Rene and Georgette Magritte with Their Dog after the War"

Graceland (Warner Bros. 25447), September 1986

Rhythm of the Saints (Warner Bros. 26098), November 1990:
   5. "Further to Fly"

Notes

A portion of this essay was presented to the 1991 meeting of the Society for Music Theory in Cincinnati.

1. From an interview in *Musician* 65 (Mar. 1984): 66–68. Paul Simon has long criticized the great proportion of rock music that has no appeal to thinking adults. Also see Loraine Alterman, "There Goes Rhymin' Simon," *New York Times*, Arts & Leisure (sec. 2), (6 May 1973): 30–31.

2. Israels was a longtime bassist with the Bill Evans Trio and director of the National Jazz Ensemble; at this writing he is associate professor of music at Western Washington University.

3. Facts of Simon's biography, career history, and discography are presented in the following sources, in addition to those cited elsewhere in this essay: Loraine Alterman, "Paul Simon," *Rolling Stone*, 28 May 1970: 36–39; Jon Landau, interview, *Rolling Stone*, 20 July 1972: 32–38; reprinted in *The Rolling Stone Interviews, 1967–1980* (New York: Rolling Stone Press, 1981), 208–22; Chris Charlesworth, "The Art of Paul Simon," *Melody Maker*, 22 Nov. 1975: 30–31; and Joe Smith, "Paul Simon," in *Off the Record: An Oral History of Popular Music*, ed. Mitchell Fink (New York: Warner Books, 1988), 281–84.

4. Richard Albero and Fred Styles, "Paul Simon's Workshop at the Guitar Study Center," *Guitar Player* 9/4 (Apr. 1975): 20. The Guitar Study Center was founded by Paul's brother Eddie.

5. "Night Game," scored simply for electric guitar, bass, vocals, and harmonica, views the eighth-inning removal of a pitcher in the context of ritual sporting death in the Roman Empire, but in an oblique, nearly inscrutable text. See Timothy White, *Rock Lives* (New York: Henry Holt, 1990), 372; and Patrick Humphries, *Bookends: The Simon and Garfunkel Story* (London: Proteus Books, 1982), 94–96. The timings above this and other graphs direct the reader to timings programmed into the respective compact discs; see the discography that appends this essay for information concerning the Paul Simon songs discussed in this chapter.

6. The bass B♭ at 1:29 in the third verse, functioning differently here than in the first two verses, places the B♭/A♯ of the bridge much closer to the heart of the tonic, D major. The C♯ and E♯ spellings at 0:56–1:02 obviate the weak apparent foreground arpeggiation of d: VI⁷–IV⁷–I, in the interest of the deeper voice leading that moves to V/V/V at 1:05.

7. Albero and Styles, "Workshop," 21.

8. Albero and Styles, "Workshop," 21. "American Tune" is a recomposition of Bach's "O Haupt voll Blut und Wunden." Perhaps its "American" status betrays a hymnal as Simon's source.

9. Stephen Holden, "Dazzlin' Simon: Family Life vs. Death" [review of *There Goes Rhymin' Simon*], *Rolling Stone*, 21 June 1973: 62.

10. Tony Schwartz, Interview with Paul Simon, *Playboy*, Feb. 1984: 166.

11. Beginning in 1957 at the age of fifteen, Simon wrote, recorded, and released more than thirty songs before Columbia Records first recorded Simon and Garfunkel in 1964.

12. Paul Simon, "Songwriting," in *Making Music*, ed. George Martin (New York: Quill, 1983), 70.

13. *Still Crazy after All These Years* topped the *Billboard* album chart for one week in December 1975, yielded four top-forty singles (including the number-one hit, "50 Ways to Leave Your Lover"), and earned Grammy awards for best album and best male vocal in February 1976. Critics praised it as a "touching" and "absorbing" yet "disciplined" and "mature" work; see, for instance, *Musician* 65 (Mar. 1984): 62. *One-Trick Pony* peaked at number twelve, with two of its singles reaching the top forty (neither of which attained top-five status). Critics found the album's slow-tempo songs "tedious"; see Ed Harrison, "Closeup," *Billboard* (27 Sept. 1980): 70. *Hearts and Bones* did not show higher than number thirty-five and its only single, "Allergies," did not make the top-forty; this project was Simon's most poorly received since 1964. The film, *One-Trick Pony*, was a flop at the box office as well as with critics, who found Simon wanting as an actor; such a review appears in *Billboard* (11 Oct. 1980): 13.

14. Alterman, "Rhymin' Simon," 31.

15. Simon certainly attained his greatest reception as a solo artist in 1986–87 with the tonally undemanding *Graceland*.

16. In a 1982 conversation with me concerning the Beatles song "And I Love Her," jazz

scholar James Dapogny likened this technique of alternating relative major and minor to the modal procedure that compares the finalis and cofinalis as two different cadence points within a single diatonic system.

17. Most often, the listener can hear the "driver" engage the clutch as one phrase ends on the original dominant, then shift to a higher gear as the new dominant appears a half step higher, and finally release the clutch on the new tonic with the beginning of a new phrase.

18. The truck driver's modulation has a long history in commercial hits from the late 1950s and 1960s, usually occurring between successive verses, but not until after the second. This may often have some dramatic effect, signaling transcendence in a story line; consider, for instance, the deaths that are symbolized by the shifts from C major to D♭ major in Bobby Goldsboro's "Honey" (United Artists 50283 [1968]). In Zager and Evans's "In the Year 2525" (RCA 0174 [1969]), tonal shifts portray not only the passage of time that occurs between verses, but also adjustments in the reported intervals of time: characteristics of the years 2525, 3535, 4545, 5555, and 6565 are expressed in G♯ minor, those of the years 7510 and 8510 in A minor, and those of the year 9595 in B♭ minor. This modulation may also provide a change of color for the "big finish," as in the move from D major to E♭ major in "Traces" by the Classics IV (Imperial 66352 [1969]). Too often, the modulation appears arbitrary and shallow but takes on a life of its own; once it starts, it seems unstoppable. Good examples of this are the Toys' "A Lover's Concerto" (DynoVoice 209 [1965]) and Bobby Hebb's "Sunny" (Philips 40365 [1966]), each of which boasts four key centers rising in half steps. Worst offender? Perhaps "Opus 17 (Don't You Worry 'bout Me)" (Philips 40370 [1966]), in which the Four Seasons ascend by half step from F♯ major to B major. (Both the Toys' and Seasons' hits were composed by the team Linzer-Randell.) In the Playmates' "Beep Beep" (Roulette 4115 [1958]), the tempo increases with the V-8 Ford's ascending shifts between verses, and the hot rodder in Jan and Dean's "The Little Old Lady (from Pasadena)" (Liberty 55704 [1964]) careens abruptly and incongruously from E♭ major to F major and then directly to D♭ major!

19. Simon, "Songwriting," 67.

20. Mark Peel [review of *Hearts and Bones*], *Stereo Review* 48/3 (Mar. 1984): 88.

21. "Frank Lloyd Wright" is from *Bridge over Troubled Water*, which, with ten weeks at number one and sales of over ten million units worldwide, was Simon's most successful product. The negative correlation suggested previously between chromaticism and popularity, however, is reinforced by one review, which finds this particular song to be "their worst" ever. See Gregg Mitchell, [review of *Bridge*], *Rolling Stone*, 14 May 1970: 58.

22. In "You're Kind," the tonal shift accompanies an unexpected "goodbye" and highlights the singer's shift in attitude from sincere appreciation to flippant cynicism. This and the fact that the title is replaced in the final verse with "Goodbye" are testaments to Simon's aim to spiral back to the beginning with a new "feel" and title.

23. "Ceiling" was recorded at the Muscle Shoals studios in Alabama, as opposed to the location of most of Simon's recording work of the 1970s, New York.

24. The "IV" function in blues is both one of a subdominant neighboring chord to the following I and at the same time a consonant doubling of a passing seventh from V.

25. Chuck Israels, "Bill Evans (1929–1980): A Musical Memoir," *Musical Quarterly* 71/2 (1985): 112–13.

26. Instability is suggested by the tonicization of the remote F♯ major at 1:34, where Simon sings G♯, F♯, D♯, and C♯ as if to complete his vocal aggregate, but he never does sing F♮.

27. The d♭♭ creates a G♭ half-diminished seventh chord, which also might be heard as an "inversion" of a B♭-minor triad with added sixth—making the fourth and first scale degrees of the linear progression the only tones that seem to be supported unequivocally by root-position chords, an unusual formulation for a sequential model.

28. Example 5.8 also respells F♭ as E and D♭♭ as C, in line with the intervallic identity of the surface verticality, a seventh chord on F.

29. This change of mode frames the change from G♭ minor to G♭ major within the chorus; the "gulp" that creates the new fifth motions at the surface embellishes G♭ major with the consistent appearance of B♭, beginning with the introduction of that tone in the bass immediately following the Jonah chord.

30. The song's coda features another A♮ in the bass as a repeated neighboring leading tone to the fifth of tonic harmony.

31. Holden, "Dazzlin' Simon," 62.

32. The F♯ of the bridge was implicit in the song's opening chord, C–g♭–b♭–d, $V^9_{♭5}$/IV.

33. In the film, Jonah is persuaded to perform his 1967 antiwar hit, "Soft Parachutes," at the 1980 Radio and Records Convention in Chicago. "Jonah and the others on the bill, including the Lovin' Spoonful, Sam and Dave, and Tiny Tim, personify the movie's title: 'one-trick pony' is an act that has only one number, but can coax an entire career from it." Joseph Morella and Patricia Barey, *Simon and Garfunkel: Old Friends* (New York: Birch Lane Press, 1991), 201. (Actually, all of the Lovin' Spoonful's first seven singles were top-ten hits.)

34. The setting is the Agora Club in Cleveland; "One-Trick Pony" is one of the two songs on the album that were recorded there, live, in November 1979.

35. An analogous setting of E-minor harmony is heard in mm. 43–44, where B and D are played by violins; F♯ is heard only as a normally behaving passing tone in the Brazilian accordion-vocal solo. The oboe's only appearance in the body of the song occurs in mm. 27–29; this passage is motivically related to that of the introduction.

36. The tears seem to be a result of an emotional discharge caused by the memories related in the B section. After the first hearing of the bridge, the listener is taken through the reflective instrumental passage of mm. 33–46; the second hearing leads to the awakening to the present of m. 47.

37. Schwartz, *Playboy* interview, 164.

38. Simon, "Songwriting," 68–69. It has been pointed out that the reference to Northern and Southern hemispheres may reflect the differences between the composer (who grew up in Queens) and his wife (who was raised in Tennessee). Morella and Barey, *Old Friends,* 155.

39. See Heinrich Schenker, *Counterpoint,* book 2, trans. John Rothgeb and Jürgen Thym, ed. John Rothgeb (1922; reprint, New York: Schirmer, 1987), 194; and *Free Composition,* trans. and ed. Ernst Oster (1935; reprint, New York: Longman, 1979), 105. See also Oswald Jonas, *Introduction to the Theory of Heinrich Schenker,* trans. and ed. John Rothgeb (New York: Longman, 1982), 85–87.

40. I have discussed dramatic examples of this voice leading technique in music by Mozart and Schubert in "Voice Leading, Register, and Self-Discipline in *Die Zauberflöte,*" *Theory and Practice* 16 (1991): 103–26; and "Grief in *Winterreise*: A Schenkerian Perspective," *Music Analysis* 9/2 (July 1990): 157–75.

41. Simon, "Songwriting," 70.

42. Sliding chromatic half steps are an important structural feature of the song's voice leading. The middle section is prepared in m. 24 by a chromatic passing motion through an augmented fifth (d^{1x} over g♯); the first verse and the middle section share chromatic half-step descents in the bass involving cadential appearances of pitch-class B♭. The verse progresses from B♭ to A in m. 15, and the B section concludes with the motion B♯–B♮–A♯ in mm. 31–32.

43. Compare the roman-numeral figures below the graph for mm. 9–11 with those of 13–16; see also the similar treatment of ♯IV and ♯II by comparing the corresponding figures below mm. 25–27 with those below mm. 29–32.

44. Simon was quite cognizant of the romantic effect of a lush string section. In the film

One-Trick Pony, producer Steve Kunelian justifies his plan to add strings to Jonah's "Ace in the Hole" by declaring, "they'll tear your heart out." It was not the effect Jonah wanted in that song, but the sound is certainly appropriate to the final verse of "I Do It for Your Love."

45. White, *Rock Lives,* 375; abstracted from White, "Public Pitches and Stolen Moments with Pinin' Simon," *Crawdaddy* (Feb. 1976).

6

"Little Wing"

A Study in Musical Cognition

MATTHEW BROWN

1

After considerable resistance from the scholarly community, rock music has recently emerged as a legitimate subject for academic discourse. This newfound prestige has stemmed partly from a wave of pluralism and interdisciplinary research that has swept across campus, and partly from the sheer importance of the music. Given its popular origins and broad appeal, discussions of rock music have tended to avoid detailed musical analyses and have focused their attention, instead, on issues of social function and meaning. To quote Simon Frith: "For the last fifty years, pop music has been an important way in which we have learned to understand ourselves as historical, ethnic, classbound, gendered subjects."[1]

One area, however, in which rock music remains largely ignored is music cognition. As David Hargreaves observes: "Psychologists have woefully neglected the 'mundane,' or 'lay' aspects of musical experience. They have dealt largely with serious 'art' music, which is a minority interest relative to the many different forms of 'folk,' or popular music."[2] This state of affairs is regrettable because rock music is an important resource for evaluating and perhaps even refining current theories of musical behavior, both for listeners and composers. Among other things, it can help us test our explanations of how listeners acquire and use musical skills, how they perceive and remember music, how they discriminate between musical styles, and how they shape their responses according to various environmental constraints. As this essay will make clear, rock music may also shed light on the nature of musical composition.

Many of us, it seems, are fascinated by musical composition and the possibility of explaining some of its mysteries. Musicologists are interested because composition lies at the heart of the musical experience; they care both about the ways in which individual pieces are put together and about the people who created them. Psychologists are intrigued because composition is one of the most remarkable expressions of human thought; through studying it, they hope to gain new insights about cognitive processes in general.

Yet, for all its allure, composition remains "the least studied and least well understood of all musical processes."[3] Musicians have tried to remedy this situation in two main ways. Music theorists have focused their attention on the finished piece; by demonstrating how the final score hangs together, they have shown what decisions the composer actually made. Meanwhile, many music historians have turned toward the composers' sketches and drafts; by examining these documents in detail, they have shown why individual composers made some choices and not others.

While these approaches certainly tell us much about the composition of individual pieces, they shed little light on what goes on inside the composer's head.[4] On the contrary, many musicians are quick to claim that such processes are so complex as to be beyond our control. Some believe that, since great pieces are unique entities, the manner in which they are created must be unique as well.[5] Others insist that composition is just too complicated for rationalization.[6] Psychologists have not fared much better. Although there is growing interest in music cognition, little progress has been made toward understanding composition per se. Certainly researchers face innumerable problems. Musical composition is an extremely sophisticated form of behavior and is hard to study in the laboratory; it is not clear how to isolate one variable from another experimentally. Furthermore, explaining composition requires us to understand something about the general ways in which people perceive, encode, store, and recall music; unfortunately, we still have little idea about how these processes work. As Marvin Minsky pessimistically notes, "Surely it is premature to ask how great composers write great symphonies before we know how ordinary people think of ordinary tunes."[7]

Minsky is certainly correct to be skeptical about the prospects of explaining musical composition, but his remarks should not prompt us to give up hope altogether. Indeed, this essay will try to take a few steps in the right direction by showing how composition might be understood as a form of knowledge-based problem solving. The discussion has two main parts. The first considers problem solving in detail and focuses on the so-called information processing model. In particular, it shows how a tonal piece of music might be regarded as a successful solution to a musical problem. Having described some the difficulties that arise when applying the model, it examines how Schenkerian theory offers us one way of representing the model analytically. The second part uses the information processing model in conjunction with Schenkerian theory to explain Jimi Hendrix's celebrated tune "Little Wing," demonstrating how Hendrix solved various problems of tonal and motivic organization in this remarkable ballad.

2

Although there are many forms of human behavior, Karl Popper was surely right to point out that people are "constantly engaged, night and day, in solving problems."[8] For Popper, these problems have a definite purpose: they allow the person to anticipate future needs or impending events.[9] He is hardly alone in his appraisal; cognitive scientists have already shown how problem solving guides general mental processes, such as learning, not to mention specific tasks, such as painting a picture.[10] Since musical composition has many connections with these activities, we have every reason to suppose that it might be explained along similar lines.

But how exactly do people solve problems? Of the many ways to answer this question, cognitive scientists often draw on the information processing model.[11] According to this model, problem solvers begin with some basic material, the starting state, and some desired solution, the goal state. They then make a series of choices that transforms the starting state into the goal state. Each transformation creates an intermediate state that conforms to various external constraints. Taken together, the total number of valid transformations constitutes the problem space. The precise subset of transformations needed to change the starting state into the goal state is known as the search strategy.

Even this brief sketch makes clear that the information processing model treats problem solving as some sort of search. Allan Lesgold explains this point rather nicely: "if we think of the problem space as a sort of maze of mental activity through which we must wander, searching for a solution, we have a powerful metaphor for reflecting the nature of problem solving."[12] It is important, however, to realize that the search strategy only explains what transformations are needed to solve a problem in a particular way by showing how a successful solution fits within the problem space. The search strategy does not attempt to re-create the actual steps, successful and unsuccessful, that the problem solver took to find this answer. This process is known as the discovery procedure.

To explain tonal composition as a type of problem solving, consider the following scenario. One of the main problems facing a tonal composer is that of taking some kernel of musical material and extending it to create a coherent tonal work. In this context, the starting state is usually a motive, rhythmic pattern, or harmonic progression, and the goal state is the finished score.[13] Composers transform the starting state into the goal state in a variety of ways; since every extension must create a coherent tonal unit, the most important transformations are those defined by the tonal system itself. The problem space is the complete list of well-formed tonal pieces that could conceivably be written from a given kernel of musical material using the principles of tonal harmony and voice leading. The search strategy can be thought of as the precise string of transformations that generate the piece in question, and identifying these transformations in turn amounts to showing how the finished work is a well-formed tonal composition. The discovery procedure is the actual manner by which the composer moved from the starting state to the goal state, as for example might be recorded in his or her sketches or drafts.

As it stands, the information processing model provides a powerful way of explaining problem solving. Difficulties arise, however, in trying to use it to explain specific tasks, especially those of great complexity. It is unclear, for example, what knowledge is needed for a given task and how it should be represented mentally. For one thing, problem spaces must be general enough to contain all knowledge that might conceivably be relevant to a task, yet flexible enough to allow for inferences and analogies.[14] Unfortunately, there is no way of predicting what knowledge will be relevant or irrelevant in any given case. These matters are especially acute in real-world situations where the knowledge base is very large and constantly revised. For another thing, there are many types of knowledge; some are easier to represent as states and transformations than others. Psychologists usually differentiate between three main types of knowledge: fact-based or declarative knowledge; skill-based or procedural knowledge; and rule-based or production knowledge. Of these, production knowledge is the simplest to represent in terms of states and transformations.[15] The situation is further complicated by the fact that people do not usually treat each piece of knowledge in isolation; they usually absorb, process, and recall it in hierarchically organized packages. These packages are often referred to as frames or schemas.

These difficulties become evident if the information processing model is applied to tonal composition. It is hard to decide what knowledge a composer needs to compose a particular piece and to determine how it should be represented. Since tonal pieces are shaped by many rhythmic, thematic, formal, harmonic, contrapuntal, and textural factors, composers must surely draw on many different types of knowledge when they write. The precise nature of this knowledge depends on their individual intentions as well as on the cultural context within which they work. The snag is that it is not obvious how a particular piece of knowledge influences a specific decision. Even confined to matters of harmony and voice leading, how the composer's knowledge should be represented in an analytical form is not obvious. Over the past few centuries, music theorists have devised many different ways of explaining the harmonic and voice-leading properties of common-practice music. Most make a few basic assumptions about tonal relationships. For example, they assume (1) that tonal harmonies are fundamentally triadic; (2) that they are hierarchic; (3) that they are essentially diatonic; (4) that tonal melodies tend to fall and reach maximum closure when they descend by step to $\hat{1}$; (5) that tonal dissonances arise from motion between consonances; and (6) that parallel octaves and fifths are banned.[16] However, although we know that tonal composers undoubtedly process their knowledge hierarchically, we are not sure how to represent it as such analytically.[17]

Other difficulties arise in trying to explain search strategies. One hitch is that problem states are not always well defined; it may not be possible to fix the starting and goal states with certainty.[18] Some activities are so complicated that the main issue is to decide which problems are really capable of solution. As Robert Nozick explains, "people do not simply *face* given problems; their task is to *make* a problem, to *find* one in the inchoate situations they find themselves in."[19] To make matters worse, problems may change shape as they are being solved; all too often, their precise nature becomes apparent only after considerable effort has been expended. There may even be situations in which a goal can be satisfied in more than one way.[20] Similarly, although problem solvers sometimes work by brute force, most rely on heuristics or learned search strategies. When solving a new problem, experts see how it resembles problems they have already solved and whose search strategies are stored schematically in their long-term memories.[21]

These particular issues loom large for anyone trying to understand the nature of composition. As John Sloboda has stressed, the problems facing them are usually ill defined.[22] Given the complexity of most musical compositions, the composer often faces a network of problems, some more difficult to solve than others. Even limited to the main themes, the precise nature of this material may be hard to interpret. It may also be tricky to specify exactly when the goal state has been reached: sometimes, the same piece may exist in different versions (such as those found in autographs, first editions, revised editions, and so forth) and in various settings (such as transcriptions, arrangements, orchestrations, and so forth). In some cases, we may be unable to say which one of these is definitive.[23] It is also clear that composers rely heavily on heuristic searches.[24] Skilled composers do not consider every possible continuation of their starting material; on the contrary, they normally pick from a small number of choices. Since composers often come up with similar decisions in different pieces— they might, for example, use characteristic modulation schemes—it seems likely that they have learned search strategies. There is also good reason to suppose that these strategies are stored hierarchically as abstract frames and schemas.

Although there are many ways to represent problem spaces, search strategies, and so forth for musical composition, one that seems particularly promising is Schenkerian theory. For example, Heinrich Schenker showed how the six rules of tonal harmony and voice leading might be represented as background states (*Ursätze*), transformations (*Verwandlungen*), and levels (*Schichten*).[25] In this representation, the tonal problem space can be seen as the set of all possible well-formed pieces that can be derived from a background by Schenkerian transformations, with the sequence of levels corresponding to the string of intermediate states. The search strategy is the precise sequence of transformations found at each level, the heuristics the distinctive ways in which composers group transformations at particular levels. Of course, by showing tonal relationships at different levels, Schenkerian theory provides a way of showing how composers solve problems hierarchically, thereby balancing local and global concerns. In other words, Schenkerian graphs offer a way of representing how tonal composers store and manipulate their material in terms of frames or schemas.

3

Having identified some of the pros and cons with the information processing model and having seen how to use Schenkerian theory to represent this model for tonal composition, I will use them to shed light on a single composition, Jimi Hendrix's exquisite ballad "Little Wing." An examination of the compositional problem Hendrix faced in writing this song encounters some of the difficulties outlined above.

Although the precise composition history of "Little Wing" will probably never be reconstructed, we do know a few facts about its genesis.[26] Documentary evidence suggests that the song took several years to finish. Hendrix mentioned to interviewer Jules Freedmond that the tune grew out of a rhythm-guitar figure he came up with while playing in a club in Greenwich Village in 1965-66.[27] After further experimentation, the song took its final form when Hendrix was in Monterey in June 1967. In his words: "It's based on a very, very simple Indian style . . . I got the idea like when we were in Monterey and I was just lookin' at everything around. So I figured that I take everything I see around and put it maybe in the form of a girl, or somethin' like that, you know, and call it 'Little Wing,' and then it would just fly away."[28] He added, "It's very simple, but I like it."

Once Hendrix had figured out "Little Wing," he recorded it with the Experience in October 1967 at Olympic Studio B in Barnes, with Chas Chandler producing, Eddie Kramer engineering, and George Chkiantz assisting.[29] This version consists of four complete verses. The first is scored for rhythm guitar and has a glockenspiel doubling some of the bass notes; the second and third are vocal; and the fourth is a guitar solo. The track ends with a fadeout through a fifth verse of guitar solo. The band did not rehearse the tune before the recording session; according to the drummer, Mitch Mitchell, and the bassist, Noel Redding, Hendrix simply showed them the finished material at Regent Sound, and after a couple of run-throughs, they immediately laid down each track at Olympic Studios on 25 October.[30] Three days later, Hendrix added new vocals and overdubbed a glockenspiel part, and the next day, Kramer modified the vocals by half-phasing them and passing them through a revolving Leslie speaker.[31]

With each track on tape, Hendrix, Chandler, and Kramer picked "Little Wing" and twelve other cuts for a new album dealing with universal and human love. This album was to be called *Axis: Bold as Love*. According to Hendrix, the Axis is an all-knowing mystic who provides a bridge between the real and the spiritual worlds and through whom we can find true love.[32] Hendrix and the others then spent four days mixing each song. Unfortunately, the mixes for side one were lost, and another eleven hours were spent remixing each song from the original tracks.[33] The completed album was released in England on 1 December 1967 and in America in January 1968. Three songs were later issued as singles.[34]

It should be clear that "Little Wing" evolved over several years. The lack of rehearsals suggests that bass and drum parts were not very complicated and that Hendrix may have had a very good idea about what he wanted before the musicians arrived at the studio. This is certainly in keeping with eyewitness accounts of his working methods. It is also clear that Hendrix worked hard on processing and mixing the final cut. The fact that he took so much care and attention suggests that numerous technical issues needed to be resolved. But what precisely might these issues have been?

Obviously, Hendrix faced a large number of different problems in composing "Little Wing," many of which were clearly ill defined. Some of the most immediate were those of thematic and tonal organization: at some level Hendrix had to find a way of extending some kernel of thematic material so as to create a larger tonally satisfying whole. In terms of the information processing model, the task is to determine the nature of Hendrix's starting state and problem space, and doing this requires understanding the basic characteristics of Hendrix's music.

It is important to remember that Hendrix's musical roots were firmly planted in the blues. Born on 22 November 1942, Hendrix spent his formative years in Seattle

Figure 6.1. Jimi Hendrix, "Little Wing"

absorbing the classics of Robert Johnson, Muddy Waters, Howlin' Wolf, John Lee Hooker, Albert King, and other great bluesmen. After a stint in the army, he started his career on the Chitlin' circuit backing such well-known rhythym and blues performers as Little Richard, Wilson Pickett, the Isley Brothers, Curtis Knight, and B. B. King. These early experiences left an indelible mark on Hendrix. According to Billy Cox, who played bass with him in the army and later in the Band of Gypsies, "His style . . . reflected his youth and social awareness, but just about everything Jimi and I recorded was blues. Everything was right from the soil, right from the depth of mankind. Even the current stuff Jimi played was just amplified blues."[35] Many other experts agree, though Tony Glover perhaps said it best: "Hendrix plays Delta Blues for sure—only the Delta may have been on Mars."[36] I will return to this "interplanetary" aspect of Hendrix's style later.

Given that Hendrix worked within blues traditions, the starting state and problem space for "Little Wing" can be imagined in blues terms. The starting state for "Little Wing," as in so many blues-based compositions, is a core of predominantly pentatonic figures that we hear at the beginning of the song. In fact, Hendrix presents several distinct pentatonic formulae in measures 1–4, as shown in figure 6.1. The first (ex. 6.1a) is introduced in measure 1 and consists of four ascending notes A–B–D–E; it recurs transposed up a fourth in measure 3. The second and third figures appear in measure 2: the former consists of a simple turn figure, G–A–G (ex. 6.1b), while the latter consists of the pattern C–B–C–B–G (see ex. 6.1c). Hendrix presents a fourth formula, the undulating gesture in measure 4 (ex. 6.1d). Significantly, these four gestures do not feature prominently in measures 5–10, though we do hear a variant of the second gesture in measure 6.

Since blues pieces essentially conform to the principles of common-practice tonality, Hendrix's problem space can be defined by the rules of tonal harmony and counterpoint. As mentioned earlier, these can be represented in the form of Schenkerian backgrounds, transformations, and levels. Since "Little Wing" centers on the tonic E, the problem space will be determined by a background state in E minor. In fact, "Little Wing" also follows the basic formal constraints of many blues compositions; instead of alternating between verses and choruses, it is built from repetitions of a single harmonic pattern (ex. 6.2). The harmonic motion of the first four bars (I–III–IV–I) is, in fact, more typical of eight-bar than of twelve-bar blues: as Dave Rubin notes, the former not only have faster changes than the latter, but they often shift from I to III in minor keys.[37] Hendrix presumably learned this pattern during his years playing rhythym and blues.

But although "Little Wing" definitely has its roots in rhythm and blues, it is no ordinary blues; on the contrary, the piece has many features we associate with late-

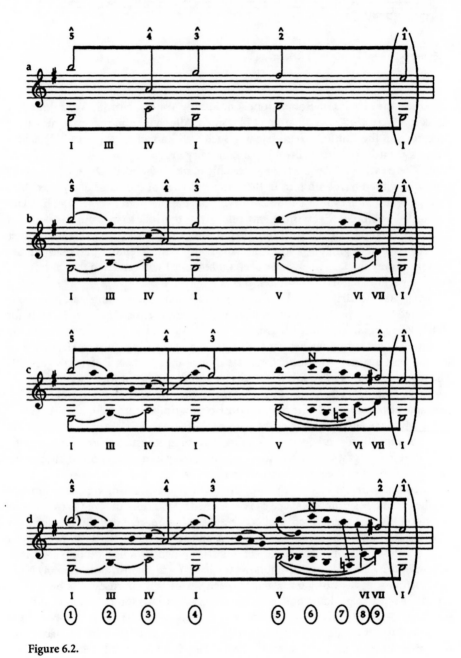

Figure 6.2.

1960s rock. These features played a decisive role in determining Hendrix's search strategy. To begin with, the imagery and style of the lyrics are clearly psychedelic. The ballad is a love song, but, as with so many of Hendrix's texts, it has an almost phantasmagorical quality. Hendrix describes how his imaginary lover walks "through the clouds" with "a circus mind that's running wild." When he is sad she comforts him and then flies away. Overall, the mood of "Little Wing" is tender and playful; it does not treat love with the passion and anguish of a slow blues, or with the superficiality and chauvinism of so-called cock rock.

Hendrix's fascination with instrumental and studio effects likewise smacks more of psychedelia than of the blues. Although "Little Wing" is considerably more restrained than the other tracks on *Axis*, the song demonstrates the composer's remarkable sensitivity to sound per se. For example, Hendrix's guitar part contains striking shifts in texture and timbre. The introductory verse is built from a subtle blend of partial chords, inversions, and hammered and pulled double stops.[38] Hendrix's sound is warm and clean; he uses out-of phase pickups on his Stratocaster and touches of univibe and octavia.[39] The solo, meanwhile, has a quite different quality. Not only does it start with a dive-bomb on the whammy bar, but the guitar tone is overdriven, phased, and passed through a rotating Leslie speaker. According to Hendrix, the results sound "like jelly bread."[40] The vocals are likewise filtered, phased, and run through a rotating Leslie speaker. The complex mélange of timbres is further highlighted by the glockenspiel. In emphasizing Hendrix's love of effects, it is important to stress that these are not simply gimmicks added to spice up an otherwise impoverished piece; on the contrary, it is clear from interviews and eyewitness accounts that electronic effects were basic elements of the composition.

Most significantly, Hendrix's melodic and harmonic idiom also shows strong psychedelic influences. Whereas bars 1-4 are built from the familiar blues progression I–III–IV–I, bars 5–10 have quite different origins. For one thing, the overall motion from a B-minor chord (m. 5) through a C-major sonority (m. 8) to a D-major chord (mm. 9–10) is not typical of a blues in E; progressions of this type, with their weak tonal functions, are far more common in rock.[41] For another, the chromatic chords on B♭ and F in measures 5 and 7 are idiomatic of psychedelic music; both chords lie outside the prevailing pentatonic collection. Lastly, many of Hendrix's voicings are decidedly unbluesy. Most striking in this regard are the ubiquitous 4–3 and 9–8 suspensions and stacked fifths. For example, the second motive (ex. 6.1b) is clearly built from a 4–3 suspension, whereas the B and C sonorities in measures 5 and 8 are both elaborated by 9–8 suspensions (C♯–B and D–C, respectively). Later, in measures 7–8, we hear a string of parallel stacked fifths: B–E–A, A–D–G, G–C–F. These sonorities have an exotic feel that may reflect the "Indian" influences Hendrix mentioned in the reminiscence cited earlier.[42]

If the motivic and harmonic characteristics of measures 5–10 are so different from those of measures 1–4, how did Hendrix manage to bind them together? In what way does the finished piece represent a discrete search through the tonal problem space? To see how the recording of "Little Wing" answers these questions, I will look more closely at the song's tonal structure. Two things become apparent. On the one hand, although measures 5–10 are usual, the progression from B minor to D major can actually be regarded as a large expansion of a dominant harmony. The intermediary chords arise from contrapuntal motion between the V chord in measure 5 and the VII chord in measures 9–10. It then becomes clear that the entire song moves from the tonic (mm. 1–4) to the dominant (mm. 5–10).

On the other hand, an examination of the layout of the opening verse makes clear not only that the guitar part encompasses a striking shift of register but also that it does so by means of a stepwise descent. From a single listening, one hears that the opening bars establish a broad pitch spectrum that extends from the E below middle C to the E three octaves higher. By the end of the verse, however, the bass part has ascended to the D above middle C, and the upper parts have descended over an octave. One of the most important strands in the contrapuntal structure descends by step from B ($\hat{5}$) through A ($\hat{4}$) and G ($\hat{3}$) to F♯ ($\hat{2}$). The pitch B appears in the opening guitar slide and on beat two. Hendrix shifts to A in measure 3 for the subdominant harmony and G in measure 4 with the return to the tonic. The pitch F♯ first appears as part of the dominant harmony in measure 5 (beat three) but is eventually confirmed with the arrival of VII in measure 9.

Based on this information, I offer a Schenkerian account of Hendrix's search strategy. To extend the core of pentatonic gestures given in example 6.1, Hendrix not only followed the rules of tonal harmony and voice leading, but he also conceived of the large-scale harmonic and melodic motion mentioned above. The graphs given in example 6.2 show how the surface structure of the song actually satisfies these requirements and constitutes a successful search through the problem space. The large-scale motion from I to V is shown in the background (ex. 6.2a), and the surface chord progression — I–III–V–I–V–VI–VII — is shown in the foreground (ex. 6.2d). The intermediate levels (exx. 6.2b and 6.2c) demonstrate how the foreground is a transformation of the background. Among other things, the stepwise descent to G is anticipated locally in measures 1–2, 4, and 7–8. In addition, the unusual parallel ninths in measure 7 actually arise from complex displacements between the outer parts (these are indicated by the diagonal lines).

In the later verses, there are significant differences between Hendrix's vocal line and his guitar solo. The voice part does not articulate the stepwise descent from B to F♯; instead, it seems to focus on members of the pentatonic scale (E–G–A–B–D–E). For example, in measures 1–2, the line outlines a retrograde of example 6.1a (E–D–A–G) and in measures 3–4 it completes the scale B–A–G–D–E. The guitar solo, meanwhile, brings out the descent from B to F♯ even more clearly than the rhythm guitar part. The solo arrives on B in measure 2 thanks to an expansion of example 6.1c (E–D–B). Hendrix emphasizes the pitch A in measure 4 with the pattern A–B–C–A–G. In measure 6 the solo begins with a complete version of example 6.1c an octave higher. Hendrix actually goes to great lengths to highlight the descent from $\hat{5}$ to $\hat{4}$ in measure 7 by a pair of wonderful parallel sixths, B–G and A–F. The descent from G to F♯ in measures 8–9 is emphasized by several versions of example 6.1b.

It would seem that Hendrix tended to repeat these processes in his live solos for "Little Wing."[43] In the three most widely available live recordings, he takes the basic outline of the studio solo and elaborates it by various pentatonic fills and extra flourishes. Significantly, they all contain the parallel sixths in measure 7, and all recycle the four pentatonic gestures, though in slightly different arrangements. The consistency between the studio and live solos suggests the extent to which the underlying counterpoint was inscribed in Hendrix's head. Besides having an extra verse of solo, the only other important divergence from this standpoint between the studio and the live solos is that the latter end with a coda. Typically, this coda does not end on E; instead, it shifts to E♭ before closing on G7. Once again, the fact that Hendrix was consistent in his solution to the problem of closure indicates that he relied on a specific search strategy and on a well-defined goal state.

4

This chapter has shown that "Little Wing" can be regarded as a successful search through a tonal problem space. The starting state is a core of pentatonic themes, the goal state is the finished piece, and the problem space is the set of all well-formed pieces that can be composed from these themes according to the principles of tonality. The search strategy itself not only balanced blues practice with psychedelic procedures, but it also traded off local and global concerns. Although we cannot reconstruct the precise way in which Hendrix discovered this search strategy, there is circumstantial evidence that it involved a long process of experimenting on the guitar as well as a period of abstract manipulation away from the fret board. Indeed, eyewitnesses have stressed the extent to which Hendrix produced overall mental images of his music. For example, according to Eddie Kramer, "There were no meetings in advance and Jimi created things in a very loose sort of fashion. *He* knew in his own head what he wanted to do and how he wanted to create—he had pages and pages of lyrics to choose from—but he knew *exactly* what he was doing. Every overdub, every backward guitar solo, every double-tracked thing was carefully worked out ... in his own head ... in a very private sense."[44] These remarks certainly conform with the general picture of knowledge-based problem solving outlined earlier, and they suggest how rock music can provide an important medium for understanding the process of composition.

This essay started by noting that current research in rock music reflects a trend toward pluralism and interdisciplinary study. In this regard, Frith is right to claim that rock and other popular music helps us "understand ourselves as historical, ethnic, classbound, gendered subjects." But besides being social animals, human beings are also complex bundles of neurons capable of the most elaborate thoughts. The ways we think are determined as much by hardwired cognitive processes as by any external social forces. As the psychologist Roy D'Andrade explains, "Cultural models are actually little *machines*. They are software *programs*, not just *data*. Of course, the brain contains a more general mental machine that runs these little cultural machines, just as there is a more general program that runs a specific Fortran program. But the little programs are important, because without them the general program, which does various universal procedures such as *search, chunk, store*, and *recall*, would have to work very hard to do very little."[45] Rock music promises to help us explain both the cultural machines and the general mental programs. As such, it can play a vital role in the most important interdisciplinary issue of all: that of understanding human behavior and the inner workings of the mind.

Notes

1. Simon Frith, "Towards an Aesthetic of Popular Music," in *Music and Society*, ed. Richard Leppert and Susan McClary (Cambridge: Cambridge University Press, 1987), 149.

2. David J. Hargreaves, *The Developmental Psychology of Music* (Cambridge: Cambridge University Press, 1986), 7–8.

3. John Sloboda, *The Musical Mind* (Oxford: Oxford University Press, 1985), 103.

4. According to Joseph Kerman, "Much ingenuity has been expended in discovering how individual works have passed through various stages to their final state, and explaining why; and by extension, to analyzing how their composers have worked as a matter of routine. By a further extension, one could go on to study musical creativity in general, at least in theory." He adds that the latter project "has not been seriously attempted since the days of Max Graf and Frederick Dorian in the 1940s." Joseph Kerman, "Sketch Studies," in *Musicology in the 1980s*, ed. D. Kern Holoman and Claude V. Palisca (New York: Da Capo Press, 1982), 58.

5. According to Felix Salzer: "There is, in a sense, no creative process as such, for the minds of different composers must have worked differently. Every composer probably had his own way of mentally 'thinking it out'; that process surely worked in different ways even within the output of a single composer." Felix Salzer, "Review: Robert Marshall, *The Compositional Process of J. S. Bach*," *Journal of Music Theory* 16 (1972): 232. This notion is common in aesthetics, see Suresh Raval, *Metacriticism* (Athens: University of Georgia Press, 1981), 39.

6. To quote Richard Kramer: "The creative act (the point needs restressing) is mysterious. If that puts it too romantically, it is an act that is so complex, motivated by so many impulses—as remote and impersonal as the entire web of knowable history, and as remote and intensely personal as the sum of one man's experience—that the material evidence (records of the act) are little more than occasional memos of a deeper, continual process." Richard Kramer, "The Sketches for Beethoven's Violin Sonatas, Opus 30: History, Transcription, Analysis" (Ph.D. diss., Princeton University, 1973), 516–17; cited in Douglas Johnson, "Beethoven Scholars and Beethoven Sketches," *Nineteenth-Century Music* 2 (1978): 15.

7. Marvin Minsky, *The Society of Mind* (New York: Simon and Schuster, 1986), 80.

8. Karl Popper, "The Place of Mind in Nature," in *Mind in Nature*, ed. Richard Q. Elvee (San Francisco: Harper and Row, 1982), 45.

9. Popper, "The Place of Mind in Nature," 45.

10. James Voss, "Problem Solving and the Educational Process," in *Foundations for a Psychology of Education*, ed. Alan Lesgold and Robert Glaser (Hillsdale, N.J.: Erlbaum, 1989), 255. For discussions of problem solving in painting, see Michael Baxandall, *Patterns of Intention: On the Historical Explanation of Pictures* (New Haven: Yale University Press, 1985), and E. H. Gombrich, *Art and Illusion: A Study in the Psychology of Pictorial Representation* (Princeton: Princeton University Press, 1960). More generally, Karl Popper has described the general role of problem solving in the acquisition of knowledge; see his *Objective Knowledge: An Evolutionary Approach* (Oxford: Oxford University Press, 1972).

11. For helpful surveys of problem solving, see Voss, "Problem Solving and the Educational Process," 251–55 and 286–94; and Richard E. Meyer, "Problem Solving," in *The Blackwell Dictionary of Cognitive Psychology*, ed. Michael W. Eysenck (Oxford: Blackwell, 1990), 284–88. More extensive accounts can be found in Allen Newell and Herbert Simon, *Human Problem Solving* (Englewood Cliffs, N.J.: Prentice-Hall Inc., 1972); Igor Aleksander and Piers Burnett, *Thinking Machines* (Oxford: Oxford Unversity Press, 1987); Avron Barr, Paul R. Cohen, Edward A. Feigenbaum, eds., *The Artificial Intelligence Handbook*, 4 vols. (Reading, Mass: Addison-Wesley Publishing Co., 1981–1989); Allan Newell, *Unified Theories of Cognition* (Cambridge: Harvard University Press, 1990); Kurt VanLehn, "Problem Solving and Cognitive Skill Acquisition," in *Foundations of Cognitive Science*, ed. Michael I. Posner (Cambridge: MIT Press, 1989), 527–79; Alan Garnham, *Artificial Intelligence: An Introduction*

(London: Routledge and Kegan Paul, 1987); Alvin I. Goldman, *Epistemology and Cognition* (Cambridge: Harvard University Press, 1986); Neil A. Stillings et al., *Cognitive Science: An Introduction* (Cambridge: MIT Press, 1987); Zenon W. Pylyshyn, *Computation and Cognition* (Cambridge: MIT Press, 1984); Zenon W. Pylyshyn, ed., *The Robot's Dilemma: The Frame Problem in Artificial Intelligence* (Norwood, N. J.: Ablex Publishing Corporation, 1987); John H. Holland et al., *Induction: Processes of Inference, Learning, and Discovery* (Cambridge: MIT Press, 1986); and Allan Lesgold, "Problem Solving," in *The Psychology of Human Thought*, ed. Robert J. Sternberg and Edward E. Smith (Cambridge: Cambridge University Press, 1988), 188–213.

12. Lesgold, "Problem Solving," 190.

13. For a discussion of problem solving in composition, see Sloboda, *The Musical Mind*, and many of the essays in *Understanding Music with AI: Perspectives on Music Cognition*, ed. Mira Balaban, Kemal Ebcioglu, and Otto Laske (Cambridge: AAAI Press/MIT Press, 1992).

14. For a general account of the Frame Problem, see Pylyshyn, *The Robot's Dilemma*. Clark Glymour describes how the frame problem articulates familiar philosophical issues in his essay entitled "Android Epistemology: Comments on Dennett's 'Cognitive Wheels,'" in *The Robot's Dilemma*, 65–75.

15. See Garnham, *Artificial Intelligence*, 48–51.

16. See Matthew Brown, "A Rational Reconstruction of Schenkerian Theory" (Ph.D. diss., Cornell University, 1989). Carl Schachter produces a similar list in his essay, "A Commentary on *Free Composition*," *Journal of Music Theory* 25 (1981): 124–25.

17. Performing and listening also involve top-down processing. For example, Deutsch and Feroe have shown that when skilled performers play a learned composition, they do so by accessing it in a top-down fashion. Similarly, Sloboda and Parker have shown that when listeners memorize a simple tonal melody, "they build a mental model of the underlying structure in which not all of its surface detail is necessarily retained." See Diana Deutsch and John Feroe, "The Internal Representation of Pitch Sequences in Tonal Music," *Psychological Review* 88 (1981): 503–22; and John A. Sloboda and David H. H. Parker, "Immediate Recall of Melodies," in *Musical Structure and Cognition* (London: Academic Press, 1985): 143–67. For further accounts of the role of top-down processing in music, see Mary Louise Serafine, *Music as Cognition: The Development of Thought in Sound* (New York: Columbia University Press, 1988), 213–22; Robert West, Peter Howell, and Ian Cross, "Modelling Perceived Musical Structure," in *Musical Structure and Cognition*, ed. Peter Howell, Ian Cross, and Robert West (London: Academic Press, 1985), 1–52; John Sloboda, "Musical Expertise," in *Toward a General Theory of Expertise*, ed. Ander Ericsson and Smith, 153–71; Carol Krumhansl, "Tonal Hierarchies and Rare Intervals in Music Cognition," *Music Perception* 7/3 (1990): 309–24; and David Butler and Helen Brown, "Describing the Mental Representation of Tonality in Music," in *Musical Perceptions*, ed. Rita Aiello with John A. Sloboda (New York and Oxford: Oxford Univeristy Press, 1994), 191–212.

18. Robert Nozick. *The Nature of Rationality* (Princeton: Princeton University Press. 1993), 165.

19. Nozick, *The Nature of Rationality*, 165.

20. See Nozick, *The Nature of Rationality*, 163–72.

21. According to Dreyfus and Dreyfus, "The expert has experienced a great number of concrete situations and as a result his brain can discriminate classes of situations. A new situation falls into one such discriminable class and the brain of the expert has learned from experience to associate an action, decisions, or plan as well as various expectations with each class of discriminable situations." Hubert L. Dreyfus and Stuart E. Dreyfus, *Mind over Machine* (New York: Free Press, 1986), 91.

22. Sloboda, *The Musical Mind*, 117.

23. Sloboda, *The Musical Mind,* 149.

24. See Sloboda, *The Musical Mind,* 117.

25. See Heinrich Schenker, *Neue musikalischen Theorien und Phantasien,* vol. 1, *Harmonielehre* (Stuttgart and Berlin: J. G. Cotta, 1906), translated as *Harmony,* ed. Oswald Jonas and trans. Elisabeth Mann Borgese (Chicago: University of Chicago Press, 1954); vol. 2: *Kontrapunkt,* part 1 (Stuttgart and Berlin: J. G. Cotta, 1910) and part 2 (Vienna: Universal, 1922), translated as *Counterpoint,* ed. and trans. John Rothgeb and Jurgen Thym (New York: Schirmer, 1987); and vol. 3, *Der freie Satz* (Vienna: Universal, 1935), translated as *Free Composition,* ed. and trans. Ernst Oster (New York: Longman, 1979).

26. Jimi Hendrix, "Little Wing," on Jimi Hendrix, *Axis: Bold as Love,* Reprise 6281 (1968). For a complete transcription, see Noe "the G" Goldwasser, ed., *Hendrix, Axis: Bold as Love* (Milwaukee: Hal Leonard, 1989), 46–51. An alternative transcription can be found in Steve Tarshis, *Original Hendrix: An Annotated Guide to the Guitar Technique of Jimi Hendrix* (Milwaukee: Hal Leonard, 1982), 55–59.

27. John McDermott and Eddie Kramer, *Hendrix: Setting the Record Straight* (New York: Warner Books, 1992), 92.

28. Harry Shapiro and Caesar Glebbeek, *Jimi Hendrix: Electric Gypsy* (New York: St. Martin's Press, 1990), 225.

29. See Shapiro and Glebbeek, *Electric Gypsy,* 529–30.

30. See Noel Redding and Carol Appleby, *Are You Experienced?* (London: Pan, 1990), 85–86; Mitch Mitchell and John Platt, *Jimi Hendrix: Inside the Experience* (New York: Harmony, 1990), 26; and John McDermott, Buddy Cox, and Eddie Kramer, *Jimi Hendrix Sessions: The Complete Studio Recording Sessions, 1963–1970* (Boston: Little, Brown, 1995), 41.

31. McDermott and Kramer, *Setting the Record Straight,* 92 and 95; and McDermott, Cox, and Kramer, *Jimi Hendrix Sessions,* 42 and 44.

32. This is made apparent in the title track, "Bold as Love." As Hendrix explained: "Well, the axis of the earth, if it changes, well, it changes the whole face of the earth, like every few thousand years. And it's like love, that a human being, if he really falls in love deep enough it will change him. It might change his whole life. So, both of them can really go together, you know." Dave Henderson, *'Scuse Me while I Kiss the Sky* (New York: Bantam, 1978), 174.

33. McDermott and Kramer, *Hendrix: Setting the Record Straight,* 97, and McDermott, Cox, and Kramer, *Jimi Hendrix Sessions,* 45–46. Allan Douglas claims that the original mixes are included in the recent record collection *Live and Unreleased* (Castle Communications, 1989). However, Shapiro and Glebbeeck deny that Douglas's version is the stolen mix, see *Electric Gypsy,* 560.

34. "Up from the Skies," Reprise 0665 (1968), "If 6 Was 9," Reprise 0853 (1968), and "One Rainy Wish," Reprise 0665 (1968).

35. Billy Cox, "Interview," *Guitar Player* 23/5 (May 1989): 47.

36. Charles Shaar Murray, *Crosstown Traffic: Jimi Hendrix and Post-War Pop* (New York: St. Martin's Press, 1990), 138.

37. Dave Rubin, "Blues Power: The Eight Bar Blues," *Guitar School* 1/2 (July 1989): 110–11. Another good case in point is J. J. Cale's tune "After Midnight."

38. According to Dave Rubin and others these techniques are reminiscent of rhythym and blues guitarists such as Floyd Cramer, Bobby Womack, Steve Cropper, Curtis Mayfield, and others. See *Guitar School* 1/3 (Sept. 1989): 118, and 1/4 (Nov. 1989): 114.

39. For detailed discussions of Hendrix's use of guitar effects, see Jon Sievert, "The Sounds of Hendrix," *Guitar Player* 23/6 (June 1989): 64–72. Many details can be found in Alan Douglas et al., *Jimi Hendrix Reference Library* (Milwaukee: Hal Leonard, 1989).

40. Michael Fairchild, Liner notes, remastered version of *Axis: Bold as Love* (MCAD-10894, 1993), 14.

41. Richard Bobbitt, *Harmonic Technique in the Rock Idiom* (Belmont, Calif.: Wadsworth, 1976), 92–110.

42. Similar examples occur in "Third Stone from the Sun" (*Are You Experienced?*) and "Castles Made of Sand" (*Axis: Bold as Love*). See Tarshis, *Original Hendrix*, 18–20. Some of Hendrix's solos seem to have exotic inflections, for example, in "If 6 Was 9," "You Got Me Floatin'," and "Castles Made of Sand." Of course, it should be remembered that Ravi Shankar performed at the Monterey Festival before Hendrix.

43. Hendrix apparently performed "Little Wing" live at least nine times. His performance at Winterland (11 Oct. 1968) is preserved on *The Hendrix Concerts* (Reprise 2306–1, 1982) and is transcribed in Noe Goldwasser, ed., *The Jimi Hendrix Concerts* (Milwaukee: Hal Leonard, 1991), 102–3. His performance at the Royal Albert Hall (24 Feb. 1969) appears (misidentified) on *Hendrix in the West* (Polydor 2303, 1972) and *Musique originale du film: Jimi Plays Berkeley* (Barclay 80.555, late 1970s), and his version in Paris (29 Jan. 1968) on *Jimi Hendrix: Stages* (Reprise 9 26732—-2). For details of these various recordings, see Shapiro and Glebbeek, *Electric Gypsy*, 493, 530, 544, 544, and 553. *Axis* made its live debut in Stockholm (8? Jan. 1968) with a rare outing of "Up from the Skies"; see Shapiro and Glebbeek, *Electric Gypsy*, 240.

44. Shapiro and Glebbeek, *Electric Gypsy*, 217. Guitarist Mike Bloomfield echoes this view: "Jimi's musical approach, as he explained it to me, was to lay out the entire song and decide how it should be . . . the way it would wind up. He would play the drum beat on a damped wah-wah pedal, and the bass part on the bass strings of his guitar, and the pattern of the song with just wah-wah pedal. Then he would flesh the pattern out by playing it with chords and syncopation. He was extremely interested in form—in a few seconds of playing, he'd let you know about the entire structure. That's why he liked rhythm guitar playing so much—the rhythm guitar could lay out the structure for the whole song." Mike Bloomfield, "Jimi Hendrix Remembered," in *Guitar Heros*, vol. 1 (1989), 71–72.

45. Roy D'Andrade, "Cultural Cognition," in Posner, *Foundations of Cognitive Science*, 824.

7

Tonal and Expressive Ambiguity in "Dark Star"

GRAEME M. BOONE

We're saying: "Let's have faith in this form that has no form.
Let's have faith in this structure that has no structure."
—Jerry Garcia, in David Gans,
Conversations with the Dead

In the vinyl Valhalla of rock, the Grateful Dead have earned a special place. Born in 1965 amid the flourishing countercultural movement of San Francisco, the Dead pioneered in the development of musical performances as druglike "experiences," featuring long, unpredictable improvisations and an eclectic mix of influences. As the hippie movement faded, the Dead provided the impetus to a vast culture of followers, known as Deadheads, whose musical and social ideals stem directly from those of the hippies, with elements of pacifism, openmindedness, hedonism, and the use of psychedelic drugs. The Deadhead movement has flourished down to the present day, showing no signs of abatement up to the disbanding of the group in November 1995 after the death of lead guitarist Jerry Garcia. In that year the Dead still ranked fourth in the country in earnings from touring, thanks to the sellout crowds at their many performances; in 1991, they ranked first.[1]

With such popular affirmation, who, then, would speak ill of the Dead? To many who do not like them, their music sounds directionless, complacent, and otherwise boring or sloppy; for others even more numerous, distaste for their psychedelic tribal image precludes any serious musical appreciation. The comments of the benchmark *Rolling Stone Album Guide*, tinged with skepticism, offer what seems to be a common mainstream assessment of the group.

As much a phenomenon as a band, the Grateful Dead have over the last quarter century gathered together the far-flung members of their massive cult for live shows that function less as musical events than as love-ins. The group for a while toured six months a year and boasted a 23–ton sound system, and it's never been the album, but rather the concert that forms the essential Dead document—a fittingly momentary one for a band whose characteristic mood is that of drifting into ether, spacing out on good vibes. Deadheads—ex-hippies or tie-dye wannabes—celebrate the Dead's myth of genial counterculturalism. The songs provide the excuse for the revelry—and they remain songs whose appeal is all but inscrutable to non-initiates.[2]

More pointedly, for those to whom rock music ideally remains a working-class rebellion against the status quo, the Dead's music does not belong in the mainstream, and perhaps not even in the picture; as Lester Bangs wrote in 1977, "The Dead aren't really a rock 'n' roll band." The growing popularity, around that time, of the stripped-down sounds of punk and Bruce Springsteen—a return, in part, to earlier rock 'n' roll values, opposed to the "genial, spaced-out counterculture" that the Dead had been seen to incarnate—gives particular resonance to his comment.[3]

If vagaries of taste are inevitable, lapses of musical understanding need not be. When one sheds dismissive or categorical stereotypes to examine the Dead's music on its own terms, its inherent qualities are better appreciated as constitutive of a style that, far from being inscrutable, can be remarkably refined, expressive, and musically satisfying.

It is to justify this statement, and to give an idea of what, to my mind, some of the best of the Dead's music is about, that this essay has been written. It offers an analysis of one version of one of their songs, namely the concert performance of "Dark Star" from 27 February 1969 that appeared on their first live album, *Live/Dead*.[4] There are several related reasons for this choice. It is one of the most highly regarded renderings of one of the Dead's best-loved songs;[5] for me, it is one of the most memorable performances in rock music. It highlights essential, enduring, and emblematic features of the group's style. It dates from their early years (1966–70), arguably their most important stylistic period, and was selected by the band for publication at that time. Above all it presents a fertile musical conception, in which aspects of local tonal construction relate to large-scale events in original ways and also relate intimately to the song's expression.

A few comments will be useful as a preamble to analysis. As good as this version of "Dark Star" is, the popularity of the song among fans and its centrality in the band's repertory is based more on a multitude of varying concert performances than on any single recording.[6] In shows the song usually does not begin a set and rarely ends one,[7] and its interior is filled with loose and variable improvisatory explorations. "Dark Star," then, is a fine example, some might say a quintessential example, of the Dead's protean approach to music making. For this reason one could approach analysis in different ways, depending on what one takes the song itself to be. If "Dark Star" is considered to be a cumulation of many performances, or a distillation of them, comparison of all available recorded versions might uncover its essential nature.[8] If, by contrast, it is considered to be a process or experience of creation rather than any finished result, analysis of recordings might be inappropriate or inadequate.[9]

My approach will be to take one particularly well-known performance, that on *Live/Dead*, as sufficiently representative, and sufficiently autonomous, to stand in its

own right as an auditory "score."[10] The analytical project will be specific: to eluci-
date certain basic tonal issues raised in the performance; to show how they are
explored and settled; and to view these tonal matters in relation to the song's expressive goals, particularly in connection with the lyrics. A concluding discussion will
raise certain points in light of this analysis concerning the broader expressive message of the band and its relationship to the Deadhead community, past and future.

Several defining moments and elements in the music will serve to orient the
analysis. In order of discussion, they are: (1) initial orientations; (2) music of the
first verse and refrain; (3) text of the first verse and refrain; (4) beginnings of two
major instrumental episodes; (5) climaxes of these episodes; (6) second verse and
end of the song. A time-flow diagram is given below, showing the placement of the
basic events just enumerated (i.e., 1-6). Time indications are based on readings from
the compact disc.

Diagram of basic events in "Dark Star" (version of 2.27.69)

```
      1     4      5     2, 3      4              5         6       6
 ...BEG..E1 ....(C1)...V1 ......E2 .........(C2)....V2 ...END...
      1:17  1:24  c.4:29  6:04    7:09           c.20:10  21:26  c.22:31
```

Key to above symbols:

1	BEG	beginning of song
4	E1	beginning of first instrumental episode
5	C1	beginning of climax to first instrumental episode
2	V1	beginning of verse 1
3	V1	text of verse 1
4	E2	beginning of second instrumental episode
5	C2	beginning of final climax to second instrumental episode
6	V2	beginning of verse 2
6	END	ending of song, i.e., beginning of transition leading to "St. Stephen"

The transcriptions of examples 7.1–7.9, illustrating the different events and
episodes named above, represent about five minutes and twenty seconds of music. It
is on these passages that my arguments will be based. They concern certain salient
moments, notably beginnings, climaxes, and endings; and they focus on melodic,
harmonic, and rhythmic features, to the near exclusion of other issues that would be
of interest in their own right, including instrumental timbres and styles, textural
patterns, and the construction of improvisatory sections. The transcriptions, made
from the compact disc, do not attempt to reproduce every nuance of the music.[11]
However, they do provide an accurate representation of pitches and rhythms of the
central tonal instruments, in all cases where they could be simply determined, and
offer, therefore, a reasonable basis for discussion.

Initial Orientations

An appropriate entry into analysis is the beginning, for it is here that the tonal point
of departure of the song is established and the first tonal questions raised. In the

Example 7.1. End of jam leading to the beginning of "Dark Star," from the performance of 27 Feb. 1969 (released on *Live/Dead*).

Example 7.1. (*continued*)

published recording the music fades in during a jam, nominally in D minor, that precedes the song proper. Example 7.1 shows the passage from the end of the jam, beginning at 0:56, that takes us into the song. The passage begins with relatively open improvisation. While Bob Weir's backup guitar maintains an F chord with what appear to be offbeat attacks, Phil Lesh's bass dominates the texture by loosely related phrases centered on D. Jerry Garcia's lead guitar, meanwhile, concentrates strongly on the note A until measure 12, where he begins to intone a brief formula beginning on B, labeled "(i)" in example 7.1. In measure 15 Lesh picks up formula i in a more complete form, and we realize that Garcia has been calling for, and waiting for, this response. Garcia states formula i once in its full form with Lesh (mm. 16–17, labeled "i") and then moves to begin a second, answering formula in measure 17, labeled "(ii)." Lesh, however, states formula i a third time (perhaps thinking that Garcia would want to state it twice). Hearing this, Garcia aborts his statement of formula ii in order to begin it again, together with Lesh, in measures 18–19 (labelled "ii"). By this time Weir has dropped out: he plays no role here until measure 20.

Notable about the formulas is the lack of clear tonal referent in formula i, based on an ornamented B and a destination note of D, as opposed to the suggestion of a clearer tonal destination in formula ii, based on E and a stronger destination note of A. In this respect the formulas bear a significant relationship to later events, as we shall see. But for the moment, together with the downbeat chord of measure 20, they mainly suggest arrival in a mixolydian A tonality. Judging by the formulas, the

1   {5}

Example 7.2. (a) Mixolydian scale basis for "Dark Star"; and
(b) Dark Star progression.

seventh degree, G, appears relatively stable in the Dead's representation of this
tonality, compared to the fourth degree D (sharped as a subsemitone to E) and even
the tonic A (sharped as a subsemitone to B).

In measure 20 the band settles on the new key, taking up a repetitive two-chord
pattern (mm. 20–24) that continues for some time. In retrospect we recognize the
two preceding formulas (mm. 16–19) as having constituted a tag, marking a new
departure in the music: this tag is the beginning of "Dark Star" proper.[12]

As this passage shows, each of the band members plays a different role in the
music. Garcia is usually the melodic leader in instrumental passages. Lesh's bass
provides harmonic support, but that role is tempered by a strong tendency to
melodic and rhythmic exploration that often results in an independent lead, or
counterpoint to Garcia. Weir plays two- and three-note chords and occasional
melodies in the upper midrange, sounding largely like a foil or companion to Garcia's melodies. Less obvious than that of Garcia or Lesh, Weir's playing cements or
undermines the harmonic and melodic ideas of the other two, and he often plays a
role not only of facilitator for the bass and lead, but also of harmonic orientation
and goad to them.[13]

The quiet and steady instrumental accompaniment of Weir and Lesh, heard in
measures 20–24 of example 7.1, is based on an alternating pair of chords which
might be defined as A–E-minor, or 1–5 in A mixolydian.[14] It will return several
times in the course of the music, and in important places: before and after the
instrumental episodes and around the beginning of both verses (see, for example,
the two lower parts in mm. 1–8 of ex. 7.4 and mm. 1–14 of ex. 7.5). It is, therefore,
a crucial element of the song's identity and a crucial point of reference for other
musical ideas in the song. I shall simply call it the "Dark Star progression." The basic
scale for the song, along with this chord progression, is illustrated in example 7.2.

As this example shows, the Dark Star progression is not without ambiguity. First
of all, given a regular alternation of triads lacking in a leading-tone relationship, a
listener could hear either (or neither) of the chords as tonic. Another possibility in
this case, then, would be to hear the progression as 1–4, and the key as E dorian. In
the passages leading up to the verses such ambiguity is eliminated by numerous
rhythmic, melodic, and contrapuntal factors which tend to establish A as the primary tonal referent. Nonetheless, the binary progression, lacking a clear tonal functionality, allows for the possibility of a blurring or recasting of tonal orientation.

Second, the changeable melodies and chordal voicings of Bob Weir's guitar and
Phil Lesh's bass produce a significant ambiguity in the second chord itself, between
minor 5 and its relative major, flat 7. For this reason the second chord name is better placed in braces: {5}. The ambiguity of the chord is reflected, in example 7.2, by

Example 7.3.   Background third chains in "Dark Star."

the parenthetical placement of two of its notes. Is D to be heard as the inessential seventh of an E-minor triad in this chord, or is E itself to be heard as the episodic "underthird" of a steadier G-major chord? It is significant that, in "Dark Star," there is never an equivalent treatment of the A chord: its relative minor, on F♯, is utterly absent from the music (as is any chord built on C♯ as root; D chords, with A as fifth, are rare). The A chord, therefore, is inherently more stable than its companion, {E}. From this pair of chords may be extrapolated a fundamental alternation, with both harmonic and melodic implications, between two stacks of thirds. The first is centered on the stable tonic A triad; the second—one might say, "the" other stack, in a diatonic sound world, although it is, in melodic terms, a prolongation of the first—is not so much a triad as a flexible grouping of thirds, which may be heard, at different times, as being built on E, G, or other notes, though never on notes that bear a simple third relationship to A (F♯ and C♯). Example 7.3 schematizes this alternation, which involves melody, counterpoint, modal traditions, and the physiology of guitar playing, as well as harmonic intuition.[15] The third chains are related to each other by step and to the principal structural degrees, E and A, by step or by leap. In sum, the basic Dark Star progression, as outlined in example 7.2, presents a gentle opposition between 1 and {5} or, broadly considered in the modal context, 1 and not-1.

Music of the First Verse and Refrain

Following the beginning of the song, illustrated in example 7.1, there is an instrumental episode of over four minutes' length. That episode will be discussed in due course; prior to addressing such improvisatory sections, however, it is worthwhile to focus on the ensuing first verse, whose melody and harmonies lie at the heart of the song and help to explain its improvisations.

As the first instrumental episode ends, the Dark Star progression recurs, and it continues as accompaniment to the first two lines of text in the first verse, shown in example 7.4, measures 1–8. The melodic phrase for this pair of lines, sung in the characteristically tremulous voice of Jerry Garcia, traces a descending scale, progressing almost entirely by step.[16] This melody presents the modal octave; but the mode it suggests is arguably E dorian rather than A mixolydian—despite the presence of A as a tonal anchor in the accompaniment—for the melody leads from the E above the tonic to E below it, giving emphasis to B on the way. The phrase also relies on third relationships as a structuring device: in its first half (poetic line 1) it falls from E to C♯, and in its second half (poetic line 2) it falls from B to G to E. Based on their rhythmic treatment, we might hear these thirds as forming part of a broader interlocking complex of third chains in the melody, in which the impression of a focus on A gradually weakens while that on E strengthens:

```
chain 1:    E      C♯     (A)     ((F♯))
chain 2:          (D)     B       G        E
```

This impression is reinforced by the presence of sustained appoggiaturas on downbeats in the melody, which challenge the 1 chord in all but its first statement (m. 3: D–C♯; m. 5: B–A; m. 7: G–E, forming the third-chain D–A–G). By contrast, the downbeats of measures containing the {5} chord tend to receive a consonant note, but it is most often held over from the preceding measure (m. 2: E; m. 6: G; m. 8: E). The one exception is in measure 4, where Garcia's B sounds (or echoes) against the {5} chord; but this is the sole moment of repose within the two phrases, and Garcia's voice "dies" as the {5} chord sounds. The melody for lines 1–2 of the song, therefore, is relying on A as tonal referent but also playing against it.[17]

In the second and third melodic phrases, corresponding to poetic lines 3–6, the suspicion of tonal ambiguity is strengthened considerably. The melody of both of these phrases is the same as that of line 1, which establishes it as an even more crucial feature of the song and makes its properties all the more compelling, even haunting: what kind of song consists of repetitions of the same open-ended tune? The accompaniment, meanwhile, reverses the previous order of chords and introduces a new bass riff to emphasize 5, instead of 1, as a distinct point of tonal orientation, as shown in example 7.4, measures 9–16. Although the cumulative power of A clearly maintains the status of this chord as primary tonal referent, it can also clearly be heard, locally, as 4 in relation to a newly emphasized E. The old melody sits fairly well on this new harmonic orientation, but there is a heightened sticking point in measures 11–12, where Garcia's voice hits D over the E chord, falls to C♯, and drops out, leaving a hanging dissonance that seems only partly resolved by the ensuing A chord of measure 12.

In measures 17–22 the chordal identity of A is weakened or eliminated entirely in favor of a prolongation of E. In measure 23, however, the bass suggests an imminent recentering on A instead of E, a recentering that indeed occurs in measure 25. The backup guitar chords of measures 19–24 act as a holding pattern but ultimately lead also back to A as well in measure 25. It is notable, in this respect, that these guitar voicings are so similar to those that originally defined the {5} harmony as secondary (mm. 2, 4, and so forth): they suggest that here, too, the E harmony will not last. In sum, although the second and third phrases of the verse center on E, it is not an entirely comfortable orientation either, and it is progressively blurred.

The two poetic lines following the verse constitute a refrain, which will recur after verse 2. One might expect that the music for these lines will make sense of what has gone before, giving direction to the melody and a satisfying conclusion to the play of harmonies. Neither of these conditions, however, is satisfied, at least at the end of verse 1, if by that is meant a comfortable resolution on A as the tonic. On the contrary the refrain suggests, more than ever, the loss of A as a definitive orientation.

The two lines of the refrain are set to two musical phrases, which trace similar paths but end differently. The first phrase, shown in example 7.4, measures 25–31, begins as a simple melodic and harmonic refocusing on A as 1, with a slowing of

Example 7.4. "Dark Star," first verse and refrain, from the performance of 27 Feb. 1969 (released on *Live/Dead*).

Example 7.4. (*continued*)

Example 7.4. (*continued*)

rhythm that promises something new (m. 25). The melody here begins solidly on A and rises to E; but it then settles on D in measure 29, while its accompaniment settles, more slowly, on a true 5 chord one measure later (moving to {5} in m. 29, and arriving on 5 in m. 30). The melodic arrival on D is, therefore, opposable to the arrival chord on 5 that follows, both in its goal note and in its timing. Despite its quietness, the arrival in measure 30 is the stronger one, due to the melodic phrasing of the bass and backup guitar, and due also to the metrical rhythm of the phrase as a whole, which gradually slows down from 4/4, to 9/8, to 6/4, to a seemingly complete stop at measure 30. This phrase, then, follows a pattern similar to that of measures 1–15, in passing from an emphasis on 1 to an emphasis on 5, but it does so in a more concise and dramatic fashion, even though it does not achieve melodic closure in the voice part.

Other things about this phrase are worthy of attention. In particular, the pattern of simultaneous thirds, in homorhythmic, equal, and slightly detached dotted rhythms, stated in measures 27–28 (E/C♯, F♯/D, G/E, F♯/D, E/C♯), lends an element of precision and deliberateness to the counterpoint that stands out sharply against the more woven, changeable sound of earlier passages. These chords not only emphasize the arrivals in measures 29 and 30 but also give a heightened purpose to the refrain as an "answer" to the verse. Sounded together with a repeated A in the backup-guitar part, the chords prolong the 1 harmony begun in measure 25, so that the phrase as a whole, with the accompanimental flourishes that follow, falls into two halves of almost exactly even length: measures 25–28 (on the 1 harmony) and the slower measures 29–31 (on, or around, 5).

Notable, finally, in measures 25–30 is the broader melodic structure of thirds that emerges when we consider the melodies of voice and bass together. Once again, as in the verse, we can hear a pair of third chains; this time, however, they are not so much interlocking as sequential. The voice traces an upward-moving A triad and then settles, at the change of harmony, on the fourth degree, where it stops. At that point, the bass takes over, sounding B against the voice's D and dropping from there to G and E.

```
chain 1:   A  C♯ E
chain 2:          D  B  G  E
```

The fifth degree, climax of the melody, occurring in the midst of the dotted rhythm pattern (m. 28), stands at the center of the matter. While it "belongs" to the 1 harmony in this measure, the chord is stated there in fragile form, as a seventh chord in second inversion, with E sounding in all three transcribed voices. Melodically and harmonically, the note and its chord do not return to a stable A harmony. Instead the melody pivots to D (the fifth of G) at the point of harmonic shift, as the harmonies move forward toward the E chord of measure 30. The voice's E in measure 28, therefore, looks both forward and backward as a hinge between the harmonic spheres of A and E. Whereas the verse melody simply dropped through the octave from E to E, with passing reference to an A that was more strongly stated in the harmony, this phrase makes a stronger and more dramatic beginning on A, only to end up with a still stronger arrival on E. The bass notes trace an octave descent that recalls the verse melody (E–C♯–B–G–E) while introducing a chromatic touch, reinforced by the backup guitar, that also dramatizes the E arrival of measure 30.

After a flourish in the bass suggestive of an E-minor seventh chord (m. 31), the second refrain phrase begins (mm. 32–37). It is similar to the preceding phrase in most ways, but with important differences. It begins with the same idea (mm. 32–35 versus mm. 25–28), although in measure 33 the backup guitar adds no fills, as if to enhance the gravity of the moment. Then, in measures 36–37, the voice adds a new ending to the refrain melody, proceeding beyond D in a descent down to E that follows the second of the third chains (D–B–G–E) and recalls the verse phrase (including, now, a clear F♯). The gingerly counterpoint we heard in measures 27–29, restated in measures 34–36, now ends with a strong bass attack (on at least two notes), reinforced by a distinct percussive thump, at the downbeat of measure 37. Here, then, is melodic closure, with an even more complete stop on E, marking the end of the refrain and completing this part of the song.

What, in retrospect, has happened in the verse and refrain? Beginning with the basis of an alternating 1–{5} progression, the music has kept the terms of that progression intact in some respect, pitting 1 against 5; but it has eroded the progression itself, and its tonic emphasis, in favor of a strong final arrival on 5. Given the prominence of the Dark Star progression as a relatively stable beginning, and thus orientation, to the song and to the verse, it is hard to hear the arrival on 5 as definitive for the song as a whole; and yet here it is all the same, posed as a conclusion.

The music finds a way out of this dilemma, and it is a clever one. Following upon the "definitive" arrival on E in measure 37, a reshaping of the earlier bass flourish (m. 31) in measure 38 leads to a tag (bass line, mm. 38–41) that guides us back to the original 1–{5} progression and to stability (mm. 42 and after). This tag is not new: it is a reprise of the tag that began the song (ex. 7.1, mm. 16–19).[18] But there it served to project the music out of nonidentity into identity. Is that its function here? It is indeed, inasmuch as the verse and refrain's movement away from the defining Dark Star progression, and toward 5, does suggest the loss of a certain tonal orientation, and thus, of a certain identity. In this sense, the not-1 of the verse ending is brought into parallel, by means of the tag, with the "not-song" at the very beginning of the recording. An opposition is thus established between two competing tonal identities for the song: on one hand, the instrumental presentation of the 1–{5} chord progression, with its relatively stable 1-centeredness, and on the other, the dissolution of that progression in the sung verse, with its relatively unstable 5-centeredness.[19] Significantly, this opposition is already contained, in embryo, within the Dark Star progression itself: 1–{5}, or 1–not-1; and also within the tag, whose two formulas suggest a reverse progression: not-1–1.

Text of the First Verse and Refrain

It has seemed appropriate to speak of the music of the first verse before discussing the text itself, in order to make clear the suggestiveness of the music on its own. The lyrics are, in fact, so perfectly suited to the music, and so suggestive in their own right, that had I begun with a textual analysis it might have seemed too strongly to dominate or color the musical analysis that followed.

The musical shifting between stability and instability, between identity and otherness, between place and loss of place, finds an eloquent parallel in Robert Hunter's lyrics for this verse and refrain:

V. Dark star crashes
    Pouring its light into ashes
    Reason tatters
    The forces tear loose from the axis
    Searchlight casting
    For faults in the clouds of delusion.
R. Shall we go, you and I while we can
    Through the transitive nightfall of diamonds?

The lyrics are couched in psychedelic images, appropriate both to an important part of the Dead's audiences of the period and to the band's own lifestyle in the later sixties. Perched somewhere between science fantasy and what some might call paranoid schizophrenia, they evoke physical and psychological disaster of cosmic proportions, but with a concision that relies on the evocativeness of individual words, in a distinctly playful, even humorous fashion.

No clear distinction is made between hallucination, metaphor, and inner or outer reality. While a star implodes (nearby?) and social and even psychological foundations disintegrate, the speaker proposes a romantic evening. Within their psychedelic context such lyrics beautifully evoke the conflict, or overlap, between a volatile, drug-induced internal reality, on the one hand, and a more stable, mundane outer-world reality, on the other. But there are other messages in the lyrics as well, which serve to organize them thematically and bind them together. Light is opposed to darkness, in the signature image itself (dark star) and in the verse as a whole. Order is opposed to chaos. Meaning, perhaps truth, is opposed to falsehood and non-meaning. Through all of these we sense an implicit opposition of life to death, and the speaker to a hostile world, in which something is, and will be, lost.

The refrain personalizes and reinforces this opposition and sense of impending loss. But, in so doing, it suggests a possible inversion of the sense of the preceding lines. The speaker leaves the image of cosmic catastrophe behind; instead he turns to address a companion, or perhaps even the listener, proposing that they go forth, together, through a world that is not so much threatening as it is exquisite.[20] Is this the same world? Perhaps, but perhaps not: to the dark star of the hallucinatory mind, we might oppose the bright-star diamonds of the nighttime sky, transitive, not because of pending cosmic doom, but because day will follow. Just the same, the psychedelic experience, and the intimacy of companionship, will end, as life will end. The moment of shared beauty cannot last.

In this manner the first verse and refrain of Hunter's brief poem brightly and subtly evoke the issue of loss: loss of what we have that makes us what we are, whether it is order, reason, truth, love, experience, or life itself. At the center of the poem, it might seem, is the lapidary theme of a dark star, which as a metaphor for mental experience is both powerful and dangerously paradoxical. But in the end that theme is overlaid by another, even more important one, namely the sweetness and ephemerality of existence.

The music offers a fitting companion to these themes, not least because it, too, dwells on matters of identity and loss and is based on a bittersweet major-minor progression. Without returning to discuss the music in depth, I would like to take note of three aspects of the text-music relationship. First, in the verse, the descending vocal line seems appropriate to the repeated imagery of loss that is expressed across its three lines. In particular, the broad movement from high to low E corresponds, in the text, to a movement from posited images (dark star, reason, searchlight) to their nemeses (ashes, tearing loose, delusion). Second, in the refrain, the slowed rhythm, the more delicate counterpoint, and the contrasting treatment of closure in measures 29 and 37, followed by moments of near silence, serve quite effectively to highlight the existential cry represented in the lyrics. In particular the high E, reached now in the middle of the melodic phrase rather than at its beginning, is joined to the word "I" in the first line of the refrain and to the word "transitive" in the second line. By contrast, the melodic descent at the end of the refrain leads to "diamonds" and low E, at the other end of the text, melody, and scale from "dark star." Is the dark star itself a protagonist, or antagonist? Is it the cause of the cosmic catastrophe, or one of its symptoms? The ambiguity of relationships remains intact, leaving the mind free to ponder on these matters and on other, more serious ones that they evoke. Finally, the paradox of the "dark star" itself might be reflected in the Dark Star progression, to which these two words are sung (ex. 7.4, mm. 1–2): both are strong points of orientation which, at the same time, harbor an essential ambiguity that is explored in the course of the poetry and music.[21]

Beginnings of Two Instrumental Episodes

The song lasts for over twenty-two minutes, but the first and second verses take up only two minutes of that time. There remain twenty minutes of instrumental jamming, in two instrumental episodes: the first leads from the opening tag to the first verse, and the second leads from the tag following that verse to the second verse. Both begin with the Dark Star progression and then abandon it, to pursue a freer exploration of the tension suggested by that progression, namely the tension of an ambiguous 5, {5}, or not-1 harmony in relation to the point of departure, 1. Following the explorations, both episodes return to the Dark Star progression; but this does not mean that they resolve the issue of not-1. In fact, the climaxes of the two episodes provide different answers to the question of how, ultimately, 1 and not-1 should be heard to relate.

Examples 7.5 and 7.6 show the beginning of the solos in each of the two major episodes, leading away from the Dark Star progression and toward harmonic ambiguity.[22] The first solo begins calmly, with Garcia's guitar repeating and varying a rising line over the Dark Star progression (ex. 7.5). For fourteen measures, as Garcia works with the line, the progression is maintained; in measure 15, when he leaves the line behind for another, it is abandoned for a loose play on {5}, which lasts until the end of the climax to this episode, two minutes later. The {5} harmony is realized in the following manner (mm. 15–26): while Garcia and Lesh suggest E, A, G, and other notes as structural pitches, Bob Weir sounds a steady G chord through offbeat comping, thereby insuring that the harmony returns neither to 1 nor to the accompanimental figure of the Dark Star progression.

Example 7.5. "Dark Star," Jerry Garcia's first guitar solo, from the performance of 27 Feb. 1969 (released on *Live/Dead*).

Example 7.5. (*continued*)

Notable in this passage are the pitch structures of Garcia's solo: solidly anchored to the mode's final and fifth, they also rely on third chains as extrapolations around, and means to reach, these pitches. From measures 1 through 14, high E is the goal note. It is approached from a rising scalar line that builds to a local climax on A in measures 10–12 before settling back on E in measure 14. Through rhythmic position, the line also suggests a third chain leading upward past E, ultimately to the climax note (G–B–D–[E]–F♯–A). In the remainder of the passage, the solo drops down, via E an octave below (m. 19), to A below that (m. 24). Here, the same chain leads down to E (mm. 15–19: F♯–D–B–G–E); then, in a cascade of intensified motion, the chain may be perceived to continue (judging by salient notes) down to A, below it, and back (mm. 19–26: G–E–C–A–F♯–D–F♯–A). In sum, Garcia has gradually opened up the guitar range, upward to high A and downward to low A and beyond, in a set of related opening gestures.

Example 7.6. "Dark Star," beginning of Jerry Garcia's second guitar solo, from the performance of 27 Feb. 1969 (released on *Live/Dead*).

Example 7.6. (*continued*)

The beginning of the second episode, shown in example 7.6, follows a stronger textural buildup and develops, rather than introduces, the playing of Garcia and the others. It is distinctly more restless in rhythm, melody, and counterpoint. At first the harmony follows the model of the sung verse: for about eight measures, it keeps roughly to the Dark Star progression (mm. 1–8), and for about eight measures following (mm. 9–16), it shifts to 5. These measures demonstrate an awareness, on the part of the musicians, of the verse harmonies as a harmonic model (ex. 7.4, mm. 1–16), distinct from the vaguer notion of movement away from 1 exemplified by the earlier episode (ex. 7.5). The strong movement to 5, however, does not prevent the measures that follow (ex. 7.6, mm. 17–24) from settling back on that vaguer harmonic notion. In fact this is to be expected, since 5 is too clearly defined to serve as a vehicle for the wide-ranging contrapuntal working-out that follows. But it demonstrates that the harmonic conclusion of the verse and refrain on 5 cannot contain the improvisations that surround them. The 5 and 1 harmonies, then, appear as poles between which the music flows, 1 as a well-recognized and eventually recurring "home" chord, and 5 as a fleeting, if powerful, distillation of non-1 harmony.

Garcia's solo in example 7.6 adds nuance to the observations made above concerning structural pitches and third chains in example 7.5. Again, A and E are the principal orienting pitches, and the same third chain governs much of the melody (E–G–B–D–F♯–A). But around high E appear stronger elements of the other chain (A–C♯–E–G), through which E and the A below it can be emphasized. The combination of third chains and structural E/A orientation helps to give Garcia's solos clarity, directedness, and consistency here and elsewhere in the music. Similarly to the other players, he limits his pitch spectrum to focus strongly on the mixolydian mode; his use of other pitches is limited, with episodic exceptions, to sliding and bent notes, which are particularly common around E and A. Emphasis on these two degrees, set into melodic third chains and supported by a fluid harmonic play on 1 and {5}, explains a significant part of the mixolydian tonal dynamic of the song.

Climaxes of Two Instrumental Episodes

The climaxes of the two major episodes differ from one another in both form and content. Both climaxes are loud, and both occur at the end of the episode, capping an extended improvisatory exploration and preceding a return to calm, to the Dark Star progression, and to the singing of a verse. But the first episode is three minutes long and is strongly unified: its climax appears as a logical conclusion to a sustained musical searching, whose intensity is steadily increased and in which the tonic chord and Dark Star progression do not reappear until the end. The second episode, by contrast, is seventeen minutes long and falls into several loosely opposable passages or subepisodes. What unifies this open-ended jamming into a single broader episode is its containment between the two verses, rather than a gradual, fully sustained intensification. Unlike the first episode, it does contain both a return to 1 and a return to the Dark Star progression before its final climax; and it settles on tonal and textural environments that are, if not fully stable, at least distinct from each other and amply prolonged. Throughout the second episode, therefore, we listen for new ideas and relate them to ideas already heard; but our expectations regarding the resolution of the initial, fundamental tonal issue are sometimes deferred or seemingly ignored.[23] As a result, the climax to the second episode appears as the conclusion to a far broader but far looser musical exploration. As will become clear, the content of this climax reflects its distinct role in the music.

In climax 1, shown in example 7.7, Garcia does two things that are characteristic of his playing during moments of particular expressive intensity. Having, with the other players, gradually increased the level of excitement in the music over the space of three minutes, he focuses increasingly on short repeated riffs as a means to heighten the climactic effect until he reaches and then leans hard on the peak of his range for this song, namely high A and its neighbor B (mm. 20–26). His note choices resemble those of examples 7.5 and particularly 7.6, showing use of both third chains (B–D–F♯–A and C♯–E–G; the beginning phrases in exx. 7.6 and 7.7 are nearly identical). But in his climactic riffing, Garcia's melodic conception in thirds and in stepwise-related thirds becomes particularly exposed (D–B, mm. 9–12; G–E and F♯–D, mm. 12–19). At this point Weir's backup guitar also reaches the top of its range for the song, and he, too, repeats brief musical ideas. However, rather than settle on the tonic chord here, Weir maintains what amounts to a steady 2 chord, based on the third chain B–D–F♯ (mm. 13–30): thanks to this, the passage cannot be heard as suggesting a 1 chord. Lesh's bass, meanwhile, roams over a wide range of notes, with a certain emphasis on A; he rises to a peak on high D (m. 18), begins a strong descent at the moment of climax (mm. 21 ff.), and plunges down to a very low E toward its end (m. 27). Climax, therefore, in this case, signifies a peak of textural intensity but not resolution of the tonal conflict; different players can and do go in different directions, which combine to create an effect that is, to a certain extent, unpredictable but remains in the domain of not-1. The use of the note A, here and elsewhere, as the melodic peak in Garcia's playing is particularly significant. While it serves, most broadly, as the fundamental tonal grounding of the song and of the Dark Star progression, it also serves as the peak note of melodic, climactic tension. In this manner the combined third chains of "Dark Star"'s mixolydian tonality, hinging on E, are bounded on one end by the low A as tonal ground and on the other by the high A as dissonant peak (A–C♯–E–G–B–D–F♯–A).

It is only in the next phrase (mm. 30–33), when Garcia drops down from his climax to begin a new phrase on a lower A, that Weir falls back on the Dark Star progression, for the first time in three minutes (since m. 13 of ex. 7.5). Garcia and Lesh, however, are not yet entirely ready to calm down: under Garcia's next phrase (mm. 34–43), spinning out his descent from B to E, Lesh also spins out his return to A. Finally, at measure 42, the band settles back onto the progression in something approximating its original form (as heard in ex. 7.1, mm. 20–24). The climax is over, the episode is over, and the first verse (transcribed in ex. 7.4) may now be sung.[24] In this episode, then, the Dark Star progression appears as an agent of calm, rather than climax.

What I am calling climax 2, occurring sixteen minutes later, arises in a different manner and leads to another dénouement. Rather than a natural peak after a series of passages of rising intensity, this climax follows a series of lengthy passages that go in various directions, including one that dwells at great length on an E-minor broken triad, played by Garcia (11:15–13:09), and another where he slips, via a growling distortion of tone, into A minor for a few seconds (the minor part lasts from 13:27 to 13:49; Weir drops out here, while Lesh flirts with A ionian). A consideration of other performances of the song would show how common such unpredictable or riff-based passages are; they illustrate the extent to which the Dead, in their improvisations, are open-minded about where they might go, depending upon the inspiration of the moment and the mood of the different players. In this recording the different passages create a feeling of depth, or wandering, or of distance traversed; they leave us floating in a vast modal space, not knowing what will transpire next, and wondering what solutions the players will find.[25]

Climax 2 begins to take shape at a curious moment in this space. After a buildup of intensity (14:41–17:00) that could have served as a final climax before verse 2 in a manner similar to that of the first climax, the players calm down onto scattered chords. Out of this, Garcia intones on his guitar the first line of the verse, prompting a momentary return of the Dark Star progression (18:18). This leads to a 5 harmony, as in the verse itself, which leads to further exploration until another settling onto the Dark Star progression (19:02). At that point, on top of light, playful chords, Garcia, unsatisfied, begins to drive toward yet another climax. This one proves to be the biggest of all and transforms the experience of the song as a whole. Garcia moves right up to the peak note, high A, and builds a long series of descending riffs from

Example 7.7. "Dark Star," climax of the first improvisational episode, from the performance of 27 Feb. 1969 (released on *Live/Dead*).

Example 7.7. (continued)

Example 7.7. (continued)

that note to the E below it (incorporating the thirds A–F#–D and G–E) that grow steadily louder and more insistent. Weir's backup guitar, having maintained a semblance of the Dark Star progression for some time, shifts over to the expected {5} chords in a counterrhythm that reinforces Garcia's riffs; Lesh's bass moves restlessly beneath. Then, the intensity of the passage leads to something new, shown in example 7.8. After seconds of heightened expectancy, Garcia breaks into a distinct pattern of climax riffs centered on A and E, solidly backed up by a simultaneous switch by Weir back to the Dark Star progression and also supported by a strong arrival on A by Lesh (m. 5). The significance of this moment, after twenty minutes of musical probing, is great. The progression is at last allied to the climactic tensions of the piece, rather than acting as a meditative foil to them; and Garcia's powerful melodic searching has landed, at long last, on the crowning summit of a chordally rooted A, to which E is clearly subservient. In this manner the tonal enigma of the song is resolved, by force; the progression triumphs over its nemesis of tonal insecurity.

The climactic arrival is not fleeting: on the contrary, it is strengthened by ensuing melodic, harmonic, and rhythmic contributions from all three players. Garcia's riffing picks up speed and intensity in the following manner. He first presents A and E as sequential goal tones in a descending phrase that lasts for two measures, with G and, more weakly, F# as intermediaries (mm. 5–7). He then restates the latter part of that phrase but concludes it by binding the arrival tone of E to the high A in a repeated eighth-note formula (mm. 8–9). This formula serves both to conclude the descending phrase A–G–F#–E and to begin that same phrase. By conflating the function of E and A as arrival and departure tones, he both reaffirms the movement to E that has characterized much of the song and reasserts its dependence on the stronger A. The formula will be restated in identical or slightly varying form eight times in the next fifteen measures, as part of a riff that settles into its most complex and definitive form in mm. 17–18.

Weir's playing in this passage is related to his playing in the verse: he holds to the Dark Star progression for eight measures (mm. 5–12) and then switches over to {5} chords for eight measures (mm. 13–20). Remarkably, though, he then *returns* to evoke the Dark Star progression once again (mm. 20–26), a harmonic move that is unprecedented in the song and that reaffirms the primacy of that progression. Weir's idea is supported by Lesh. In the course of measures 5–20 the bassist settles on a riff related to the Dark Star progression but which works also in the context of Weir's {5} chords. Then, in measure 20, as Weir returns to the progression, Lesh hits A on a downbeat for the first time in fifteen measures.

The conclusion of this climax begins at the downbeat of measure 25. At this point Garcia finally begins to quiet down on a sustained, stable high-A arrival, backed up by its neighbor B. Lesh, having let out a brief soaring line that hit high E—his own moment of climax—drops down to a sustained A at the same point. Weir continues his slowly rising chords to settle, four measures later, on a quiet, repeated, high A-major chord. The music continues its decrescendo, despite a rising line by Lesh, through to measure 33, where Garcia intones the same riff he intoned after the climax to the first episode (ex. 7.7, mm. 44–46). Finally the Dark Star progression picks up again, for the last time, in measure 35, preparatory to the singing of verse 2.

Example 7.8. "Dark Star," climax of the last improvisational episode, from the performance of 27 Feb. 1969 (released on *Live/Dead*).

Example 7.8. (*continued*)

One wonders what the relationship could be between this climax of climaxes and the issues raised in first sung verse (ex. 7.4; we shall take up the second verse in a moment). By comparison with the long, wandering, and tonally searching improvisations, the Dark Star progression seems to represent a kind of order, reason, and containment. In climax 2, then, perhaps the "forces" have indeed been recentered on the "axis," and the "searchlight" has pierced the "clouds of delusion." At the same time, however, joining the progression to climactic musical tension may suggest a connection between it and the hallucinatory night, or dark star, of psychedelia, where resolutions are fleeting in the ongoing turmoil of images. The original presentation of the Dark Star progression, with its gentle, understated manner, seemed to offer a certain perspective on that turmoil, perhaps evoking the beauty of the actual nighttime sky, or a connection to a background of calm reality or stability, even if it could be overwhelmed by the volatile foreground of drug experience. Does this climax, and the romantic identification it suggests, resolve the conflict of reality and unreality, or perpetuate it?

The question could be answered in one way by consulting other recordings of the song. In fact no other recording I have heard presents quite this romantic a reading of a final climax, if indeed there is a climax at all; there is no systematic joining of the progression to a peak moment of intensity. The choice made by the Dead in this case, therefore, represents only one reading or rendering of the song. Accepting this recording as a sufficient text, we have another element to consider before answering the question, namely, the second verse that follows the climax.

Second Verse and End of the Song

The first verse of "Dark Star" projected the listener into tonal doubt, necessitating a rescue by means of the instrumental tag which itself marked a new beginning. After the tonal recentering of the last climax, must there be a return to the haunting ambiguities already experienced? The music of the second verse is almost identical to that of the first, while the text offers a certain change of perspective.

V.   Mirror shatters
     In formless reflections of matter
     Glass hand dissolving
     In ice petal flowers revolving
     Lady in velvet
     Recedes in the nights of good bye.

The scale of images has diminished greatly, to reach a more intimate, human level (mirror, hand, flowers, velvet); their character is more familiar than epic. But hallucination, distortion, chaos, ephemerality, and loss are still the rule, and another person (lady in velvet) slips away, as if to amplify with loneliness the hint of melancholy or nostalgia in the call for companionship of the first refrain.

Since the particular qualities of the second verse do not change its basic agreement with the underlying themes of the first verse, the music is equally appropriate here. One might say even more so, since the quietness of the music, matched by the more tender intimacy of the words, makes a fitting aftermath to the intensity of the instrumental climaxes, which have, in effect, drawn off the violence suggested by the first verse's lyrics. However, since the music is the same, the tonal problem of verse 1 is precisely restated: here again the point of departure, A, is opposed to an arrival on E. This repeated harmonic, textural, and melodic framework sounds like a reality check in relation to the shifting, indistinct, or searching qualities of the improvisations; even a grand tonal "victory" such as that of the second climax has little effect on it. It remains, then, for the final refrain to confirm or change the inevitable tonal "loss" in the music. The music for this refrain is shown in example 7.9.

Instead of a simple restatement of the first refrain melody, this time the refrain is amplified by added voices; its second phrase is lengthened also, to permit a more emphatic conclusion that now includes a strong *tonicization* of 1, with raised leading tone on G♯, backed up by a tonicization of 5 as well (through 5 of 5), with raised leading tone on D♯ (mm. 12–16).[26] Garcia's lead melody for the second phrase is likewise changed: after the peak note of E (m. 14: "*transitive*"), the important arrival on D—which, in the first refrain, ended the first phrase and preceded the descent down to low E in the second phrase—has been eliminated in favor of a new peak note on F♯ (m. 15: "*night*fall"). This heightened arrival draws particular attention to the final phrase of the song and its harmonies, which effectively call into question, in a single gesture, the entire preceding mixolydian tonal framework.

The passage, with its precise vocal polyphony and its cadential functionality, is curiously reminiscent of eighteenth-century vocal counterpoint. The fact that it does not seem entirely out of place reflects the playful and contrapuntal nature of the Dead's style, in which many different musical influences may be sensed. But it is, at the same time, a bit jarring, due both to its unexpected vocalizing and its unexpected tonal shift: the players are dwelling on and leaning on the final line of the refrain, as if to celebrate or amplify its meaning. We have heard the words before; partly for this reason, and partly because of their new setting, they make an even stronger statement about companionship, ephemerality, beauty, and loss. This time, however, it is the song itself that is ending. The reference to classical music adds an element of rhetorical formality to this closure, which resonates with the somewhat heightened, obscure language of these lines.

Shall we go, you and I while we can
Through *the transitive nightfall of diamonds?*

The refrain is followed by a new, even quieter, precomposed transitional passage (mm. 18–22 and beyond), leading out of "Dark Star" and into another song that often follows it, namely "St. Stephen." The tag we heard at the beginning of the song, the regenerator of the Dark Star progression, is notably absent, and the "song," therefore, no longer recurs: its tonal and expressive topic has evaporated, like a fleeting vision or dream.

The group has effectively resolved any harmonic ambiguity between 1 and 5 at the end of the song by establishing a clearly hierarchical dominant-tonic relationship; but, by the same token, the mixolydian scale basis of the song has been removed. Now we may return to the question posed by the climax of example 7.8. Does it resolve the issues of identity or, rather, compound them? The answer depends on one's point of view; but I tend to the latter conclusion, for it better reflects the floating, transitory

Example 7.9. "Dark Star," second (and final) refrain, from the performance of 27 Feb. 1969 (released on *Live/Dead*).

Example 7.9. (continued)

qualities of the music that most broadly define it and that are reaffirmed in verse 2. Ultimately, there is no clear distinction between the elements of musical intensification and the volatile psychedelic foreground suggested by the lyrics; the struggle for meaning may as well plunge us further into that foreground as gain us any perspective on it. In fact this climax, perhaps even more than the others, seems *opposed* to the Dark Star progression in its tranquil, quiet form, which begins and anchors the song: it is that calm state that orients us and suggests peace of mind. By the same token, Garcia's climactic high A's lie at the opposite end of the song's expressive range from the low A's that underpin the Dark Star progression.

In the end, the listener does float away from that progression definitively, but its calmness still remains, as if to suggest that, in letting go of attachment to fixed identity, one can find greater stability in the movement itself.

Conclusion

In the foregoing analysis I have tried to show some of the ways in which the Dead's music functions, based on close listening to one recording, and I have proposed some interpretations of its meaning. In conclusion I shall comment briefly on the implications of this analysis for an appreciation of the Grateful Dead as a band, and of the social phenomenon that surrounds it.

First of all, this recording of "Dark Star" illustrates the Dead's combination of concentrated, organized musical thought and loose, unpredictable interaction. These qualities affect various aspects of the music, ranging from the smallest moment to the broadest sequence of events. The fluidity of harmony, counterpoint, and musical episode encourages the listener to hear the music itself as a fluid, changeable object, embracing various kinds of musical convergence and divergence to arrive at a broad, open-ended sense of what is possible. The Dead enthusiast is therefore likely to be a tolerant listener, prepared to accept many different kinds of sounds and prepared also to listen for clues to form and direction in a long-winded, somewhat unpredictable musical flow.[27]

Dead fans must also be tolerant of the vagaries of the music in its effect. The recording I have discussed is a strong performance, but it is also common for fans and band members too to speak of high and low points in concerts and entire seasons. As one fan said to me, "I'll wait for a whole concert, a whole *series* of concerts, just to get that one special moment," that moment where the music comes together and transcends ordinary experience.[28] As the foregoing analysis of "Dark Star" shows, the Dead's music can have many such meaningful moments, framed by the constant, flowing qualities of their style. While such moments are, to some extent, normal for any music, the emphasis of the Dead on open-mindedness and spontaneous freedom and on the constant, shifting possibilities of meaning arising from ambiguity gives this factor of imminent transcendence a particular importance.

The searching quality, the quality of being on the edge of a special, unpredictable, and highly meaningful experience in the moment, might be called *virtuality*. This word is not to be confused with "virtual reality," which, as commonly used, is nearly opposite to the virtuality of which I speak, even if the latter could, in its broadest sense, be said to embrace the former. Virtual reality tends to emphasize the approximation of an implicitly stable, external, "actual" reality through novel intermediaries, usually mechanized. Virtuality, as I am using it, emphasizes the far more open-ended approximation of an internal, intuitive reality, distinct from the externally tangible and the mundanely real. Virtual reality directs us to a fixed, replicable end, based on connection to known or concrete things. Virtuality invites us to an inward leap of faith, imagination, or experience that is inherently unpredictable and unique unto itself. Virtual reality objectifies; virtuality subjectifies. Virtual reality manipulates; virtuality suggests.

Jerry Garcia has evoked something of this quality at various times when describing the Dead's music, as, for example, in the following excerpt from an interview of 1972:

> I think of the Grateful Dead as being a crossroads or a pointer sign, and what we're pointing to is that there's a lot of universe available, that there's a lot of experience available over here. We're kinda like a signpost and we're also pointing to danger, to difficulty, to bummers. We're pointing to whatever there is, when we're on—whatever's happening. . . . We play rock and roll music, and it's part of our form—our vehicle, so to speak—but it's not who we are totally. Like Moondog in New York City, who walks around, he's a sign post to otherness, a sign post to something that's not concrete. It's the same thing. . . . Formlessness and chaos lead to new forms and new order. Closer to, probably, what the real order is. When you break down the old orders and the old forms and leave them broken and shattered, you suddenly find yourself a new space with new form and new order which are more like the way it is. More like the flow. And we just *found* ourselves in that place. [29]

Of course, all experience involves a component of virtuality, inasmuch as consciousness is distinguishable from experience and must project meaning on it. All experience involves a component of actuality as well. There are many experiences of the Dead's music that have served to actualize the hopes and dreams of Deadheads or prompted the Deadheads to actualize them; the "special moment" referred to above is a good example. But in the Dead's psychedelic, intuitive world, the margin between real and unreal, the suggestive connections and barriers between them, and the fleeting, intimate nature of experience are particularly at issue and make the precise, edgelike quality of virtuality particularly relevant. For the Dead, music is a doorway to a different, heightened reality—what its detractors would surely call an *unreality*, opposed to everyday reality. Through the vernacular spirituality of the group and its fans, that other reality can be a positive, uplifting thing, and the doorway to it becomes an essential, permanent Sign.[30]

"Dark Star" provides an excellent illustration of these qualities, both in its lyrics, which evoke a subtle, complex relation between the inner and outer worlds, and in its music, which balances identity against an open-ended searching for meaning on different levels.[31] It is in that improvised balancing act, constantly subject to question, that a good part of the genius of the music lies.

Qualities such as these have been explained as the result of drug influence, on band members and audience alike. It would be wrong to minimize the importance of drugs in the history of the Dead and of the Deadhead movement; the Dead are considered by many to be the ultimate psychedelic band, and the qualities of virtuality and of transcendence seem appropriate in that context. Still more important, however, is the music itself, and the particular sense of community that it, and the band, have generated. Simon Frith once suggested that "[t]he question we should be asking is not what does popular music *reveal* about 'the people' but how does it *construct* them."[32] Such construction is readily visible in the Deadhead phenomenon. The Dead is a band whose creative ideology not only helped to define an era but resulted in a unique listening and concertgoing public whose chief bonds are those same qualities we have heard in the music. For those who dislike them, Deadheads may represent aimless, drug-crazed hedonism; but for those who believe in them, they represent a rare acceptance and appreciation of diversity and faith in the power of transcendence.

At the present time, following Jerry Garcia's death, the sprawling Deadhead movement faces a moment of truth. It will organize itself in some new way or else find various new points of focus; but in the process, some of the qualities that previously defined it will come into question. One of these is its quality of floating on such a grand scale, of being simultaneously formed and formless, of suggesting profound social changes without tending to realize them in clear political terms or impose them on the broader society—in other words, its own virtuality, which is, of course, in perfect relation to the Dead's music. For now, the element of balance in motion appears to be missing; at least, the constant state of becoming, as specifically embodied in the Dead's musical performances, is no more. What the Deadheads have left is a stark choice, or diluted combination of choices, between two alternatives: to look back for meaning into the grand tape loop of recorded shows or to look forward into a future devoid of the original, guiding manifestation of the Sign. The foregoing analysis of "Dark Star," the recording, takes the former course; but "Dark Star," the performance, argues at least as eloquently for the latter.

When Garcia was alive it was easier to say, of an analysis such as this, that the next performance of the song made it irrelevant. His death is one more reminder that, when caught in the frame of art or human life, even paradox and transitoriness have their limits; even the Dead die. Regarded in this light, the words to "Dark Star" take on additional meaning. We have gone through the nightfall of diamonds and beyond it to a new day. The forces have indeed torn loose from the axis. The mirror is shattered, the message of "Dark Star" scattered. Again, one might ask: better scattered to the winds, or to an endless mechanized redundancy? Perhaps the answer lies in neither of these but, instead, in a slight change of consciousness, involving heightened vernacular faith, openmindedness, and perhaps even thoughtfulness about our intimate and collective memories. In an age of obsessive mechanical reproduction and transient fame, history becomes depthless and flat; perhaps the Deadheads could make a dent in the past as well as the future.

By contrast, however, consider Garcia's own thoughts about dying. His answer is consistent with his approach to music and to life; it is consistent with the expressive message of "Dark Star." But it is glaringly inconsistent with the mythic world the Dead have engendered, inasmuch as that world seeks to survive and to maintain its past identity as its inhabitants come and go. To the extent that the Deadheads fade away or move on to other things, Jerry's words will have been appropriate and prophetic.

I'm hoping to leave a clean field—nothing, not a thing. I'm hoping they bury it all with me. I don't feel that there's this body of work that must exist. I'd just as soon take it all with me. There's enough stuff—who needs the clutter, you know? I'd rather have my immortality while I'm alive.[33]

Appendix: Reactions of members of the Grateful Dead

Partly through the good efforts of Thomas Vennum, senior ethnomusicologist at the Folklife Program of the Smithsonian Institution, and Dennis McNally, manager of the Grateful Dead, I obtained a number of reactions from members of the band to a copy of, or arguments in, the original, shorter version of this chapter. As presented here, the statements are paraphrases.

JERRY GARCIA: *The song is tonally ambiguous. If pressed, I would say it is not in A mixoly-dian but rather E dorian.* [Garcia later said it could be in A.]

PHIL LESH AND BOB WEIR: *The song is in A.*

TOM CONSTANTEN: *The paper sounds like a weather report in French, delivered perfectly by someone who doesn't speak a word of the language. While the points made are all true, the spirit of the paper has nothing to do with the spirit in which the music was made.*

To these might be compared the following comment by Frederic Lieberman, ethno-musicologist and longtime associate of the band: *This is the most "etic" analysis I've ever heard. If you ask the band members, they'll say the song is just two chords.*

Notes

1. Concerning the Dead's earnings in 1995, see "1995 Top Tours," *Pollstar*, 31 Dec. 1995: 7. Concerning their earnings in 1991, see "Year of the Dead" and "1991 Top 50 Tours," *Pollstar*, 31 Dec. 1991: 5 and 7, respectively. Also reported in Sandy Troy, *Captain Trips: A Biography of Jerry Garcia* (New York: Thunder's Mouth, 1994), 245. In recent years, a Deadhead-related following has also been attaching itself increasingly to other, younger bands, including Phish, Blues Traveler, and Rusted Root. According to *Pollstar's* "Concert Pulse" of 22 Jan. 1996, Phish, Blues Traveler, and Rusted Root ranked seventh, seventeenth, and twenty-third, respectively, in overall concert earnings for the preceding three months; see *Pollstar*, 22 Jan. 1996: 2. Phish was ranked fifteenth in overall earnings for 1995; Blues Traveler was ranked forty-seventh ("1995 Top Tours," *Pollstar*, 31 Dec. 1995: 7).

2. *The Rolling Stone Album Guide*, ed. Anthony DeCurtis and James Henke (New York: Random House, 1992), s.v. "Grateful Dead," by Paul Evans, 288.

3. Lester Bangs, "The Clash," *New Musical Express*, 10 Dec. 1977; reprinted. in *Psychotic Reactions and Carburetor Dung*, ed. Greil Marcus (New York: Knopf, 1987), 233. Seven years earlier, his views were essentially the same: "the Dead seemed more like a group of ex-folkies just dabbling in distortion (as their albums eventually bore out)" ("Of Pop and Pies and Fun," *Creem* [Nov. and Dec. 1970]; reprinted in *Psychotic Reactions*, 42). In 1983, Bob Weir, in a facetious moment, put it somewhat differently: "Let's face it: we're a jazz band." Quoted in David Gans, *Conversations with the Dead: The Grateful Dead Interview Book* (New York: Citadel, 1992), 182.

4. *Live/Dead*, Warner Brothers 2WS-1830 (1969); recently rereleased on compact disc (Warner Brothers 1830–2). The date of recording is provided in *Deadbase 4: The Complete Guide to Grateful Dead Song Lists*, ed. John W. Scott, Mike Dolgushkin, and Stu Nixon (Hanover, N.H.: Deadbase, 1990), 485. Concerning the composition and performance history of this song, see Rob Bowman's important liner notes to John Oswald's compact disc, *Gray-folded*, Swell/Artifact 1969 (1996), partially reprinted as "Dark Star: The Legend Continues," *Dupree's Diamond News* 32 (Fall 1995): 32–35.

5. As Robert Hunter, who wrote the lyrics for "Dark Star," said recently, "What the Dead

do on 'Dark Star' is what the Dead are, that's what they do best. What defines the Dead is 'Dark Star'" (quoted in Bowman's liner notes to *Grayfolded*, [2]; reprinted in "Dark Star: The Legend Continues," 32). Jerry Garcia called the performance released on *Live/Dead*, "a real good version." See Jann S. Wenner and Charles Reich, "The Rolling Stone Interview with Jerry Garcia and Mountain Girl," *Rolling Stone*, 20 Jan. 1972; reprinted in *Garcia: By the Editors of Rolling Stone*, ed. Holly George-Warren (New York: Rolling Stone/Little, Brown, 1995), 92. Garcia has also praised the continuous medley of songs released on the album ("Dark Star," followed by "St. Stephen," "The Eleven," and "Turn On Your Lovelight"), considered as a single musical unit: "In the sense of being a serious long composition, musically, and then a recording of it, it's our music at one of its really good moments" (quoted in Troy, *Captain Trips*, 125).

6. There is a studio version, appearing on an early single, which is not well liked by the band ("Dark Star," b/w "Born Cross-Eyed," Warner Bros. 7186 [1968]). For a discussion of the single, including comments about it by Jerry Garcia, see Bowman, liner notes to *Grayfolded*, [4].

7. Judging by the data presented in *DeadBase 4*, p. 225, there were 153 performances of "Dark Star" through 31 Dec. 1989 (the chronological endpoint of that edition of the database). Among these, the song opens a set 7 percent of the time (eleven performances) and opens a song list within a set 10 percent of the time (sixteen performances). It closes an encore once and closes a list 5% of the time (eight performances).

8. John Oswald's recent composition *Grayfolded* was made electronically by splicing, overlaying, and manipulating parts of one hundred recorded performances of the song. Reaction from the Deadhead public has been enthusiastic but also mixed; some find it to be the "ultimate" or "best" "Dark Star," while others think the opposite, repelled by the thought that the Dead's music could be improved by outside tinkering.

9. As Bob Weir once remarked, "The tapes always lie." Quoted in Gans, *Conversations with the Dead*, 182.

10. While my analysis of this recording will be tempered (at times implicitly, at other times explicitly) by acquaintance with other recordings, I shall nonetheless consider it to be adequate unto itself. Such an approach does impose a certain fixity or finality on this particular performance, and some might reasonably argue that the spirit of the band runs counter to such a stance. This is a point that merits serious consideration, and I shall return to it at the end of this essay. Nonetheless, recordings of the Dead's performances exist and are listened to, even studied, to the point of memorization by many fans. It is, to say the least, reasonable to examine these recordings for the structures and meanings that they suggest to the listener, all the more so in the case of highly regarded "classic" instances such as this one. By analyzing this recording in depth, however, I do not mean to suggest that it is more than one rendering of the song. In another essay, forthcoming as an article, I examine sixteen early recordings of "Dark Star" in order to categorize the style, content, and interrelationships of its various episodes across different performances ("Dark Star: What's the Score?" read at the conference in Honor of Rulan Chao Pian, Harvard University, April 1992).

11. For transcription in this article, I used a Panasonic SL-PS352 CD player with an Edcor HA 400 headphone amplifier and Koss Pro 4 AAA Plus headphones. Other equipment may cause the music to sound different as to relative loudness of instruments at different moments and even, more frequently than one might think, as to precise notes and rhythms played. Beyond equalization and other matters of high-fidelity sound reproduction, this is due partly to the conditions of the original live recording, including saturation caused by the bass and other instruments, which occasionally clouds the sound. The dynamic indications are simple and are intended only to give some sense of the relative apparent loudness of different passages. In fact, the dynamics depend more on the band as a whole (including percus-

sion and organ) than on the instrumental lines transcribed. In addition, I have not systematically indicated the slides, pulls, and other subtle features of guitar and bass playing that occur from time to time; I have resolved occasional rhythmic ambiguities; I have resolved the often gently swinging rhythm to straight eighth notes; and, as is explained later, I have not transcribed the playing of every musician in the band.

12. Other performances confirm that this tag marks the beginning of "Dark Star." In instances I have heard where the song has been located at the beginning of a set and has, therefore, lacked a preceding jam, the tag is still present.

13. Three other musicians in the band, Tom Constanten on electric organ and Mickey Hart and Bill Kreutzmann on percussion, contribute significantly to the texture, rhythm, dynamics, and mood of the song (another band member, Pigpen [a.k.a. Ron McKernan], may also be playing percussion). The percussion has an important role in establishing an introspective atmosphere: unlike much rock drumming of the time, it is muted and even reticent, relying for much of the time on Latin hand instruments and gently swinging cymbal work and adding stronger accents during climactic or otherwise salient passages. In this respect, it recalls certain styles of jazz playing; together with the repetitive modal chords and the swinging rhythm that often obtains in the music, it is particularly evocative of the style of *Kind of Blue* by the Miles Davis Quintet (Columbia PC 8163 [1959]). Constanten's sinous organ lines, based largely on right-hand pentatonic arpeggios, weave lightly and episodically through the texture, at certain times rising to the surface of the music and at others receding or disappearing altogether. Since I am primarily concerned with tonal sensibility in the analysis that follows, I shall not dwell on the percussion; and since the organ part is so much more episodic and less audible than the guitar trio of Garcia, Weir, and Lesh in the recording, I shall not dwell on it either.

14. For the sake of clarity, and in order to avoid improper parallels with chordal functionality in common-practice music, I am naming chords in this essay by either upper-case letters (A, E, and so forth) or simple arabic numerals (1, 5, and so forth). Pitches are named by upper-case letters only, never numbers. Roman numerals and caret-topped arabic numerals are not used.

15. Garcia recently described the Dark Star progression as follows: "[It's] like a two-bar honk. That's like the fundamental rhythmic piece . . . You can think of that as figured bass. It's early counterpoint in the same sense that 'Cold Rain and Snow' is." Lesh made a related observation: "Some reviewer described the way I play as being 'Like a sandworm in heat wrapped around Garcia's guitar line.' I love that line and it does describe that really because it's like we're playing chasing the train which is a lot of fun. I try to do that all the time but 'Dark Star' is *supposed to do that*." Both quotes from Bowman, liner notes to *Grayfolded*, [3]; reprinted in "Dark Star: The Legend Continues," 33, emphasis is Bowman's.

16. There is one minor-third leap, from G to E; but the voice evokes the intervening F♯ without clearly singing it, by means of a slight dip from G. Not transcribed in example 7.4 (or in ex. 7.9) are the many nuances of Garcia's singing; also untranscribed is Garcia's guitar part here, which plays, very quietly, the same melody he sings.

17. Garcia has said of this melody, apparently in reference to the possibilities it suggests for improvisation: "Something about the structure of it meant that you could open up any part of it. You could take [the first half of the melody] and stop and then you could play for 5000 bars and then come back with [the second half of the melody] for example. You could open it almost after every note and come back and it'll be fairly graceful. . . . It's so simple, it doesn't have any rules. It's really simple and also as complicated as you could possibly get. It's both things at the same time." Quoted in Bowman, liner notes to *Grayfolded*, [5]. The two half-lines of melody are transcribed there; but they were either mistranscribed or rendered in two different keys by Garcia.

18. The juxtaposition of the tag and the preceding bass line here reveals or at least casts the first tag formula (marked "i" in ex. 7.1, bass line, mm. 15ff.) as part of the third chain rising up from E (E-G-B-D). That, in turn, reinforces the impression of harmonic movement in the tag from {5} to 1.

19. In discussing his ideas for the early, single version of the song, which he later decided was flawed, Garcia has expressed explicit awareness of the opposition of 1 and 5 harmonies in the verse and drawn an implicit connection between that opposition and the character of the song as a whole. His comment also shows that the opposition is less explicit and focused, and more open-ended, in the mature versions of the song than it could have been: "I wanted the bass figure to be more powerful. Then when it drops down to the E-minor part, that would have been much stronger and much darker and it would have had an E-minor ninth feel, almost like E-minor as a dominant chord . . . As always with Grateful Dead stuff, my version usually just dies somewhere and the Grateful Dead version takes over . . . At the time I was panicked a little because I thought, 'What happened to my song . . .?' But, as it opened and we got really risky, when we started to drop the rhythm and just went all over the place, by then I realized that the Grateful Dead version, the x version, was way more interesting both to me as a player and to me as an audience." Quoted in Bowman, liner notes to *Grayfolded*, [4].

20. The text for the first refrain line paraphrases the opening line of T. S. Eliot's poem, "The Love Song of J. Alfred Prufrock" (1915; *The Wasteland and Other Poems* [New York: Harcourt, Brace, 1934; reprint, 1988]). The second line of the refrain is also related, in its "nighttime" theme, to the second line of Eliot's poem, albeit distantly.

21. When asked whether the lyrics' exploratory imagery had influenced the music, Garcia recently said: "No question. The reason the music is the way it is, is because those lyrics did suggest that to me. That's what happened. They are saying 'this universe is truly far out.' That's about it. You could take whatever you will from that suggestion. For me, that suggestion always means, 'Great, let's look around; let's see how weird it really gets.'" Lesh agreed that the lyrics might have had a "subliminal" effect but placed more emphasis on the chord structure: "My feeling is the reason that that song became the archetypal Grateful Dead jamming song is because of the chord changes to it. It was a kind of a drone song. It didn't have a lot of chord changes in it. Generally speaking, those kind of songs are easier to really stretch out on because there's so little to adhere to." Both quotes from Bowman, liner notes to *Grayfolded*, [4].

22. In both cases, due to space constraints, I am leaving out the passage that occurs prior to the entry of Garcia's guitar as melodic lead. In the first episode (ex. 7.5) that preceding passage is tranquil and based firmly on the Dark Star progression. In the second episode (ex. 7.6), by contrast, it involves a strong buildup that leaves the progression behind, while still remaining anticipatory of Garcia's solo. In this episode, then, his entry (m. 1) coincides with a momentary return to the progression, before further harmonic exploration.

23. Regarding the open conception of these episodes in performances of "Dark Star," organist Tom Constanten has characterized it in the following terms: "[It's an] exploratory venture—possibly you could use the word *experimental* for that—it's not so much a set piece, that you know where you are in it and know where you're gonna go, as you're out on an ocean in a boat and you can choose your landmarks and response to things and move in certain directions as you wish—of course, always interacting." Quoted in Troy, *Captain Trips*, 123.

24. Garcia's riff of mm. 44–46 (repeated and varied several times thereafter) is, in fact, a signal, following the settling down of the musical texture, for movement toward the singing of the verse. It recurs at the end of the second instrumental episode, before the second verse (see ex. 7.8, mm. 33–35), and can be heard in other performances of the song in analogous places.

25. In performances where the band goes into an atonal "space jam" in this second episode, the improvisations leave modality behind as well, in order to explore feedback, free percussion, and other open-ended possibilities. In this performance, there is no space jam.

26. The 5 of 5 tonicization may be the result of a fortuitous slip of the voice: the bass below plays a note (quietly) that may be D natural, and on other recordings of the song I have heard, the voice sings D natural rather than D♯.

27. It has often been said that Dead shows have, over time, become relatively formulaic and predictable, with a tendency to relegate certain categories of music to specific points in the sets (notably the exploratory sections that have come to be called "Drums" and "Space"). While that is true, it also remains true that the range of music and of sheer sound played by the band is extraordinary; and they have often invited other musicians to play with them, such as Bob Dylan, jazz saxophonist Branford Marsalis, percussionist Kitaro, and many others, further broadening their stylistic horizons.

28. The phenomenon of the special moment has been noted many times as an essential aspect of Dead concerts, by band members as well as fans. In 1981, Garcia remarked: "People have reported to us so many times that experience: 'You looked at me and I knew what you were going to play,' or 'I knew what you were going to play before you played it,' or 'I was making you play'—all those variations. It's like flying saucer reports. Thousands of 'em, so much so that I can't pretend it doesn't happen." Quoted in Gans, *Conversations with the Dead*, 73. In the same year, Lesh remarked: "After all these years, man, there's nothing awesome about it all, except the moments. Those moments, when you're not even human anymore—you're not a musician, you're not even a person—you're just there." Quoted in Gans, *Conversations with the Dead*, 110.

29. Wenner and Reich, "The Rolling Stone Interview with Jerry Garcia and Mountain Girl"; reprinted in George-Warren, *Garcia*, 95.

30. As Garcia put it, in 1983: "it's a religion to me, too, on a certain level . . . I don't like the word *religion*. It's a bad word. I'd like to not have that concept . . . I don't want to assign any word to it. Why limit it? I want it to surprise me. I don't want to know anything about it." In the same interview, Lesh was more succinct: "For us, myself, it's faith . . . I have faith in this thing, whatever the fuck it is." Gans, *Conversations with the Dead*, 214.

31. A Deadhead view of the matter, not untypical in my experience, is provided by Steve Silberman, coauthor of a book on the Deadheads. Explaining why "Dark Star" is his favorite music by the group, Silberman comments: "Hearing *Live/Dead* when I was in high school was like a can opener to worlds of spirituality, introspection, philosophy, and improvisation for me. So when I specifically hear the 'Dark Star' on *Live/Dead,* I hear the sound of the door to the universe opening for me" ("30 Years upon Our Heads: Roundtable Discussion with John Dwork, David Gans, Blair Jackson, and Steve Silberman," *Dupree's Diamond News* 32 [Fall 1995]: 46).

32. Simon Frith, "Towards an Aesthetic of Popular Music," in *Music and Society: The Politics of Composition, Performance, and Reception,* ed. Richard Leppert and Susan McClary (Cambridge: Cambridge University Press, 1987), 137.

33. From Anthony DeCurtis, "The Music Never Stops: The Rolling Stone Interview with Jerry Garcia," *Rolling Stone,* 2 Sept. 1993; reprinted in *George-Warren Garcia,* 197. The centrality and distinctiveness of Garcia's vision and personality within the band, opposable in some sense to those of the other band members, is illustrated in a recent article by David Gans, which describes projects of the remaining members after Garcia's death. These include the accelerated release of archival recordings and videos, a "Deadapalooza" tour, and the founding of a permanent gathering place in San Francisco where Deadheads can "recapture as much of that spirit as possible." Such plans are understandable, given that the rest of the band is alive, committed to making music, and central to such a large phenomenon (with its com-

mercial, as well as musical and spiritual, forces). The Grateful Dead, Mickey Hart noted, "has been our home for our whole adult lives," and Weir comments that "I'm doing what I believe he [Garcia] would have me doing: bringing music to people" (David Gans, "Dead End," *Rolling Stone*, 25 Jan. 1996: 23–24). But they also leave behind many of the qualities that this essay has attempted to evoke. It seems that, like the death of John Lennon in relationship to the Beatles, Garcia's passing unequivocally signals the end of the Dead.

Outside of the band, the recent comments of a leading Deadhead figure, John Dwork, reflect the combination of open-ended spirituality and hope that characterizes an optimistic Deadhead view of life after the Dead: "the Grateful Dead Experience has become, for so many of us, the closest we may ever get to having a spiritual path. . . . How do we keep our scene alive and continue along our path without Jerry? . . . we must accept the reality that we'll never see Jerry up there on stage again. We must, therefore, learn every day how to summon the love, joy, and sense of adventure we felt at Dead shows. We must learn how to spread this energy out into the rest of the world. . . . Now that the Grateful Dead as we've known it has ended, we, the Deadhead community at large, need to be our own source of light" (John Dwork, "Deadication," *Dupree's Diamond News* 32 [Fall 1995]: 2–3).

Index

Printed in the United States
83096LV00003B/114/A

9 780195 100051